The Presidential Elections of Trump and Bolsonaro, Whiteness, and the Nation

The Presidential Elections of Trump and Bolsonaro, Whiteness, and the Nation

Vânia Penha-Lopes

LEXINGTON BOOKS
Lanham • Boulder • New York • London

Published by Lexington Books
An imprint of The Rowman & Littlefield Publishing Group, Inc.
4501 Forbes Boulevard, Suite 200, Lanham, Maryland 20706
www.rowman.com

86-90 Paul Street, London EC2A 4NE

British Library Cataloguing in Publication Information Available

Library of Congress Cataloging-in-Publication Data Available

ISBN 978-1-7936-1130-7 (cloth : alk. paper)
ISBN 978-1-7936-1132-1 (pbk. : alk. paper)
ISBN 978-1-7936-1131-4 (electronic)

Contents

Preface

The idea for this book was born in 2018. Having written two books on affirmative action in Brazil (2013; 2017), I was thinking of inquiring about Whiteness in the United States, which I understood had gained even more prominence with the election of Donald J. Trump to the presidency two years earlier. His campaign promise to "Make America Great Again," which included the construction of a wall between the United States and Mexico in order to prevent immigration from a country which, according to him, sent mostly criminals, and efforts to curtail the entry of Middle Easterners and Africans, all of whom are non-Whites, fit into a history of racial exclusion only at times interrupted in the United States.

Meanwhile, in Brazil, Jair Messias Bolsonaro, a former army captain with a parliamentary career nearly three decades old, was elected president in 2018. The year before, Bolsonaro had made an incendiary speech during which he referred to non-White Brazilians with disdain: he equated the residents of *quilombos*, communities which had been created by fugitive slaves, to cattle and vowed to appropriate indigenous land in order to explore it commercially. In saying so, Bolsonaro ignored the Constitution of 1988, which guaranteed both groups territorial rights to their areas. Again, the fact that neither *quilombo* residents nor Brazilian Indians are White brought to mind the century-old struggle by Brazilian elites to make the country Whiter.

Then, on October 7, 2018, the first round of the Brazilian presidential election took place. As a legal resident of the United States who lives in New York City, I stood in line to cast my vote. The long line afforded me the opportunity to hear several fellow Brazilians chant "Seventeen! Seventeen!" That was the number of Bolsonaro's political party, Partido Social Liberal, or PSL (Social Liberal Party). Turning toward the sounds, I saw that they were wearing T-shirts emblazoned with a picture of Bolsonaro and the saying,

"MAKE BRAZIL GREAT AGAIN!" Not all of them were White, even by Brazilian standards, although, given Brazil's fluid racial classification, it is possible that they identified as such in their native country and tried to pass as such, or perhaps take on a Latina identity, in their adopted country.

To the shock of many, Bolsonaro won the second round on October 28, 2018. The next day, President Trump tweeted that he had congratulated president-elect Bolsonaro by telephone and that he expected "to work closely with him." Soon, newspaper analysis appeared about the "alarming similarities" between the presidents of the two largest countries of the continent. I decided then to analyze sociologically the similarities that voters and journalists had pinpointed between Trump and Bolsonaro. My research showed me that, far from outliers, both presidents fit into age-old conceptions of nation that characterized their countries.

I watched both inaugurations when they were broadcast on television in their respective countries, in 2017 and 2019, and divided my time between the United States and Brazil thereafter. My reflections on the two tenures are in part based on my own observations, a content analysis of historical events as they unfolded. In 2019, I presented earlier formulations of my argument at the annual meeting of the American Sociological Association (ASA) in New York in August, the biannual meeting of the Association of Brazilianists in Europe (ABRE) in Paris in the following month, and at the Columbia University Seminar on Brazil in December. Soon after, I left for Rio de Janeiro, where I was to spend the spring semester of 2020 writing my manuscript.

I was in Rio when the coronavirus pandemic, the so-called "Covid-19" pandemic, first reached Brazil and spread throughout the country. Although Brazil had received scores of international tourists for New Year's Eve 2019–2020 and Carnival, the coronavirus officially arrived there in March 2020, traced to a well-to-do White Brazilian woman who had traveled in Europe. According to epidemiological authorities, she contaminated her maid, who then spread the virus in her low-income community in a nearby town, where she later died. As is common in Brazil, the maid was Afro-Brazilian. Pretty soon, although I heard Rio de Janeiro inhabitants conclude that the virus was "democratic" in that it contaminated people equally, without regard to race or class, and had emerged in order to teach humans to have more solidarity toward one another, it was the non-White and the poor who were most likely to succumb to the infection as a result of their limited access to health care.

I returned to the United States in August 2020 and remained here while President Trump campaigned for reelection in November amid his defensive stance toward the pandemic. At first he negated the gravity of the contamination, then proposed inefficient medications to combat it, and openly fought specialists, including Dr. Anthony Fauci, the director of the Center for

Disease Control, a path that placed the United States at the top of the list of casualties in the world. The fact that Latinos and African Americans were the most affected, relatively speaking, did not escape me.

President Bolsonaro openly copied President Trump's dismissive attitude and behavior toward the spread of the contamination, including promoting the same medications that Trump had recommended. In time, Brazil occupied the unenviable position of second place in the world in mortality rates.

It is for that reason that I conclude this book with a discussion of the coronavirus pandemic. Not only has the pandemic highlighted racial-ethnic inequality in the United States and Brazil, but it has also illustrated yet another similarity between the presidents of the two countries. Bolsonaro's defense of and convergence toward Trump's reaction to the pandemic was so pronounced that, when Trump lost reelection, Bolsonaro was among the last statespersons to congratulate his successor, Joe Biden. Ultimately, however, Bolsonaro's emulation did not go far enough, for, unlike Trump, he took so long to negotiate the purchase of vaccines that Brazil ended up surpassing the United States in mortality rates. As of this writing (June 2021), relatively few Brazilians have been vaccinated and the dearth of new batches of vaccines looms large.

Acknowledgments

Writing a book is arduous enough; writing a book during a viral pandemic was physically and mentally challenging.

I am thankful to the Committee on Tenure and Advancement at Bloomfield College for having awarded me a study leave in the spring of 2020, which freed me to write most of my manuscript.

I presented the first iterations of my argument at the annual meeting of the American Sociological Association (ASA) in New York in 2019, at the biennial meeting of the Association of Brazilianists in Europe (ABRE) in Paris a month later, and at the Columbia University Seminar on Brazil in December of the same year. I appreciate the comments by Chandra Reyna, Charles A. Gallagher, and Daniel A. Sherwood, who participated in the Section on Racial and Ethnic Minorities Refereed Roundtables at the ASA. Thanks are due to Angela Alonso and Stéphane Boisard, cochairs of the ABRE session in which I presented my paper, my fellow session members, and the audience. I am thankful to my cochairs at the Brazil Seminar—Sidney Greenfield, Diana Brown, and John Collins—for once again providing me with a forum for my ideas. They, together with Mario Bick, Marcia Contins, Ken Erickson, José Reginaldo Gonçalves, Ellie Greenfield, Miriam Grossi, Jack Hammond, Elizabeth Hansen, Maxine Margolis, Sean Mitchell, Laura Randall, Carmen Rial, and Peta Kelenka, afforded me a stimulating debate with lots of useful suggestions.

Thomas J. Trebat, director of the Columbia University Global Centersin Latin America, generously offered me the use of the conference room at the Rio de Janeiro office as a writing space. Yuri Alvarenga, a former member of my expert social media team, quickly helped me find the photograph I chose for the cover of this book.

I acknowledge the on-point comments by an anonymous reviewer; I also thank Erica Simone de Almeida Resende for lending me crucial material with which I could address the reviewer's comments.

My colleague and friend Deidre H. Crumbley, who has championed my work ever since we met in 1996 as fellows at the Carter G. Woodson Institute for Afro-American and African Studies at the University of Virginia, lit the proverbial light at the end of the tunnel. Her expert advice was fundamental for concluding my manuscript. Of course, as always, I am solely responsible for its content.

Once again, I am indebted to my editor at Lexington Books, Nicolette Amstutz. From my book prospectus to my delivery of the final draft, she was the utmost professional; she was also sympathetic to my dealing with the obstacles brought on by the viral pandemic. It feels good to let the world know of my appreciation of her. Thanks are also due to Alexandra Rallo, the new acquisitions director for Latin America, who came in just in time for the final stretch.

Living during a time when so many fellow human beings have lost their loved ones to an unprecedented pandemic, I know how fortunate I am to have had my mother, Diva Penha Lopes, and my sister, Dilma Penha Lopes Pavlidis, by my side through my writing this book. Amid all the changes the pandemic has brought to life as we used to know it, being able to count on their love and support has been a blessing.

Introduction

Race, the Media, and the Far Right in the United States and Brazil

In 2016, a New York businessman turned reality TV star named Donald Trump was elected president of the United States. Two years later, Jair Messias Bolsonaro, a congressman and retired army captain, was elected president of Brazil. Astute observers quickly noted their many similarities, to the point of calling their styles "Trumpism" and "Bolsonarism" (Millikan 2018) and categorizing Bolsonaro as "part Donald Trump, part Rodrigo Duterte," that is, the president of the Philippines (Anderson, J. 2018). The similarities were not lost on Brazilians either. In Brazil, Bolsonaro sympathizers often displayed signs in rallies that evoked Trump's name. In the United States, in the polling place in New York, which serves Brazilian nationals who live in that state as well as in New Jersey, Pennsylvania, and Bermuda, a vociferous mass of Brazilians chanted "Make Brazil Great Again!" while wearing green T-shirts with that phrase printed under a picture of Bolsonaro in the first round of Brazilian presidential elections, on October 7, 2018. Given that "Make America Great Again" had been the slogan of Trump's presidential campaign two years earlier, there was no doubt as to who their role model was. The voters followed Bolsonaro himself, who had no qualms about verbalizing his admiration of Trump. Once elected, Bolsonaro selected the United States to be the first country he would visit as president. The day after Bolsonaro's victory on October 28, 2018, Trump tweeted that he expected to work closely with him.

Both presidents stand clearly to the Far Right of the political spectrum and have succeeded in taking advantage of "frustrated expectations of millions of people in situations of increasing social and economic vulnerability" (Millikan 2018). In that sense, they ride the wave to the right that has risen in the world, such as in Italy, Poland, Hungary, and the Philippines, to name a few countries. In an interview to a Brazilian magazine published in early

2018, Kenneth Maxwell, a history professor at Harvard who is a specialist in Brazil, declared that Bolsonaro

> is an unprepared person, but also extremely attractive to part of the population that is disillusioned with politics in general and with the current leadership in Congress. He could be compared with a tropical Silvio Berlusconi. In fact, Berlusconi's government in Italy was the political result of the Clean Hands campaign, an anti-mafia operation of honest judges who destroyed corrupt politicians and businessmen, but who ultimately also destroyed the political system as such. (in St.-Clair 2018, 12)[1]

In addition, even though Bolsonaro had had a 28-year career as a congressman affiliated with a number of political parties, both he and Trump were touted as unconventional candidates and promoted themselves as "saviors" of their countries, which appealed to the many voters who had become disenchanted with traditional politicians. Moreover, throughout their presidential campaigns and tenures, Trump and Bolsonaro have had contentious relationships with the news media, often labeling opposing reports as "fake news," but also flooding social media with made-up stories about their opponents. Both sported misogynist attitudes and behavior, had a tremendous appeal to Evangelical voters, and professed an intimate relationship with Israel. Last but not least, both relied on racial tensions to boost their campaigns.

This book is a sociological analysis of the notable similarities between the elections of Donald Trump and Jair Bolsonaro, based on biographies, academic sources, newspaper, television, and internet reports published in the United States and Brazil between 2014 and 2021. I argue that the success of each candidate reflects the racially hierarchical structure of their societies as well as the strength of the ideology of White supremacy that is necessary for that structure to remain in place despite efforts to dismantle it. According to that logic, regardless of class and gender, Whites responded to Trump's nativist call to exclude "undesirable" immigrants, especially Mexicans and Muslims, both of whom are racialized as non-White, and "Make America Great Again." In Brazil, the country with the largest population of African descent outside of Africa and the largest miscegenation rates in the world, the votes for Bolsonaro pointed to the social wish to achieve Whiteness and thus eliminate (or at least abate) the insecurity that comes from a belief in the racial inferiority of non-Whites. Based on that argument, I suggest that the results of the presidential elections reflect a fear by Whites that their higher status was being threatened after decades of gains by minorities, women, and the poor in both countries.

The two largest countries in the Americas have grappled with racial and social inequality from their inceptions, as both have racially and ethnically heterogeneous populations (Degler 1971; Daniel 2006). Even though the U.S. Constitution famously starts with the phrase "We the People," it referred only to landowning White men. As for Brazil, its well propagated "racial democracy" has yet to come to fruition; rather, that ideology summarizes a collective aspiration to become a White majority through systematic miscegenation, while maintaining a racial hierarchy with Whites at the top (Penha-Lopes 1996; Telles 2004). In the United States, "the pursuit of fairness" (Anderson, T. 2004) in 50 years of affirmative action policies and advances toward gender equality and more inclusion of LGBTQIA+ persons,[2] in addition to the election and reelection of the first Black president, have led to claims that White men were losing ground. From allegations that the election of Barack Obama was a fraud because he had not been born in U.S. soil to terrorist attacks against Blacks and Jews and the dismantling of affirmative action programs, White supremacy has maintained its power. In Brazil, 10 years of university racial and social quotas as part of an affirmative action program as well as anti-poverty programs are being followed by attacks on minorities, including Blacks, indigenous peoples, women, and LGBTQIA+. In sum, both the United States and Brazil are examples of "racialized social systems," that is, "societies in which economic, political, social, and ideological levels are partially structured by the placement of actors in racial categories or races. . . . In all racialized social systems the placement of people in racial categories involves some form of hierarchy that produces definite social relations between the races" (Bonilla-Silva 1997, 469).

WHITENESS, WHITE PRIVILEGE, AND WHITE SUPREMACY

In 1946, Richard Wright, recognized as one of "the first African American writers to protest white treatment of Blacks" (The Editors of Encyclopaedia Britannica September 25, 2020), emigrated to France to escape the rampant racism that characterized his native land. In that same year, Wright was interviewed by Raphaël Tardon, a French journalist, who asked him what he thought about the "Negro problem" in the United States. He replied, "There isn't any Negro problem; there is only a white problem" (in Lipsitz 2006, 1; 250 n1). Evidently, by that he meant it was Whites in power who had created a system that left Negroes disenfranchised, vulnerable to underemployment and unemployment, and in constant fear for their lives. Still, it would take decades for social scientists to start to focus on the attitudes and behavior of Whites as Whites, not just as generic "people."

The maintenance of Whites' dominant racial status since the dawn of the United States makes them "normal" and "normative" against whom all other groups are measured and blamed for social problems, such as the interviewer's question to Richard Wright implied. The intersection of race with class frames the issue further, such as when sociologist Talcott Parsons categorized "the normal American family" as the one composed of a breadwinning father, a stay-at-home mother, and their children, even though, when he first argued that in the 1940s, only middle- and upper-class Whites could afford it.

Whiteness per se continued to be ignored in the 1960s. *Beyond the Melting Pot* (1963) concerned the ethnic groups in New York that, according to Glazer and Moynihan, had not and could not assimilate into the dominant group. However, as Steinberg (1981) counterargued, they were already on their way to assimilation. Therefore, studies of White ethnicity held on to cultural diversity instead of focusing on the social construction of Whiteness. As Dyer (2012, 12) puts it,

> It is studying whiteness *qua* whiteness. Attention is sometimes paid to "white ethnicity" . . . , but this always means an identity based on cultural origins such as British, Italian or Polish, or Catholic or Jewish, or Polish-American, Irish-American, Catholic-American and so on. These however are variations on white ethnicity (though some are more securely white than others), and the examination of them tends to lead away from a consideration of whiteness itself, John Ibson . . . , in a discussion of research on white US ethnicity, concludes that being, say, Polish, Catholic or Irish may not be as important to white Americans as some might wish. But being White is.

The social construction of Whiteness focuses on how Whites have retained most of the power by securing their privilege and, over time, extending it to selected groups. Certainly during slavery (1619–1865), and then again during Jim Crow (1896–1964), Whiteness was akin to White supremacy, since to be White meant to have access to all areas of society denied to non-Whites. As Cox (1948) noted, class oppression was not enough to unite poor and working-class Whites with Negroes; being White granted the former a privilege that was denied to the latter regardless of class, even though lower-class Whites were not nearly as privileged as their higher-class counterparts. Roediger (1991) showed how Irish Americans, long regarded as an "inferior race," were later re-racialized as Whites in part by adopting anti-Black attitudes and behavior.

Feagin (2003) credits W. E. B. Du Bois as the first sociologist to conceptualize White supremacy. Morris (2015) adds that, running against the eugenist current at the turn of the twentieth century, Du Bois had already argued, in his classic *The Souls of Black Folk* (1903), that race is a historical and social construct rather than a biological given and that racism was not only a major problem in the United States, but a global phenomenon. Later, in "The Souls of White Folk" (1920), Du Bois elaborated on the concept of Whiteness as a social construct of the nineteenth and twentieth centuries; the way Whiteness is taken for granted as the best race promotes the continuation of racism:

> This assumption that of all the hues of God whiteness alone is inherently and obviously better than brownness or tan leads to curious acts. . . .
> . . . "But what on earth is whiteness that one should so desire it?" Then always, somehow, some way, silently but clearly, I am given to understand that whiteness is the ownership of the earth forever and ever, Amen!. . . .
> . . . Everything considered, the title to the universe claimed by White Folk is faulty. It ought, at least, to look plausible. How easy, then, by emphasis and omission to make children believe that every great soul the world ever saw was a white man's soul; that every great thought the world ever knew was a white man's thought; that every great deed the world ever did was a white man's deed; that every great dream the world ever sang was a white man's dream. In fine, that if from the world were dropped everything that could not fairly be attributed to White Folk, the world would, if anything, be even greater, truer, better than now. And if all this be a lie, is it not a lie in a great cause?

Du Bois observes that the novelty of White supremacy is to determine social inequality by color; while social inequality has characterized human interaction since the ancient world, assigning a rigid social status to interpretations of skin color was "a modern thing" Europeans developed from the colonization of peoples in Africa, Asia, and the Americas. Because the United States was first a European colony, it too espoused those ideas and that structure once it became an independent country.

Academic interest in Whiteness grew after the gains of the civil rights movement. With the outlawing of legal racial segregation, Blacks and other non-Whites have conquered more space in education, employment, political participation, and housing; the growth of the Black middle class is undeniable (Wilson 1978). However, racism has persisted, albeit in a different form, from overt to veiled.

Frankenberg (1995) is recognized as a pioneer in Whiteness studies thanks to her research on U.S. White women. She showed how those women saw themselves as neutral and claimed to be color-blind, while attributing race to non-Whites. Therefore, at the same time they alleged that it did not matter whether one was "green, striped, or purple," they saw non-Whites as "different" and the "other." Frankenberg concluded that the social construction of Whiteness is grounded in privilege, that the privilege is structural, and that it continues via behavior and attitudes that are taken for granted.

Bobo (1997, 1998, 2008) called the veiled form of racial inequality "laissez-faire racism," or the type of racism that relies on nonracial language to explain away racism; it is "ostensibly color-blind" (Bobo 2008, 157), such as the claim that the concentration of African Americans in the lower socioeconomic strata is not due to racism because affirmative action policies have leveled the field. Therefore, the explanation must be African Americans' faulty work ethic. An illustration of that reasoning occurred on October 26, 2020, a few days before the presidential elections, when Jared Kushner, President Trump's son-in-law and senior adviser, declared,

> One thing we've seen in a lot of the Black community, which is mostly Democrat, is that President Trump's policies are the policies that can help people break out of the problems that they're complaining about. . . .But he can't want them to be successful more than they want to be successful. (in Jacobs and Egkolfopoulou October 26, 2020)

According to that logic, the opportunities for success exist, but individual lack of motivation prevents them to materialize. Bobo (2008, 163) presented data from the National African American Election Study in 2000 that show that Whites were almost six times more likely than Blacks to think that racial equality had already been achieved; in addition, 19 percent of Blacks, but only 3 percent of Whites, thought that racial equality would never be achieved. This attitudinal racial gap signals "the crystallization of a new racial ideology here in the United States" (Bobo 2008, 156), one based on the neoliberal notion of minimal state intervention on a free market where individuals can all compete on an equal basis. As a matter of fact, part of the platforms in Trump's and Bolsonaro's presidential campaigns was the divestment of the state, exemplified by the dismantling of social policies on health and education, and, in the case of Brazil, the selling of state companies to foreign investors. Bobo warns, "But make no mistake—the current social structure and attendant ideology reproduce, sustain, and rationalize enormous black-white inequality" (157).

Based on over 1,000 interviews with Blacks and Whites, Bonilla-Silva (2003, 28–30) identified four components ("central frames") of the ideology of color-blind racism: "abstract liberalism," "naturalization," "cultural racism," and "minimization of racism." Abstract liberalism emphasizes the values of individuality and merit, according to which society rewards anyone who has initiative and works hard with success; Jared Kushner's aforementioned contention and the charge that affirmative action policies constitute "reverse discrimination" illustrate that argument. Naturalization is the tendency to view social phenomena as "almost biologically driven," which justifies the status quo. For example, the fact that less than 10 percent of all marriages in the United States are interracial even after more than 50 years of the ban on anti-miscegenation laws would be due not to the persistence of prejudice, but to natural preferences that people have for staying within their own group. Cultural racism is the attribution of inferior values and behaviors to non-Whites; in my view, it is akin to the "cultural deficit" model that once predominated in studies of Black families that did not fit the "normal" nuclear arrangement (Penha-Lopes 1999). Finally, minimization of racism is the belief that, because racial discrimination is no longer legal, racism is much less commonplace, so that racist incidents are seen as the exception, regardless of their level of violence. For instance, the "Black Lives Matter" movement is dismissed because "all lives matter."

Color-blind racism "maintains white privilege by negating racial inequality" (Gallagher 2009, 101). When Whites are the majority of consumers of rap and hip-hop, musical genres that were created by inner city Blacks, and middle-class youth from every racial/ethnic group imitate the dress style of poor Black youth, Whites get the impression that racial and even class inequalities are things of the past. For Gallagher, color-blind ideology reduces race to commodities consumption. Of course, while they may all dress alike, the origins of that style and the stereotypes associated with it may surface at any moment, with dire consequences. Chances are White and Black teenagers in hoodies will be treated quite differently, as the murder of Trayvon Martin by a Latino vigilante in Florida in 2012 attested.

In sum, color-blind racism is racism nonetheless. It, however, ignores past discrimination, masks current racial inequality, and sees that inequality as an individual problem—both from the standpoint of victims and of perpetrators (Guinier and Torres 2009). Consider the "Executive Order on Combating Race and Sex Stereotyping," which President Trump signed on September 22, 2020. He cites the Constitution, the Founding Fathers, Abraham Lincoln, and Martin Luther King Jr. to admonish against a new ideology that

> is rooted in the pernicious and false belief that America is an irredeemably racist and sexist country; that some people, simply on account of their race or sex, are oppressors; and that racial and sexual identities are more important than our common status as human beings and Americans.

The text proceeds to turn history around by claiming that, rather than new, that ideology is a rehashing of the antebellum belief that the country was made for and by White men. The order supports diversity training that fosters inclusive job environments and champions individual merit, but condemns any mentioning of collectivities, group oppression, or White male privilege. It even blames social scientific research for the circulation of such ideas, as if the omission of racism were proof that it does not exist:

> But training like that discussed above perpetuates racial stereotypes and division and can use subtle coercive pressure to ensure conformity of viewpoint. Such

ideas may be fashionable in the academy, but they have no place in programs and activities supported by Federal taxpayer dollars. Research also suggests that blame-focused diversity training reinforces biases and decreases opportunities for minorities.

The manifestation of that type of racism in the United States is a sign of its convergence toward the Brazilian racial ideology (Daniel 2006). At least since the early twentieth century, Brazil has promoted itself as a racial democracy. Even though there is plenty of historical and contemporary evidence of deep-seated racial inequality, many Brazilians still resist admitting it. One glaring example took place in 2020 on November 19, the eve of Black Consciousness Day, the holiday that marks the assassination of Zumbi of Palmares in 1695. Zumbi was the leader of the largest *quilombo*, a society of runaway and former slaves who resisted slavery and colonization. The acknowledgment of that date was a victory of the Black movement in Brazil. Although the date has been commemorated since 1988, the centennial of Abolition, every year statements are made that it is a mistake because "there is only the human race." On November 19, 2020, a Black man who was shopping at a Carrefour supermarket in Porto Alegre, the capital of the southernmost Brazilian state of Rio Grande do Sul, was beaten and asphyxiated by two White security guards after he had had a disagreement with a White cashier. Demonstrations erupted throughout the country. The next day, while the minister of Women, Family and Human Rights, Damares Alves, condemned the "barbaric" nature of the murder, Vice President General Hamilton Mourão categorically denied it had anything to do with racism. To reporters, he declared the United States from the pre–civil rights movement era as the true home of racism:

> I tell you with the utmost tranquility: there is no racism in Brazil. . . . I say that because I have lived in the United States. . . . Here, there is inequality, the result of a series of problems. (Exame.com.br November 20, 2020)

It took President Jair Bolsonaro two days to make any pronouncements about the murder. He finally tweeted that he was "colorblind" and that the murder had nothing to do with race:

> Let us not be manipulated by political groups. As a man and as the President, I am colorblind: all have the same color. No color is better than the others. There are good men and bad men. It is our choices and values that make the difference. . . . Those who instigate the people to discord, fabricating and promoting conflict, go against not only the nation, but against our own history. Whoever preaches that is in the wrong place; their place is in the garbage. (noticias.uol .com.br November 21, 2020)

Bolsonaro added that the country was racially mixed and cordial; to insist to the contrary was an attempt to divide its people in order to usurp its sovereignty. That was quite different from his pronouncements during his presidential campaign in 2017, when he clamored that "the minorities must bow to the majority." Instead, Brazil had a much more serious problem than race to contend with: the "moral, political, and economic corruption. . . . Those who negate that fact contribute to its persistence" (noticias.uol.com.br November 21, 2020). Never mind that the president himself had declared, in the previous month, that corruption no longer existed in Brazil (Jornal GGN October 7, 2020).

We see that while in the United States color-blind ideology claims the end of racism because affirmative action policies have opened up opportunities for all and have even dispensed preferential treatment to Blacks, in Brazil color-blind ideology claims that the country has never been racist because its people is racially mixed and because of the absence of legal racial discrimination. Therefore, affirmative action policies, which were instituted early in the twenty-first century, are illegitimate, alien instigators of racial hatred, and should never have been implemented. Color-blind racism in Brazil relies on miscegenation to claim that it is impossible to know who is Black. However, at least since the First Republic (1889–1930), Brazil has aimed at increasing its White population by promoting European immigration, encouraging systematic miscegenation, and keeping White at the top of the racial hierarchy (Penha-Lopes 2017).

In Brazil, studies of Whiteness date back to the 1990s, in the psychology department at the University of São Paulo (Carone 2003, 17–22). Like Richard Wright decades earlier, Bento (2003a, 41) charges that the disregard of studies on Whites places the nature of race relations in Brazil solely on Blacks, by either denying the existence of racial discrimination or by admitting it, but rationalizing it as the product of Black inferiority or a legacy of slavery. That in itself points to the strength of White privilege in Brazil. Bento (2003) has captured the tension between the negation of racism in Brazil and its favoring of Whitening (*embranquecimento*), thus affording the greatest prestige to Whiteness (*branquitude*) by . Piza (2003) found that the White women she interviewed in a country town in the state of São Paulo recognize the privilege they enjoy (e.g., the ability to frequent clubs that are closed to Blacks), but do not see it as stemming from racial inequality. At the same time, they place Blacks in an inferior status whenever they are asked to compare themselves with the other, which leads Piza to conclude that "it is the non-demarcation or racial nomination that most strongly deceives in the process of Whiteness" (85). More recently, Pinho (2009) showed how in Brazil, even Whiteness is a gradation rather than an absolute. Telles and Flores (2013) add that, throughout Latin America, Whiteness is contextual, just as Blackness is.

In sum, in contrast with the United States, which established a racial dichotomy (Daniel 2006; Nogueira 1954; Penha-Lopes 1996), and South American countries such as Chile and Argentina, which have White majorities (Telles and Flores 2013), Brazil aims at achieving Whiteness, so it allows for White racial classification and identity to be more fluid and contextual. As I show in my analysis of university quota students (2013; 2017), a number of those who entered the State University of Rio de Janeiro via quotas for Afro-descendants used to identify as *pardos* (i.e., Brown) and even as *brancos* (i.e., White) if they were the lightest-skinned person in a gathering. When they were in a mostly White gathering, however, they tended to see themselves and be classified as *pardos* or even as *negros* (i.e., Black), which illustrates the point that White is the more exclusive and hierarchical racial category.

In the United States, the election of Barack Obama in 2008 and his reelection four years later made some believe that the country had become "post-racial." After all, given that Whites constituted almost three-quarters of the U.S. population in 2008 and Blacks, only 13 percent, Obama needed White support in order to be elected. However, as it turned out, 95 percent of Blacks, but only 43 percent of Whites voted for him (Roper Center 2020). In 2012, "Barack Obama lost the white vote by 20 percentage points . . . an astonishing margin, and by far the largest deficit among white voters of any successful Democratic presidential candidate" (Abramowitz 2018, 128). In both elections, Obama's victories were guaranteed by the strength of the Latino and Asian votes.

By 2016, any semblance of racial neutrality had disappeared. Examining the election results through the lens of his work on White organizations throughout the country, Hughey (2017) suggests that White identity leads to specific behaviors. Donald Trump's campaign discourse appeal to the White working class, two-thirds of whom voted for him and over one-third claimed "that their Whiteness is 'very' or 'extremely important to their identity'" (Hughey 2017, 17), had to do with their hope of taking back from non-Whites and immigrants what they consider theirs by virtue of their Whiteness, which Hughey labels "hegemonic Whiteness":

> Much ink has been spilled in pondering Trump's supposed "economic populism" and the power of political ideologies to magnetize the White working class. But what measures of White attitudes fail to acknowledge is that racism against people of color correlated *much* more closely with support for Trump than did attitudes about economic dissatisfaction, even after controlling for political partisanship and political ideology. It's not a matter of whether race trumps (pardon the pun) either economics or political ideology (or vice versa), but how these voters interpret the world through the lens of Whiteness. (Emphasis in original.)

The interpretation of the world through the lens of Whiteness goes beyond personal identity. Hegemonic Whiteness is anchored in definitions of nationhood, or who is allowed to belong to a given nation. As I show in chapters 1 and 2, the social construction of Whiteness has also helped to construct nationhood both in the United States and in Brazil.

THEORETICAL CONSIDERATIONS ON THE IDEA OF NATION

In his classic book *Imagined Communities* (1991, 6, 7), Benedict Anderson defines nation as "an imagined political community—and imagined as both inherently limited and sovereign." Nation is a creation, "limited" in that it encompasses only certain people, not the entire species. It is "sovereign" because it seeks to govern itself. Finally, it is a "community" because "the nation is always conceived as a deep, horizontal comradeship," thus masking in its conception the deep cleavages that exist within it. According to Anderson, nation as we understand it today emerged in France, as the Enlightenment (eighteenth century) did away with divine right. From there, it spread to other areas, including the Americas, where former colonies such as the United States and Brazil adopted those ideas. Anderson further argues that "print-capitalism" allowed the former colonies to become nations by reporting on social, economic, and political life, thus fomenting in people the sense that they belonged to a community even when they could not possibly know all of its members.

Anderson's definition is quite optimistic. In all fairness, Anderson recognizes the existence of elites in former colonies that identified with the hierarchical relations imposed by the former colonizers even after independence. For example, both the United States and Brazil maintained slavery systems once they became nations. However, that does not seem to be enough for Anderson to undermine the notion of "comradeship."

Among the critics of Anderson's argument, Balakrishnan (1999) takes issue with the idea that comradeship always outweighs the cleavages. As examples, he cites "the Nazi, the Khmer Rouge guerilla or the Serbian militiaman" (207). Balakrishnan asserts that Anderson unconvincingly resorts to "nationalistic poetry and anthems" to substantiate his claim that nationalism deemphasizes hatred. In addition, Balakrishnan reminds us that,

for Weber, like Hegel, the modern state possesses a historical purpose and collective meaning because it organizes a community into a sovereign polity ready for war. It is during war that the nation is imagined as a community embodying ultimate values.

Indeed, as I mention in the next chapter, the participation of the United States in World Wars I and II inspired Negroes to act toward achieving full civil rights. After having served under segregated and humiliating conditions and, especially during World War II, "liberating" the world from "oppression," Negro soldiers returned to their country only to be treated just as badly as before they had left. In other words, the war effort strengthened Negroes' national spirit, but the nation continued to exclude them from its community. Charles Hamilton Houston, who had vowed he would work toward dismantling Jim Crow if he survived World War I, went on to have a brilliant career as the lawyer who contested the "separate but equal" doctrine in the courts. It was he who trained Thurgood Marshall, who would later be the chief attorney in *Brown v. Board of Education* (1954) and the first Negro Supreme Court justice. In turn, the denial of jobs upon return to Mississippi from World War II (i.e., the denial of full participation in the nation) led Medgar Evers (1925–1963) to join the National Association for the Advancement of Colored People and fight for desegregation, a fight he paid with his own life one year before the Civil Rights Act of 1964 outlawed racial discrimination in employment, education, and public places.

Another critic, Verdery (1999), differentiates between "nation" and "nationalism": the former is a symbol, whereas the latter is "the political utilization" of that symbol. Because symbols can have different meanings for different people at different times and places, so can the idea of nation. Therefore, we can conclude that comradeship may happen in a hierarchical, rather than horizontal, context. National symbols may be invoked for political purposes, for example, to impose on the whole that which interests only certain groups. For instance, the official slogan during the military dictatorship in Brazil (1964–1985) was "Brazil: Love it or Leave it." The implication was, those who went against the dictatorship were branded as haters of the nation, as not enough nationalistic; they should either leave out of their own accord or risk being imprisoned as "subversive," expelled from the country, or tortured and even murdered by the state. During his presidential campaign in 2017 to 2018, Jair Bolsonaro appropriated national symbols such as the colors of the Brazilian flag and a verse from the national anthem, *Pátria Amada, Brasil* (beloved country, Brazil), and then used them to exclude those who did not fit his own idea of nation, which, as I show in later chapters, is quite exclusive; he also repeatedly referred to the dictatorship with longing.

Reitner (2013, xvii) considers Anderson's understanding of "nationalism as an anthropological category." His aim is to "explore what it means to be a citizen, and how different people and groups flesh out its meaning in their mutual and daily interactions." For Reiter, the crux of citizenship is exclusion. While he agrees with Anderson about the origins of nations as imagined communities, Reiter instead argues that the ideals of the French Revolution ended up being about "defending white privilege," given that they were not extended either to former slaves or fully to contemporary "nonwhite French citizens" (xx). As a result, citizenship is a product of White privilege, in that it divides people into first- and second-class citizens. In other words, for Reiter, "Racism is at the core of this exclusion" (25). Whiteness is a scarce resource, a type of "symbolic capital." Those who are most successful at acquiring it—be it through behavior, through historical membership, or economically—are the most successful at achieving citizenship and avoiding exclusion.

European countries and countries colonized by Europeans see Whiteness not only as a powerful symbolic capital for citizenship, but also as capable of interacting with other types of capital in such a way that the presence of one signals the presence of the others. That would explain why, to this day, not being White is associated with lower income, lower education, and any other lower status in Brazil and the United States. Reiter (2013, 39) concludes,

> To the white elites of the Americas, nonwhites are not really part of "their" nation; they remain suspicious, foreign, alien, and "others within," in the case of blacks, and a nation apart, or "others outside," in the case of indigenous people.

Reitner singles out Brazil as the typical case of exclusion. There, exclusion is centered around formality, especially formal education, which helps to perpetuate formal codes, especially the legal system, characterized by "archaic language" (127). The strong separation between formal and informal language is ever more apparent in the legal system. Functional illiteracy affects over 20 percent of the population, who, without access to the formal codes, are effectively excluded from the nation. Moreover, functional illiteracy interacts with "economic informality, illiteracy, poverty, and blackness" (125–126), even after the current Brazilian Constitution was adopted in 1988. We can conclude that second-class citizens may be part of a nation without really belonging, that is, without being treated like full-fledged citizens. Whether or not they have the right to vote, they are constantly excluded from political decisions, so that, according to Reiter, the election and reelection of a presidential candidate from the Workers' Party in 2002 and 2009—and, I would add, again in 2010 and 2014—were deviations from politics as usual, that is, the election of candidates outside of "the traditional political elites" (131).

I agree with Reiter about the strong separation between formal and informal language in Brazil that interacts with race and class and helps to exclude the large mass of functionally illiterates from full participation in the nation. As I have mentioned, university quotas were adopted in part as a result of pressure by segments of the Black movement to open up opportunities for Brazilians of African descent and the poor. The issue is not particular to Brazil, however. The same argument could be made of any country whose language derives from Latin, such as Spain and France and their former colonies. Latin languages have notoriously complex grammatical systems that intimidate even some who possess high educational and professional credentials.

To a certain extent, a similar argument could also be made about language in the United States. Even though American English is relatively much simpler than Brazilian Portuguese and less class-based than British English, it is heavily affected by race, to the point that a version of it has been developed. Black English, sometimes called "Ebonics" and "African American Vernacular English," not only differs markedly from formal English, but is also less prestigious, so that its speakers have historically been excluded from social relations on the basis of it. As a matter of fact, prior to the signing of the Voting Rights Act of 1965, it was common for southern states to require Negro voters to pass "literacy tests" that involved reading passages from the U.S. Constitution with the thinly veiled intention of their failing them. To this day, Black English is often seen as "inarticulate" and of low status. Standard American English is, for all intents and purposes, middle-class White English; entry into and permanence in positions of prestige require mastery of it.

Anderson argues that capitalism and the print technology made nations a possibility. Therefore, if a large portion of the population of a country is illiterate or even functionally illiterate, then it will be excluded from the nation for all intents and purposes. In that case, language is all important for the idea of nation. Resende (2012) raises the question as to how members of a nation feel a sense of belonging given that a nation is an "imagined community." She relies on Stuart Hall, for whom language and culture give "mental codes with which we signify nation" (112), and concludes that nation is "a system of cultural representations" built on the "symbolic" and the "imaginary." A nation is a collectivity brought together by "the myth of a unified, coherent, stable and homogeneous national identity which sustains itself only on the discursive plane" (Resende 2012, 120).

In sum, the idea of nation is neither "homogeneous" nor "horizontal." The more power groups have, the more effective they are in trying to make their own ethos appear to be in the interest of the whole society while excluding those who do not fit that ethos. Having been born as nations which give primacy to those they regard as "White," both the United States and Brazil have treated "non-Whites" either as second-class citizens or excluded them altogether. Therefore, the elections of Donald Trump and Jair Bolsonaro fit historical expectations rather than being exceptions to the rule.

SOCIAL MEDIA, FAKE NEWS, AND
PRESIDENTIAL ELECTIONS

In her reflection on the continuing difficulty in forming and maintaining inter-racial friendships in the United States, Plummer (2019, 180–181) addresses the role of "post-truth" in the way people see themselves and others across races:

> In 2016, the word of the year, as designated by the Oxford Dictionaries, was "post-truth"—an adjective defined as "relating to or denoting circumstances in which objective facts are less influential in shaping public opinion than appeals to emotion and personal belief." When we live in racially segregated environments and socialize in segregated settings, get information filtered through news media aligned with our interpretation and then add racial distrust, that becomes a perfect formula for a separatist society. *Fox & Friends* cable news program consistently ranks as number one in viewers, though reportedly only 1 percent of those viewers are black and the percentage of other viewers of color is most likely as low. With the lack of diversity in its viewership and in its staff representation, the news program sets up the kind of all-white environment that Derek Black observes easily leads to white nationalist beliefs. Getting information from trusted, fact-checked media sources, interacting with diverse friends, and exercising multicultural competences is a formula for democracy.

"Post-truth" is intimately tied to "fake news." In *The Social Dilemma*, a 2020 documentary about the production and reproduction of internet data-bases and social media, Tristan Harris, a former Google design ethicist, cofounder and current president for the Center for Humane Technology, had this to say about the power of fake news: "There's a study, an MIT study, that fake news on Twitter spreads six times faster than true news. What is the world gonna look like when one has a six times advantage to the other one?" (Orlowski 2020). The same documentary mentions the election of Jair Bolsonaro as the result of Facebook and accuses Russia of employing Facebook to destabilize the 2016 U.S. presidential election. In turn, Moura and Corbellini (2019) called Bolsonaro's election "the WhatsApp election." Indeed, one major similarity between Donald Trump's and Jair Bolsonaro's campaigns was how successful they were in using social media to propagate their ideas and attract voters.

Historically, the mass means of communication have been fundamental for electoral campaigns. The famous photograph of Harry Truman smiling with the *Chicago Daily Tribune* in hand whose headline read "DEWEY WINS" is an example. Surveys had predicted the presidential victory of Thomas Dewey based on telephone interviews. However, in 1948, only about 60 percent of households owned telephones, which were still luxury items.[3] Therefore, the prediction failed to tap into the majority of voters.

In 1960, a new mass medium had supplanted radio to play a prominent role on the presidential election: television. By then, close to 90 percent of households contained a television set (Jordan 1996, 798). In what was to be the first televised presidential debate, a cool, camera-friendly John F. Kennedy won over a sweaty Richard M. Nixon. From then on, television debates that emphasized good screen presence became de rigueur.

In 2016, presidential candidate Trump, who had for years anchored a successful television show, appeared more at ease in front of the cameras than former senator and secretary of state Hillary Clinton. Moreover, his constant controversial statements made it for entertainment, so that he got more media exposure than his opponent, which generated high revenues for television stations and the print media. As Moura and Corbellini (2019, 145) note,

> Researchers Jack Beckwith and Nick Sorscher analyzed about 22,000 texts published on the sites of some of the main newspapers in the USA during the campaign. According to their study . . . , Trump was cited in the titles of nearly 15,000 articles, more than double of Hillary mentions. . . .
>
> According to research from the Shorenstein Center on Media, Politics, and Public Policy at Harvard Kennedy School, the journalistic coverage of Trump in the eight largest U.S. newspapers and channels, in the primaries alone, yielded the equivalent of US$55 million in advertising.

In Brazil in 2018, presidential candidate Bolsonaro had had plenty of television time due to his constant guest appearances on shows over the years, but he did not participate in most televised debates. His stabbing during a campaign stop in the state of Minas Gerais on September 6, 2018, just a month before the first round, was the justification for his absence. However, the frequent updates on his medical condition gave him plenty of airtime in absentia.

The impact of television, however, pales in comparison with the strength of social media. The *Merriam-Webster Dictionary* traces the first use of that term to 2004 to mean "forms of electronic communication (such as Web sites) through which people create online communities to share information, ideas, personal messages, etc." Sociologically, Schneider (2014, 207) defines the term as

> a hybrid of social interaction and media. Interactions in this realm rely on user-generated content, a process that can occur in real time. Types of social media can include websites that host user-generated content, such as text, audio, or video and, of course, social networking.

Murthy (2012) differentiates between "social media" and "social networks." An example of the latter is Facebook, that is, a service through which persons can connect with each other and share information. In turn, "social media are mainly conceived of as a medium wherein 'ordinary' people in ordinary social networks (as opposed to professional journalists) can create user-generated 'news' (in a broadly defined sense)." The innovation of social media is that they allow anyone who is connected to a platform to create and disseminate information. An example of social media is Twitter, famous for limiting texts ("tweets") to 140 characters. Unlike Facebook posts, tweets are always public and may be disseminated by anyone. According to Murthy (1062), social media activity "is about self-reproduction," that is, it requires the constant generation of information about one's life to the point where it defines one's identity.

Social media production, consumption, and reproduction of information have been greatly facilitated by smartphones, due to their portability vis-à-vis other electronic devices such as computers and tablets. That type of cellular telephones, whose state-of-the-art technology connects us to information instantly, has become ubiquitous. In 2016, smartphones were present in the majority of U.S. households (76 percent), regardless of race/ethnicity and class, unlike computers and tablets, which were more common in higher income, White, and Asian American households (Ryan August 2018). In Brazil, 66 percent of individuals own cellular phones, most of whom use it over all other devices to have access to the internet (Moura and Corbellini 2019, 112). In both countries, smartphones are increasingly the preferred method for access to the news.

It is no wonder, then, that social media became the main conduit of information in the presidential elections of both countries. Donald Trump's preferred medium was Twiter. Moura and Corbellini (2019, 147) note that candidate Trump capitalized on his image of unconventionality and authenticity by appearing to be so accessible to the public with his constant tweets, which for them was "one of the greatest paradigmatic breaks on political communication in the world." Bolsonaro also utilized Twiter in addition to Facebook and WhatsApp, a platform easily accessible by smartphone which allows communication by text, audio, conventional telephone calls, and videocalls. After Bolsonaro was stabbed, Flávio Bolsonaro, his oldest son and also a politician, tweeted the information, to which tens of thousands reacted. So many hundreds of thousands commented on the stabbing that "Jair Bolsonaro" was the second most popular theme on Twitter worldwide (Moura and Corbellini 2019, 125–126).

Both Trump and Bolsonaro used social media to fabricate and disseminate damning "information" about their opponents. Trump, for instance, blamed Hillary Clinton for spreading the rumor that Obama's presidency was illegitimate because he was not U.S.-born, when it was Trump who had started it years before (Cheney September 16, 2016). Once Trump was in office, reporters cataloged over 13,000 instances of false information in less than one year (Kessler, Rizzo, and Kelly October 14, 2019). In turn, Bolsonaro accused Fernando Haddad, the presidential candidate from the Workers' Party, of having created and adopted a "gay kit" to turn school children into homosexuals during his tenure as mayor of the city of São Paulo (2013–2016). In fact, the Ministry of Education had elaborated pamphlets as part of a program to expose school children to diversity, including sexual diversity, but they were never distributed due to pressure from conservative sectors (Belloni 2017). Regardless, almost 85 percent of Bolsonaro voters and even over 10 percent of Haddad voters believed in the existence of a "gay kit" (Moura and Corbellini 2019, 130).

Yet, while candidates, both Trump and Bolsonaro would label any facts that went against them or tarnished their campaigns as "fake news," especially if broadcast by the professional media. Both have had extremely polemic relationships with them and have threatened to censor both individual journalists and publications. By producing their own "news" and allowing laypersons to spread them in their social networks, Trump and Bolsonaro increased their cache among those who distrusted politics and saw them as "saviors" and "unconventional" candidates.

Both campaigns were closely connected to the "alt-right," the abbreviation of "alternative right," a movement based in the United States which congregates White nationalists and the Far Right. According to Frédéric Louault (2019), a Belgian scholar, the "redefinition of the notion of truth" (post-truth), a tactic employed by the Far Right in the United States and Europe, was an important component in Bolsonaro's presidential campaign. Moreover, Messenberg (2017) found that all Brazilian right-wing digital influencers whose 2015 discourses she analyzed regard state programs such as quotas policies as antimeritocratic and promoters of racism.

The obvious similarity with Trump's slogan is not mere coincidence; Steve Bannon, Trump's campaign manager and subsequent member of President Trump's White House counsel who would fall in disgrace in 2017, denied taking part in Bolsonaro's presidential campaign. However, Bannon met with one of Bolsonaro's sons in New York City in 2018. Afterward, he declared to *BBC News Brasil* that he found the Brazilian candidate "'a leader,' 'brilliant,' 'sophisticated' and 'very similar' to Trump" (Senra October 26, 2018).

ORGANIZATION OF THE BOOK

Chapter 1 reviews the history of the United States from the standpoint of the social and racial inequality under which the country was born and with which it continues to struggle. I argue that, rather than an anomaly, Trump's presidential election fits into a history of struggles over nativism, xenophobia, and the right of non-Whites to belong to the nation.

Chapter 2 does the same for Brazil, the last country to abolish slavery in the Americas and with the largest contingent of people of African descent in the world. While the United States has relied on White supremacy to maintain its racial hierarchy, Brazil has strived to achieve Whiteness and thus eliminate (or at least abate) the insecurity that comes from a belief in the racial inferiority of non-Whites.

Chapter 3 starts with a biography of Donald Trump, including his life as a businessman, his foray into television, and his decision to run for president. It then focuses on Trump's campaign, which was characterized by a nativist rhetoric that appealed to a sizable portion of the electorate. He vowed to "make America great again" by adopting neoliberal economic policies and implicitly promising to turn the country back to a time when minorities and women had fewer rights, that is, when Whiteness reigned supreme, before the gains of the civil rights movement in the 1960s.

Chapter 4 analyzes the events leading up to Trump's victory, including the surprise of journalists and academics who had been confident that Hillary Clinton would win. I describe the characteristics of Trump voters and show the prominent role that racial resentment played on the election results. The chapter ends with an overview of President Trump's inauguration and cabinet formation.

Chapter 5 concerns Bolsonaro's biography, from his military career to his years as a congressman, up to his presidential campaign. It also considers the turbulent events that led to the impeachment of President Dilma Rousseff and signaled Brazil's turn to the Far Right, which created conditions for Bolsonaro to be a contender for the presidency.

Chapter 6 focuses on the Brazilian presidential elections of 2018. Unlike the United States, Brazilian presidential elections run for two turns, unless a candidate achieves over 50 percent of votes in the first turn. The chapter discusses the period between the two turns, between October and November of 2018, when Bolsonaro sealed his victory. It also goes over the characteristics of Bolsonaro voters, his inauguration, and the composition of his cabinet.

The conclusion draws comparisons between Trump and Bolsonaro, from their meeting in Washington, DC through the high turnover that characterized both tenures, and their other similarities. It also sums up my argument about the narrow view of nation that both presidents displayed and how it fits into the history of racial-ethnic exclusion in their respective countries.

Finally, the afterword concerns a phenomenon that affected the entire world and the ways Trump and Bolsonaro responded to it. In 2020, which marked the last year of President Trump's tenure, the world faced a pandemic the proportions of which had not been seen since a century earlier. President Trump and President Bolsonaro reacted to it in similar ways, which resulted in their countries' ranking first and second in the number of casualties. This book concludes with an analysis of the effects of the pandemic on both governments, including the polarization that both fomented over how to confront it and a comparison of Trump's and Bolsonaro's reactions to the pandemic.

NOTES

1. All translations of material published in Portuguese are by this author.

2. The acronym LGBTQIA+ is an umbrella term that stands for "lesbian, gay, bisexual trans[sexual/gender], queer, intersex, and asexual." In addition, the + sign leaves room for the inclusion of new categories that may emerge (Betts n.d.).

3. In 1940, a telephone was present in 36.9 percent of U.S. households; in 1950, the figure rose to 61.8 percent (Statista Research Department September 30, 2010).

Chapter 1

Whiteness and the Idea of Nation in the United States

The United States sees itself and is recognized the world over as a democracy and as "the land of the free." However, sociologists know that depiction is much too simplistic. In fact, even though the country had been founded in the late eighteenth century, it took until the second half of the twentieth century for all citizens to achieve full political representation. Women gained the right to vote in 1920, but have yet to receive equal pay to men. American Indians had their land taken from them, were forcibly put in reservations, and continue to have very limited access to education and other means of upward mobility. Up until the early twentieth century, only those regarded as White could become naturalized U.S. citizens. In the nineteenth century, the Chinese could migrate to the United States to work in gold mines and railroads, but were not allowed to establish roots here; the Chinese Exclusion Act (1882) finally barred their entry. Japanese immigrants were routinely harassed, as they were taken to be Chinese. During World War II (1939–1945), Japanese Americans were the only racial/ethnic group to be isolated in "internment camps" and to have their businesses confiscated. African Americans were enfranchised in the entire territory only by the Voting Rights Act of 1965. During slavery, enslaved people were not considered fully human, but beasts of burden. After the 1857 Dred Scott Supreme Court decision, a slave was legally worth three-fifths of a man. Despite Emancipation in 1865, former enslaved persons and their descendants enjoyed civil rights for a relatively short period, not only because they were terrorized by the explicitly racist Ku Klux Klan from 1865 on, but also because they were relegated to second-class status in 1896 with *Plessy v. Ferguson*, the Supreme Court decision that institutionalized legal racial segregation; "separate but equal" often meant isolated and unequal. In sum, if voting is a major mark of a democracy, for a

considerable time, only White men had all the rights that come with belonging to a democratic nation. As Lipsitz (2006, 99) summarized,

> "Whiteness" emerged as a relevant category in U.S. life and culture largely as
> a result of slavery and segregation, Native American policy and immigration
> restrictions, conquest and colonialism. Economics and politics relegated vari-
> ous racial groups to unequal access to property and citizenship, while cultural
> practices institutionalized racism in everyday life by uniting diverse European
> American subjects into an imagined community called into being through
> appeals to white supremacy.

"WE THE PEOPLE": WHITENESS AND THE FOUNDATION OF THE UNITED STATES

The independence of the North American colonies from British rule on
July 4, 1776 is celebrated as the triumph of the revolutionary forces over
the European colonizer, guided by the ideas of freedom and equality put
forth by the Enlightenment thinkers and realized 13 years before the French
Revolution. Participants in the revolutionary campaign (1775–1783) included
members of the American elite, that is, wealthy White landowners, such as
George Washington and Thomas Jefferson, who would be named "founding
fathers" of the new nation, though young, poor, and landless White men made
up the bulk of those who actually fought in the battlefields (Brooks December
26, 2017; Ferling 2010).

The men who plotted and led the American Revolution were all Anglo-
Saxon Protestants, descendants from the religious Puritans (who had settled
in Massachusetts in the first half of the seventeenth century), the aristocratic
Cavaliers (who had settled in Virginia from the mid- to late seventeenth centuries), and the religiously tolerant Quakers (who had settled in Pennsylvania in
the latter part of the seventeenth century and early eighteenth century). Much
less affluent were the Scotch Irish, who migrated to the colonies through
most of the eighteenth century and occupied the Appalachian Mountains;
they were the ones who would get involved in "frontier politics" in search of
land the following century (Kivisto 1995, 118–119). Over a relatively short
time, those different strands forged a British American culture that forms the
basis for majority-minority relations (Kivisto 1995, 117–120). Even though
in colonial times wealth and religion were the main criteria to establish social
status, Whiteness gained increased importance as the European settlers and
their descendants got in contact with the indigenous population and enslaved
Africans and managed to overpower them both politically and economically.

In sum, the dominant U.S. culture is White Anglo-Saxon Protestant, or "WASP" (Baltzell 1964).

The revolutionary troops were by no means all White, however. Some American Indian peoples, such as the Catawba of North and South Carolina, the Maliseet and the Passamaquoddy of Maine, the Delaware, and the Oneida and the Tuscarora of New York joined the campaign, as many of them had hoped the Americans would respect their rights to the land more than the British (Brooks November 17, 2017). In addition, people of African descent, both free and enslaved, served in the independence effort in various capacities, in hope that the abolition of slavery would follow (Foner 1976: 43); it is estimated that they amounted to ". . . some 5,000 blacks . . . , approximately 5 percent of the total number of men who served in the Continental Army" (Ferling 2010). Despite protests from the part of slave owners, who feared the war might lead to slave rebellions, slaves were indeed recruited both in the northern and southern colonies (Foner 1976). According to Dobyns (2007), "The Continentals, including George Washington's troops, had such a mixture of black and white soldiers that a French staff officer referred to them as 'speckled.' American combat troops were not integrated as they were in the 1770s and 1780s until the Korean War 170 years later."

Of course, the promise of manumission was not delivered. Not only did slavery persist after independence, but, after a series of state-level measures that excluded people of African descent from the military, Congress formally passed the resolution that restricted military service to "free able-bodied white male citizens" (Lanning 2000). In other words, the nascent country made it clear that its Negro population was good enough to die for it, but not to live in it as full-fledged citizens. Such idea would remain a driving force for nearly 200 years: even after the Civil War (1863–1865) rectified Emancipation, African Americans who served in World War I (1914–1918), World War II (1941–1945), the Korean War (1950–1953), and the Vietnam War (1965–1975)[1] confronted the same reality both in the troops and once they went back home and tried to resume their lives.

Approved on July 4, 1776 and signed on August 2 of the same year, the Declaration of Independence appeared to cover the rights of all who had contributed to the success of turning the colonies into a sovereign nation by using an inclusive language:

> We hold these truths to be self-evident, that all men are created equal, that they are endowed by their Creator with certain unalienable Rights, that among these are Life, Liberty and the pursuit of Happiness.—That to secure these rights, Governments are instituted among Men, deriving their just powers from the consent of the governed. . . . (Declaration of Independence: A Transcript)

By the practice of the eighteenth century, "men" meant both sexes. However, women did not enjoy the same rights as men then; prohibited from voting and from owning property,[2] they were for all intents and purposes inferior to men.[3] In fact, all 56 signatures of the representatives of the 13 colonies that declared independence from the British crown were of men. All were also wealthy and well-educated, thus bringing into question the assertion that "all men are created equal." Finally, although no mention to race or skin color is made, all were White. The only reference to any categorization coming close to race or ethnicity is the passage about the use of the British rulers of Native Americans to destabilize the American revolutionaries: "He has excited domestic insurrections amongst us, and has endeavoured to bring on the inhabitants of our frontiers, the merciless Indian Savages, whose known rule of warfare, is an undistinguished destruction of all ages, sexes and conditions" (Declaration of Independence: A Transcript). In other words, the very first document of the United States regards the original dwellers of the North American continent as uncivilized and cruel usurpers of the land, an interpretation that would justify the later expansion of the territory "from sea to shining sea" by expulsion, warfare, and genocide well into the twentieth century. The image of American Indians as "merciless savages" would be imprinted on the national mind by Hollywood film depictions that showed "frontier families" as victims who needed to be protected by (White) cowboys from screaming Indians; never mind that so many of the cowboys were African American men who had ventured into the far west away from the blatant racial oppression of the American south (Durham and Jones 1965).[4] The characterization of American Indians as "savages" excluded them from "all men" to whom, according to the same document, God had bestowed "unalienable rights"; "all men," then, is a shortcut to "only White men."

The other group excluded from "all men" were people of African descent, most of whom were enslaved at that time. As has been well-documented, slavery was the law of the land; many of the signers of the Declaration of Independence, such as George Washington and Thomas Jefferson, were slave owners who regarded slaves as "chattel," that is, not fully human. George Washington vetoed Blacks from enlisting in the Revolutionary War until 1775 (Schenawolf 2013). Although slaves were finally recruited to fight for the revolutionary forces, there was no intention to extend "unalienable rights" to them. Again, the founding of the nation took Whiteness for granted and excluded those who did not fit into that category. Centuries later, Gunnar Myrdal would call the discrepancy between the belief in freedom and the practice of racial oppression "an American dilemma" (1944). That discrepancy has been so glaring for most U.S. history that it is no wonder that Frederick Douglass, the former slave who excelled as an abolitionist, orator, writer, and ambassador, reflected in 1852 on the meaninglessness of the Fourth of July celebration for slaves:

> What, to the American slave, is your Fourth of July? I answer: a day that reveals to him, more than all other days in the years, the gross injustice and cruelty to which he is the constant victim. To him, your celebration is a sham; your boasted liberty, an unholy license; your national greatness, swelling vanity; your sounds of rejoicing are empty and heartless; your denunciation of tyrants, brass fronted impudence; your shouts of liberty and equality, hollow mockery; your prayers and hymns, your sermons and thanksgivings, with all your religious parade, and solemnity, are, to him, mere bombast, fraud, deception, impiety, and hypocrisy—a thin veil to cover up crimes which would disgrace a nation of savages. There is not a nation on the earth guilty of practices, more shocking and bloody, than are the people of these United States, at this very hour. (1997, 127)

Ratified in Philadelphia in 1787, the Constitution of the United States kept the same tone of the Declaration of Independence in regard to its narrow definition of citizenship: "We the People" is equally exclusionary. For starters, the Constitution put an end to the debate over slavery that had characterized its convention. According to Feagin (2019, 2), on the one hand, "The northern states were moving away from chattel slavery as a part of their local economies, and some were seeing a growing abolitionist sentiment"; Benjamin Franklin, for example, one of the eight signers from Pennsylvania, was "the president of the Pennsylvania Society for Promoting the Abolition of Slavery" at the time (ConstitutionFacts.com). On the other hand,

> a great many northern white merchants, shippers, and consumers still depended on products produced by enslaved workers on southern and border-state plantations, and many merchants sold manufactured goods to the plantations. Northern shipbuilders and bankers were also central to the U.S. slavery economy. (Feagin 2019, 2)

Eventually, as we know, slavery prevailed in the new nation. The delegates reached the compromise that slaves were private property worth three-fifths of a (White) man, at once divested of citizen rights and counted as such "for the purpose of white representation" (Feagin 2019, 3). Feagin concludes that, by maintaining the slavery system, the Constitution established "a racist foundation" for the nascent nation, the repercussions of which are felt to this day:

> While most Americans have thought of this document and the sociopolitical structure it created as keeping the new nation together, in fact this structure was

created to maintain racial separation and oppression at the time and for the fore-seeable future. The elite framers reinforced and legitimated a system of racial oppression that they thought would ensure that whites, especially men of means, would rule for centuries. (Feagin 2019, 6)

Feagin (2019, 8) calls the structure built on that exclusionary foundation "systemic racism," a perspective he formulated based on the works of African American thinkers from Frederick Douglass, Ida B. Wells-Barnett, and W. E. B. Du Bois to Oliver Cox and Kwame Ture: an enduring, society-wide system that maintains White privilege through practice and ideas. In that sense, systemic racism promotes White supremacy, an idea that, Feagin notes, was first developed by Du Bois in "The Souls of White Folk" (1920).

As I have mentioned, the establishment of the United States as a nation centered on White supremacy. In fact, as early as 1790, with the Naturalization Act, Congress determined that U.S. citizenship would be restricted to "free white persons." According to Glenn (2000), the U.S. Constitution had not stipulated the parameters of citizenship:

It left to each state the authority to determine qualifications for citizenship and citizens' rights, e.g., suffrage requirements, qualifications for sitting on juries, etc. Individuals were, first, citizens of the states in which they resided and only secondarily, through their citizenship in the state, citizens of the United States. The concept of national citizenship was, therefore, quite weak.

If that was so, it is particularly curious that the one overarching criterion for naturalization was Whiteness. That the establishment of the new nation would, on the one hand, define citizenship so loosely and, on the other, center it around Whiteness points to the long-lasting power of White supremacy in the development of the idea of nation in the United States.

As I show here, throughout the history of this country, from denying non-Whites full social representation, be it through disenfranchisement or through lynching, White supremacy has imposed its existence. I would conclude that, as much as the United States is heralded as a democratic nation based on modern ideals, its narrow use of the term "people" is quite similar to the view of so many so-called primitive societies, such as the Inuit, whose names mean "the people" (Goldi Productions 2007).

The same men who founded the independent United States sought to justify the preservation of their class and racial interests by establishing racial inequality as "natural." In the second part of the PBS documentary *Race: The Power of an Illusion* (California Newsreel 2003), historian Paul Finkelman credits Thomas Jefferson, the wealthy Virginian slave owner, with writing the first treatise on race in North America, part of his *Notes on the State of Virginia* (1785). Despite his lack of any reliable empirical evidence, he asserted, "I advance it, as a suspicion only, that the blacks, whether originally a distinct race, or made distinct by time and circumstances, are inferior to the whites in the endowments both of body and mind." Ira Berlin, also a historian, identifies Jefferson's argument as fundamental in the formation of the new nation:

> The moment when we become a nation is critical for our understanding of both American nationality and race. We accept the notion that all men are created equal, but then, perhaps, some of those people who are enslaved are not quite men. That is, we'll keep our ideas of American nationality, but we'll write certain people out of the human family.

That Jefferson maintained that public argument while fathering three children with the slave Sally Hemmings, his late wife's half sister, but never recognized them as such further attests to his dismissal of people of African descent as full-fledged human beings.

Jefferson's view of American Indians was more ambiguous. Although he had referred to them as "merciless Indian savages" in the Declaration of Independence, in *Notes* he approaches them to his own image of "civilized beings": "Their vivacity and activity of mind is equal to ours in the same situation. We shall probably find that they are formed in mind as well as in body, on the same module with the 'Homo sapiens Europaeus'" (California Newsreel 2003). In retrospect, historians suggest that Jefferson's more respectful image of the native population was due to the influence of Enlightenment ideas of the "noble savage" and also the fact that "he had little contact with them. Most Virginia tribes had been pushed west or killed off by war and European diseases" (California Newsreel 2003). However, during his presidency (1801–1809), Jefferson promoted the destruction of native cultures by ordering the forced relocation of the American Indians farther and farther west (Jewett 2019). That would set the precedent for their massive expulsion years later, in what came to be known as the "Trail of Tears" (1836–1839).

"GO WEST, YOUNG MAN!": WHITENESS AS JUSTIFICATION FOR NATIONAL EXPANSION

The marriage of Whiteness, civilization, and God-given rights would emerge in the nineteenth century as the ideology of "Manifest Destiny," that is, the idea that God had intended for Whites to claim the entire North American territory because it was a waste to leave it in the hands of inferior peoples such as American Indians (Knowles and Prewitt 2008, 19). By declaring independence from Great Britain, the new nation had "inherited" the right to rule over the territory that had once belonged to the colonizers. According to that logic, Indians retained only "the right of occupancy," but the U.S. government could nullify that as well. And nullify it, it did. In his inauguration speech during his first tenure as president of the United States, Thomas Jefferson declared, "A rising nation spread over a wide and fruitful land traversing all the seas with the rich productions of their industry advancing rapidly to destinies beyond the reach of mortal eye" (California Newsreel 2003). He partially accomplished that with the Louisiana Purchase from France in 1803, thus increasing the area of the country from 864,746 square miles to 1,681,828 square miles (U.S. History.com). In order for that plan to work, the Indians would have to be "civilized," that is, assimilate into White culture, and relinquish their territory, either willingly or by force. The Supreme Court decision in *Johnson v. Mcintosh* on February 28, 1823, in the words of Chief Justice Marshall, well illustrates this point:

> It has never been doubted that either the United States, or the several states, had a clear title to all the lands within the boundary lines described in the treaty, subject only to the Indian right of occupancy, and that the exclusive power to extinguish that right, was vested in that government which might constitutionally exercise it. . . .
>
> But the tribes of Indians inhabiting this country were fierce savages, whose occupation was war, and whose subsistence was drawn chiefly from the forest. To leave them in possession of their country, was to leave the country a wilderness; to govern them as a distinct people, was impossible, because they were as brave and as high spirited as they were fierce, and were ready to repel by arms every attempt on their independence. (in Aguirre, Jr. and Baker 2008, 11; 12)

Many U.S. presidents have espoused such a restrictive view. For instance, during his first presidential campaign in 1828, Andrew Jackson (1829–1837) promised poor Whites that he would secure them landownership, the main source of wealth at the time. That populist agenda was carried out at the expense of American Indians: once Jackson was elected, he encouraged landless Whites to take land from American Indians, especially from the Cherokee, who, according to historian Scott Malcomson, had become "more and more prosperous along more or less classic, white southern lines" (*Race: The Power of an Illusion, Episode 2*). While they had occupied "parts of what is now Kentucky, Virginia, Tennessee, the Carolinas, Alabama, and Georgia," they ended up adhering to the "Civilization plan" by signing treaties with the U.S. government, becoming farmers, and adopting Christianity; the Cherokee, together with the Seminole of present-day Florida; the Choctaw of the southeast; the Chiokasaw of Mississippi, Alabama, and Tennessee; and the Creek, also from Alabama and Georgia, became the "Five Civilized Tribes" (History.com editors September 30, 2019). As Richard Allen, a Cherokee policy analyst, put it, "The civilization policy was actually designed to assimilate us into America. It was ultimately to make us farmers . . . , to live like the colonists lived. The civilization policy was to make us brown white men" (*Race: The Power of an Illusion, Episode 2*). However, during Andrew Jackson's tenure, and after the Gold Rush of 1829 in their land (Pauls n.d.), the Cherokee saw their treaties nullified under the Indian Removal Act of 1830, which stipulated that Indians in the southeastern states be transferred to "Indian Territory" (later Oklahoma). Jackson's speech left no doubt about his desire for the extermination of Indians as an inferior "race":

> They have neither the intelligence, the industry, the moral habits, nor the desire of improvement which are essential to any change in their condition. Established in the midst of another and superior race, they must necessarily yield to the force of circumstances and ere long disappear. (*Race: The Power of an Illusion, Episode 2*)

According to Theda Purdue, a historian,

> Nationalism begins to be, in many respects, equated to race. People began to think that nations should be composed of people who had inherent qualities in common: they thought the same way; they believed the same things; they spoke the same language; *they looked the same*. (*Race: The Power of an Illusion, Episode 2*; emphasis added)

Having converted to Christianity and learned English was not enough for the members of the "civilized tribes" to be thought of as belonging to the United States. Ultimately, their "transfer" was in practice an expulsion and a genocide:

> In the winter of 1831, under threat of invasion by the U.S. Army, the Choctaw became the first nation to be expelled from its land altogether. They made the journey to Indian Territory on foot (some "bound in chains and marched double file," one historian writes) and without any food, supplies or other help from the government. Thousands of people died along the way. It was, one Choctaw leader told an Alabama newspaper, a "trail of tears and death." (History.com editors September 30, 2019)

It seems obvious, then, that the "civilization plan" was nothing more than a ruse to weaken Indian resolve and, thus, facilitate the confiscation of their lands. The expulsion continued in the following year, this time targeting "the Sauk, Fox and other native nations," who lost their lands in the Black Hawk War in Illinois and Wisconsin (History.com editors September 30, 2019). Curiously, in that same year the Supreme Court upheld the natives' right to keep their lands in *Worcester v. Georgia*, but that right was not enforced (History.com editors September 30, 2019).

The Trail of Tears officially started in the penultimate year of Andrew Jackson's tenure as president, in 1836. During the forced relocation of 15,000 Creek to Indian Territory, over a third perished (History.com editors September 30, 2019). In 1837, the Chickasaw were pushed out of Tennessee. In 1838, already in Martin Van Buren's presidency (1837–1841), Congress ignored the Cherokee's pleas for respect for the treaties, thus sending them at gunpoint to the Trail, selling them as slaves, and placing them in camps. Between exhaustion, disease, and starvation, it is estimated that 8,000 Cherokee died during the yearslong 1,000-mile trek (Snipp 2016).

With the territory expanded well into the west after the Louisiana Purchase and the Trail of Tears, the U.S. government turned its attention to the far west. According to Kivisto (1995, 171), "As early as the Louisiana Purchase of 1803 it became increasingly clear to [Mexican] government officials that the United States, and not the European powers, posed the greatest threat to the region." After having failed to convince Mexico to sell part of its territory to the United States, President James K. Polk (1845–1849) engaged the country in the Mexican American War between 1846 and 1848. By then, the supposed racial inferiority of non-Whites was justified by anthropometrics and pseudoscientific theories. In other words, conquering the North American territory by force was no longer only "God's will," but also a "scientific" necessity: "Supporters of the war argued that Mexicans were an inferior, mongrel race. A popular guide for homesteaders described them as 'mere Indian,' barbarous 'savages' who 'intend to hold this delightful region against the civilized world'" (*Race: The Power of an Illusion, Episode 2*). That led the Mexican president, General Porfirio Díaz, to utter, "Poor Mexico! So far from God, so close to the United States." Over 13,000 Americans perished in the war, mostly due to disease; nearly twice as many Mexicans died (Andrews 2018). Mexico capitulated by signing the Treaty of Guadalupe Hidalgo, through which the United States annexed one-third of Mexican territory at the price of US$15 million and revoked the rights of the existing population. In other words, even though Mexicans lived in the U.S. territory from then on, they were not treated as U.S. citizens and were subjected to legal segregation. In 1848, gold was discovered in San Francisco, California, a former Mexican territory; previous owners of the land no longer had any rights to it.[5] Throughout the nineteenth century and well into the twentieth century, Mexican Americans would continue to be treated as second-class citizens. As a matter of fact, seven years before the landmark 1954 Supreme Court decision in *Brown v. Board of Education*, which overruled legal racial segregation in schools, Mexican Americans had successfully challenged that in *Mendez v. Westminster* (Strum 2010). In sum, ideas and policies that favored Whiteness guided the formation and expansion of the U.S. territory and solidified it as a nation.

Territorial expansion and the Gold Rush introduced yet another group of non-Whites to the polity. The construction of cross-country railroads and mining in San Francisco opened up job opportunities in the United States; flooding and famine encouraged Chinese men to migrate to the United States in search of those jobs. While their numbers grew with each decade until 1890, most Chinese "came as sojourners intent on making money in the gold fields and then returning to China" (Kivisto 1995, 103). At the same time, the U.S. government had no intention of allowing them to become naturalized citizens. All the cities with a sizable Chinese contingent, such as San Francisco in California, and Tacoma and Seattle in Washington, passed laws that curtailed their economic prosperity. The Chinese were made into a "bachelor society," forbidden from marrying both Chinese and American women, as a way of preventing their setting roots in the new country. Evidently, if the Chinese could not become U.S. citizens, they had no civil rights. Nativist animosity against them culminated with the Chinese Exclusion Act of 1882:

> The nation's first restrictive immigration legislation directed at particular nationality or ethnic groups. Provisions called for barring additional Chinese from entering the country for ten years and forbade the naturalization of those already in the country. . . . This prohibition was subsequently extended every ten years until 1904, when an unlimited extension was instituted. This situation did not change until World War II. (Kivisto 1995, 104)

There is no doubt that the basis for such prohibition was racist. The White majority in the United States regarded the Chinese as racially inferior, good for labor, but not for assimilating into the larger population, relying as they were on nineteenth-century racial "theories." In 1905, the Asiatic Exclusion League was created with the specific purpose of preserving the White race (Polenberg 1991). It is also evident that most White Americans could not and would not differentiate among Asian nationalities. Thus, when the Japanese began to arrive in the United States in large numbers in 1880, they too were subjected to prejudice and discrimination and devoid of rights, as they were taken to be Chinese. One of the characteristics of racism is the reliance on stereotypes. Notwithstanding the fact that the Japanese immigrants had passed through a meticulous process at home that would allow only exemplary citizens to leave their home country, they fell prey to anti-Chinese attacks once in the United States.[6] That led to the "Gentlemen's Agreement" (1907): Japan would cut down the number of emigrants and the United States would guarantee better treatment to the Japanese citizens already in its territory. The following year, Japan began to allow emigration to Brazil instead. With the closing of the U.S. borders in 1924, Japanese emigration to the United States officially came to an end (Kivisto 1995); those who had already been here and wished to become naturalized U.S. citizens were denied that specifically because they were not White. As Higginbotham and Andersen (2016, 35) recount,

> In the early twentieth century, although most were literate, Japanese immigrants could not become citizens and vote. Consider the case of Takao Ozawa, originally from Japan. Ozawa arrived in California in 1894, graduated from high school, and attended the University of California, Berkeley. After that, he worked for an American company, living with his family in the U.S. territory of Honolulu. Because he was not legally classified as White, he could not become a U.S. citizen, though he very much wanted to and filed for citizenship in 1914. Ozawa argued that he was a "true American," a person of good character who neither drank, smoked, nor gambled. His family went to an American church; his children went to American schools; he spoke only English at home and raised his children as Americans. In 1922, the U.S. Supreme Court denied his eligibility for citizenship based on the claim that he was not "Caucasian."

Anti-Asian prejudice and discrimination would be extended to Filipinos and Indians as well. When the United States won the war over Spain in 1898, it made its own the Philippines and Guam, in the Pacific Ocean (in addition to Puerto Rico, in the Caribbean Sea), all former Spanish colonies. With that, Filipinos and Puerto Ricans were allowed to enter the United States, but they came in with the status of non-White, as "brown" and "colored" in a country that more and more relied on racial "theories" to justify racial inequality. According to historian Robert Rydell, "If you look at the way Filipinos are represented, they are represented not as Filipinos. Some Filipinos are portrayed as being akin to African Americans. Some are portrayed as being akin to Native Americans" (*Race: The Power of an Illusion, Episode 2*). In 1929 to 1930, anti-Filipino riots erupted on the West Coast. That fueled the passage of the Tydings-McDuffie Act of 1934, which granted independence to the Philippines and whose real purpose was to limit their immigration quota to 50 persons per year (Ngai 2004). Finally, in 1917, the United States denied entry to Asian Indians (Lipsitz 2006, 2). Four years later, Bhagat Singh Thind took his naturalization petition to the Supreme Court. He argued that was eligible under current racial theories, which categorized Indians as Caucasian, and the Court's recent conclusion that "Caucasian" meant "White." However, the

Court denied his appeal, by turning against those same theories: "The ruling contended that Asian Indians were not what was commonly understood to be white and as such scientists had erred in including such a wide range within the Caucasian group" (Halley, Eshleman, and Vijaya 2011, 170).

THE "PECULIAR INSTITUTION": SLAVERY, EMANCIPATION, AND WHITENESS

The United States had inherited the slavery system from Great Britain and continued to rely on it as an economic system well into its period of territorial expansion. In comparison with Brazil, however, slavery in the United States was restricted to a smaller area, mainly the south. The first antislavery society was founded in Pennsylvania in 1775; the slave trade was abolished in 1808; the abolitionist movement expanded both in the United States and abroad; by the mid-nineteenth century, not only had all northern states abolished slavery, but they also depended on manufacture and industrialization. As the United States expanded westward, the question as to whether slavery would extend to the new territory took on national proportions, as did the tension between the two economic systems.

The future of slavery was a major issue in the 1860 presidential elections. They were won by Abraham Lincoln (1809–1865), who

> ran . . . on the Republican platform under which slavery would remain legal in the states where it was already established but would limit its expansion. He was not an abolitionist as many in his party were and was considered a moderate within his own party. (Abraham Lincoln Historical Society)

In other words, Lincoln advocated for the curbing of slavery while maintaining it where it already existed. The southern states did not accept that compromise, severed ties with the federal government (the Union), and organized themselves as the Confederacy. According to Feagin (2019, 7),

> Lincoln suggested a constitutional amendment making slavery permanent in the existing southern states if that would prevent a civil war. Such a projected pro-slavery amendment was supported by many of his fellow Republicans and was actually approved by the U.S. Congress in early 1861.

Instead, the Civil War began when the Confederacy army "captured Fort Sumter in 1861, and rose its own Confederate flag" (Reference.com).

As the war waged on, Lincoln issued an executive order in 1863, the Emancipation Proclamation, "which declared that slaves in all areas under the control of the confederacy were free" (Kivisto 1995, 223). However, not only did the war continue, but also no slave was freed by the decree. The bloody conflict would end with the victory of the Union only two years later, when slavery would be finally abolished by the Thirteenth Amendment. In the same year, Lincoln would be assassinated by a disgruntled southerner, John Wilkes Booth, and be recognized as a martyr.

The Civil War is remembered as the conflict that almost tore the country apart over the issue of freedom for all regardless of race or color and Lincoln is revered as "the Great Emancipator." However, Emancipation did not grant former slaves full civil rights; notwithstanding the Civil Rights Act of 1866, that is, the Fourteenth Amendment, which made Negroes U.S. citizens, and the Fifteenth Amendment (1869), which granted them suffrage, their civil liberties were consistently denied. As for Lincoln, he was not fully in favor of equality for Negroes. Enamored by the ideas of Louis Agassiz, a European scientist who became famous in the United States for defending the thesis of the racial superiority of Whites in the 1850s (*Race: The Power of an Illusion, Episode 2*), Lincoln had espoused very similar views in a speech during his campaign for the senate in 1858: he was against interracial marriage and suffrage for Negroes. He ended his speech, however, claiming that he still believed in the granting of some rights for them: "I say upon this occasion I do not perceive that because the white man is to have the superior position the negro should be denied every thing" (Abraham Lincoln Historical Society). Even though Lincoln signed the Emancipation Proclamation already as president, he continued to rely on Agassiz's racist ideas about what to do with the former slaves. In fact, "Agassiz advised, 'Beware of how we give to the blacks rights by virtue of which they may endanger the progress of whites. They are incapable of living on a footing of social equality'" (*Race: The Power of an Illusion, Episode 2*). As a result, until 1864, Lincoln seriously considered sending former slaves to live in Africa and Central America, a "colonization" plan that he ended up abandoning: "This plan never worked as freedmen did not consider Africa their homeland, they were born and raised in America" (Abraham Lincoln Historical Society). Given that the transatlantic slave trade had ended over half a century earlier, it is safe to assume that the majority of slaves freed in the 1860s had indeed been born and raised in the United States. However, the president of the nation disregarded that.

In 1857, a few years before the beginning of the Civil War, the Supreme Court had upheld the constitutional view that slaves were worth three-fifths of a man in *Dred Scott v Sandford*. The Emancipation and subsequent Reconstruction period (1865–1877) raised hope that Negroes would finally be treated as full-fledged human beings, as they had the right to vote, to private property, and to an education. In 1869, with Reconstruction in full swing, Congress approved the Fifteenth Amendment to the Constitution, which guaranteed to Negroes the right to vote. However, because the states had control over qualifications, they were left alone to interpret the law and discriminate against eligible Negro voters. The Amendment, imposed on the Confederate states as the condition for their readmission to the Union, was also potentially significant in the north, where the Negro constituency could decide close elections (Elliott 1974, 62–63). Judging from its provisions, however, it was apparent that Negro suffrage would be hard to enforce in the south. Without barriers to literacy tests or the issue of property, the Amendment was so ambiguous that, rather than securing enfranchisement, it "merely stipulated that states could not invoke race as a ground for disfranchising people otherwise eligible to vote" (Lawson 1976, 23).

Soon terror in the south prevented Negroes from voting, in large part due to the Ku Klux Klan, an organization funded in 1865 by working-class Whites who feared competition for jobs from the recently emancipated Negroes. Those who testified against voting violations were routinely murdered, while White witnesses and jurors hardly ever convicted accused state officials. By 1877, responding to national pressure, the Republican Party withdrew interest in securing the rights of southern Negroes. Though some Negroes were able to vote in the following decade, their numbers were sharply reduced in the 1890s, when several southern states rewrote their constitutions so as to disenfranchise them (Elliott 1974, 65–68; Lawson 1976, 6–110). White supremacy was so effective that, until the early years of the twentieth century, no claims for the enforcement of Negro suffrage emerged. For instance, Booker T. Washington, a former slave, who founded the Tuskegee Institute and was a noted leader at the time, encouraged Negroes to focus on vocational training and economic improvement rather than on politics (Washington 1901). That would be the basis for a long debate with W. E. B. Du Bois, who led a group of northern Negro professionals in 1903 who argued that "voting is necessary to modern manhood." Two years later, Du Bois was part of an interracial group who organized the Niagara Movement to push for civil rights, out of which the National Association for the Advancement of Colored People (NAACP) was founded; Negro suffrage was prominent on their list (Lawson 1976, 16).

In sum, suffrage is a right only granted to the citizens of a country; therefore, the denial of suffrage on the basis of race effectively strips people of their citizenship. Negro disenfranchisement was part of a plan to return the former slaves and their descendants to the subordinate status they had occupied prior to the Civil War. Such a system of structured inequality preserved a social order in which a White agrarian elite dominated the economy and politics. In theory, if Negroes were allowed to vote, they could try to dismantle the system by voting for candidates who opposed White supremacy. Although northern Negroes had the right to vote and did exercise it, their precarious status nationwide was made clear by the end of the century. In *Plessy v. Ferguson* (1896), the Supreme Court established legal discrimination on the basis of race. Known as the "separate but equal doctrine," it actually made White supremacy the law of the land by denying Negroes basic civil rights such as the freedom to come and go as they pleased, to live wherever they wanted, to marry across racial lines, and to vote. The decision defined the races as a dichotomy by the criterion of "hypodescent," or the primacy of the so-called "inferior" race in the tracing of one's ancestry. One was either "White" or "not White," thus eliminating the gradation generated by racial mixing that had been in vogue for centuries. Also called "the one-drop rule," the Supreme Court decision established Whiteness as the supposed absence of Negro "blood." In other words, the concern was to preserve "White purity." Such arbitrary definition led to "passing," that is, the practice of light-skinned persons who lived life as White even though they knew that at least one of their ancestors was not.[7]

By federal decree, Negroes continued to be denied full access to the polity at the dawn of the twentieth century. In effect, by maintaining a racial dichotomy and rendering non-Whites inferior, the practice of White supremacy continued to exclude from the idea of nation not only Negroes, but, as we have seen, indigenous Americans, Asians, and, as I show in the next section, even certain Europeans.

THE GREAT IMMIGRATION: WHEN EUROPEANS WERE NOT WHITE

The Chinese and Japanese immigrants who arrived in the far west in the nineteenth century were part of the Great Immigration, a movement that brought about 24 million persons to the United States between 1880 and 1924. Most of the immigrants went to cities in the northeast, such as New York, Newark, Pittsburg, and Philadelphia, and in the Midwest, such as Chicago, Detroit, Milwaukee, and Cleveland, attracted by the abundant job opportunities in factories. Had society been interested in the economic integration of Negroes, it would have promoted their move northward and away from the sharecropping system of the south, and it would also have hired northern Negroes. Instead, the majority of factory jobs went to the European immigrants; at most, Negroes were employed as strikebreakers, thus creating animosity between them and the European newcomers (Cox 1948).

While immigration has been common since colonial times, what sets the Great Immigration apart from the other waves were the origins of the newcomers: if before the majority of immigrants had been northern and western Europeans, most of the newcomers came from southern and eastern

Europe. Of the eastern Europeans, 2.5 million were Jewish, primarily from the Russian Empire, from where they were fleeing to escape state-sponsored pogroms. As a result, the U.S. Jewish population, which comprised 300,000 in 1800, grew by 1,300 percent (Belth 1979, 26–28; Feingold 1981, 120).

To appreciate the impact of that migratory wave, the U.S. population in 1880 was 50 million; by 1920, it was over 105 million (U.S. Census Bureau 1921). With the ongoing flow of new immigrants, nativists feared economic competition and the defilement of the country by the newcomers (Higham 1971, 76). Mixing exacerbated nationalism with populist rhetoric, they cried for restrictions on immigration. Their cries found respite in the so-called racial theories so popular at the time, and also in the eugenics movement, according to which the newcomers belonged to several "inferior" "races" which displayed inherent personality traits that resulted in a propensity for lives of poverty and crime, both of which would be too onerous to society. The eugenics movement gained strength and momentum after Mendel developed a theory of genetics. Though Mendel's research concerned plants, eugenists applied it to human beings to justify their beliefs in the superiority of Whites over all others. According to legal scholar Silver (2008, 340–341),

> Building upon Galton and Mendel's works, eugenists studied the inheritance of social behaviors, intelligence, and personality and "carried out elaborate research programs to determine the type of inheritance these traits exhibited." . . . Eugenics proponents "develop[ed] a taxonomy of human traits," categorizing some people as "normal" and "healthy" and others as "abnormal" and "unhealthy." Harry Laughlin, a leading American eugenist, defined "socially inadequate" people to include the "feebleminded," the "inebriated or the drug addicted," the blind, deaf, or deformed, the "dependents" (i.e., orphans), and the homeless. The "accepted view" was that these groups "were reproducing more quickly than normal people, thus posing a significant threat to society." There was also a racial and ethnic component to the "science" of the eugenics movement.

The main differences between this way of thinking and earlier ones were in its definition of Whiteness and the association of Whiteness with health and high moral character that could be purportedly backed up by science. In fact, the basis of the nativist and eugenics movements was the conviction that White was the superior race and that it was "the white man's burden" to keep the country under White control. Although Europe is identified as a "White" continent, at the turn of the twentieth century the label "White" was restricted to northern Europeans, for example, British, Germans, French, and Scandinavians. Southern Europeans, such as Greeks, Italians, and Spanish, and eastern Europeans, such as Polish and Jews, were excluded from Whites.

According to Barret and Roediger (2012, 41), evidence that southern and eastern European immigrants were not considered White was the use of "guinea," which was a term for "African slaves, particularly those from the continent's northwest coast, and their descendants," to refer to "Sicilians and Italians, . . . Greeks, Jews, Portuguese, Puerto Ricans, and perhaps any new immigrant." There are also examples of Italians who were lynched in Louisiana in 1891 and of Greeks who were called "niggers." Barret and Roediger (2012, 41, 42) add that, "As late as 1937, John Dollard wrote repeatedly of the immigrant working class as 'our temporary Negroes.'" Another term was "not-yet-white ethnics," coined by John Bukowczyk, a historian. The association of "not White" with new immigrants was so strong that, for foreigners, to be "American" meant to be "White" (Barret and Roediger 2012, 40).

Yet, not all northern Europeans fitted the White label: the Irish, who had a history of subordination by the British, were also excluded from the "superior" group. Although no longer equated with Blacks as they had been in colonial times, the Irish who started coming in the 1840s to flee the potato famine were not considered White either (Halley, Eshleman, and Vijaya 2011, 67–74). Unlike the Irish who had immigrated during colonial times, the more recent immigrants were Catholic, which excluded them from WASPs, but were also subjected to harsh working and living conditions. Former peasants, they took on unskilled labor that kept most in poverty, victimized by alcoholism, and prone to criminal activity. "They became," states Kivisto (1995, 128), "America's first truly impoverished ghetto dwellers." As a result, they were stereotyped as a social problem and targeted as responsible for the potential demise of mainstream society if not contained. In fact, the practice of social work started as a movement spearheaded by well-to-do women from the large industrializing cities to try to make the Irish assimilate.

To add insult to injury, the purported racial inferiority of the new immigrants was associated with mental defectiveness. As Kivisto (1995, 39) notes,

> During the peak of mass immigration from eastern Europe in the early part of the [20th] century, race theory was employed to discredit the new arrivals. As Madison Grant's diatribe against these newcomers, *The Passing of the Great Race* (1916) illustrates, this mode of thinking was extremely pliable. Where predecessors might have viewed all Europeans as members of the same race, Grant provides a new classificatory schema that delineates the superior races (the Nordic peoples from western Europe) from the inferior, which he identifies as originating from the "Mediterranean basin and the Balkans." Here, racial theory was used in the interest of the immigration restriction movement. As Grant . . . argued, "Our jails, insane asylums, and almshouses are filled with this

human flotsam and the whole tone of American life, social, moral, and political, has been lowered and vulgarized by them."

The arbitrariness of such classification points to the power of WASPs to determine who belonged in the country and were entitled to rights. It is ironic that though European and U.S. scholars commonly attribute the "birth" of "Western civilization" to ancient Greece and Rome, the U.S. government would categorize modern Greeks and Italians as "inferior."

Between 1880 and 1924, several laws were passed which excluded from entry anarchists, paupers, "mental defectives," and epileptics, among others. The "immigrant question" led to the formation of the Dillingham Commission, a team of senators, congressmen, and experts chosen by President Theodore Roosevelt (1901–1909). In 1917, the commission issued a 42-volume report which recommended stricter immigration laws to prevent the "unfit" to enter the United States. That came to fruition with the adoption of a literacy test for immigrants and the restrictive immigration laws of 1921 and 1924, when the U.S. borders were officially closed for over 40 years (Belth 1979, 31–35; Steinberg 1981, 78; 101). The 1929 Act stipulated national quotas, the bulk of which went to northern Europeans.

To be sure, the impact of the Great Immigration was also felt in academia. The first department of sociology in the country was purportedly founded at the University of Chicago in 1896 in an attempt to understand the effects of the several immigrant cultures on mainstream culture. In 1921, Robert Park, one the founders of the "Chicago School of Sociology," and Herbert Miller published *Old World Traits Transplanted*, a treatise commissioned by the Americanization studies of the Carnegie Corporation, in which they considered which groups would become "Americanized" first; their premise was that assimilation was "inevitable and desirable." They concluded that Jews, although not Protestant, would be assimilated first because not only were they willing and able to learn English, their work ethic and education values were similar to U.S. values. To wit, consider the following praise Park and Miller (235–236) bestowed on Jews:

Other immigrant groups are usually defective in leadership and creative individuals; few intellectuals come, and those who do come are usually only intelligent enough to exploit the simpler members of their own groups, not to compete with intellectual Americans. Consequently it is in general true that the immigrant leader is able and willing to organize his people just sufficiently for his own good, but not sufficiently for their good.

The Jews, on the contrary, are conspicuous as creators and organizers in different fields—economic, scientific, artistic, etc.—and their superior members not only live without exploiting their own people, but sincerely devote their abilities and resources to the improvement of the mass of their race. Furthermore, for the first time since the dispersion the Jews have found in America a toleration which has made it possible for them to show an open interest in their own welfare and to discuss openly the improvement of their status and the realization of their ideals.

For these reasons, the Jews, far more than any other immigrant group, are resorting to reflective social activity and supplementing the old social forms, spontaneously reproduced, with new, conscious organizations.

Such enthusiasm is interesting if we consider the surge of anti-Semitism that resulted from the Great Immigration. Despite the assimilation of the descendants of previous migratory waves, such as the German Jews in mid-nineteenth century, all Jews felt the blunt: they were routinely denied hotel accommodations and club memberships and were the victims of derogatory language, such as the use of the noun "Jew" as a verb (e.g., "to Jew down") and as an adjective (e.g., "Jew boy" and "Jew banker") (Belth 1979, 24–25; Moore 1981, 104). Finally, in 1913, anti-Semitism took on deadly proportions when Leo Frank, a northern Jewish businessman, was accused of raping and murdering one of his employees in Atlanta, Georgia. At first quickly convicted despite the absence of evidence, Frank had his death sentence commuted to life in prison two years later, but he was kidnapped from prison and lynched. That episode led to the foundation of the Anti-Defamation League of B'nai B'rith, which is active to this day in the denouncement of anti-Semitism in the United States. Although Jews of German descent were instrumental in spearheading such efforts, some of them also harbored their own prejudices toward the eastern European newcomers by regarding their behavior so "inappropriate" as to cause anti-Semitism to reemerge. Consequently, some B'nai B'rith and Anti-Defamation League members rushed to help Eastern European Jews to become assimilated Jews like themselves; until that happened, however, they restricted their interactions with them (Moore 1981).

Conversely, Park and Miller predicted that Negroes, who by then had initiated the Great Migration (1914–1960) out of the south and were being forced to live in ghettoes in northeastern and midwestern cities, would be assimilated last despite their language and religious similarity to the dominant group; the difference, of course, was their race: although not regarded as White, Jews were closer to WASPs than Negroes, who, by then, had a larger native-born contingent than any other group. By taking WASP mainstream culture as the standard and measuring all others against it, the Chicago School maintained Whiteness as the standard and displayed an affinity with social

Darwinism, that is, Herbert Spencer's application of Darwin's "survival of the fittest thesis" to human societies and cultures.

WORLD WAR II AND THE REMAKING OF WHITENESS

World War II (1939–1945) was a turning point for race relations in the United States. With the country having been closed for over a decade, in 1940 the population of foreign-born was 8.5 percent, mostly from Europe, and the second generation of European Americans was nearly 18 percent (Polenberg 1991). The United States joined the Allies in late 1941, after Pearl Harbor was bombed and President Franklin D. Roosevelt (1945–1953) abandoned his isolationist position.

According to Polenberg (1991, 47), the war fostered a national unity that blurred class distinctions and deemphasized ethnic lines. The federal government promoted the rhetoric that "by making this a people's war for freedom, we can help clear up the alien problem, the Negro problem, the anti-Semitic problem." The growth of jobs related to the war effort aided in the income distribution, with a notable increase in the labor force participation of women, retirees, and Negroes.

The war effort promoted a sense of solidarity that celebrated the contributions of immigrant groups to the country as a whole, thus enforcing nationalism and opening up a path toward assimilation. Restrictions on naturalization were also lifted: in 1943, President Roosevelt revoked the 1882 Chinese Exclusion Act, and in 1946, President Harry Truman (1945–1953) lifted the ban on Filipino and Asian Indian naturalization (Taparata 2016). By 1942, restrictions on Italian Americans had also been lifted (Polenberg 1991).

Although Italy, Germany, and Japan were all members of the Axis, against whom the Allies were fighting, Italians in the United States were more accepted than Germans and Japanese. Japanese Americans were particularly targeted, so much so that even the Issei, that is, the third generation, were barred from naturalization (Polenberg 1991). Moreover, unlike any other group, the Japanese in the United States, be they immigrants or native-born, were the only group who had their property confiscated and were placed in "internment camps" (Polenberg 1991). It seems obvious that, by the 1940s, the United States was seeing people of Italian descent as White, but it continued to view the Japanese as "alien." Interestingly enough, U.S. Negroes did not share that attitude with mainstream society. Polenberg (1991, 70) indicates that Negroes opposed discrimination against Japanese Americans, for they understood the war as "being fought against one nation that preached a doctrine of racial supremacy and against another composed of colored people."

Negroes' attitude toward the Japanese made sense if we considered the fact that, while the United States fought against Nazi Germany, it maintained its own domestic system of White supremacy. As a matter of fact, it bears mentioning that Hitler found inspiration for its politics of extermination of any group that was not "Aryan" in the U.S. legal segregation system, which included the murders of Negroes with impunity. Furthermore, while the United States was promoting ethnic solidarity with European immigrants, it promoted racial segregation as a source of country unity (Polenberg 1991, 74). Thus, Negro soldiers served in segregated troops overseas, while at home President Roosevelt continued to refuse to sign an executive order outlawing lynching despite pleas by the NAACP and other organizations because he did not want to interfere with states' rights and because he did not want to lose the southern White vote (Polenberg 1991). Moreover, the job prosperity that engulfed the nation during the war kept Negroes at bay, to the point where A. Philip Randolph, head of the Pullman Union, the most prominent Negro union at the time, threatened to send 100,000 people to a march on Washington, DC in 1941 if job opportunities in the bellicose industry were not extended to Negroes.[8] After much coaxing from the First Lady, Mrs. Eleanor Roosevelt, herself a supporter of civil rights, President Roosevelt created the Committee on Fair Employment Practices to investigate complaints (Polenberg 1991). Still, White supremacy went on, especially in the south. In a speech before a wide U.S. audience in 1944, Roy Wilkins, the future assistant secretary of the NAACP, pointed out the glaring contradiction between the U.S. defense of liberty abroad and maintenance of racial inequality at home: "It sounds pretty foolish to be *against* park benches marked 'Jude' in Berlin, but to be *for* park benches marked 'Colored' in Tallahassee, Florida" (in Moore 1981, 122; emphasis in original).

If Negroes and Japanese Americans fared badly during World War II, the opposite could be said about Americans of European descent. The federal government made a "possessive investment in whiteness" (Lipsitz 2006) with a package of policies that benefited only certain categories of veterans: the GI Bill, which paid for them to go to college and offered them low-interest loans for homeownership. Since higher education is a characteristic of middle-class culture and middle-class culture in the United States is White (Halley, Eshleman, and Vijaya 2011, 68), the government paved the way for the European "races" to become White. In the 1950s, federal and state governments promoted suburbanization by displacing lower-income city dwellers in order to build highways that facilitated commuting to work. The development of "Levittowns" that discriminated against prospective Negro buyers further isolated White ethnics from non-Whites and brought them further into the mainstream (Lipsitz 2006; Oliver and Shapiro 1995). Results were noticed as early as 1944, when overt anti-Semitism started to decrease; quotas restricting university enrollment by Jews up to the 1930s (Steinberg 1971) were being lifted; Irish Americans, who wanted to distance themselves from Negroes, "took the 'wages of whiteness' instead of the greater bargaining power of organizing together with all working-class people" (Halley, Eshleman, and Vijaya 2011, 73); Polish Americans, who also had a history of conflict with Negroes over competition for jobs, experienced less prejudice and discrimination before the start of the war (Kivisto 1995, 202); rates of interethnic marriages started to go up. In sum, the once despised "aliens" assimilated into mainstream society and came to be relabeled "White." Although they did not abandon their ethnicity, that became more of an asset than a liability, a matter of choice, to be claimed mostly in festive occasions instead of determining their life chances, that is, a "symbolic ethnicity" (Gans 1979; Waters 1990).

"TO SECURE THESE RIGHTS": WHITENESS AND THE QUEST FOR CIVIL RIGHTS IN THE TWENTIETH CENTURY

The advent of World War II was a turning point for American Negros as well. The need for military material generated new jobs and brought industries to the south. As a result, over two million people migrated from rural areas to southern cities and to the north. Since 1910, large numbers of Negroes had been leaving the south, first in response to the labor shortage that World War I created, and then to replace European immigrants when the U.S. borders were closed in the 1920s. In the north, where they were allowed to vote, the new migrants "strengthened the political hand of the black community already established there" (Bloom 1987, 68). By 1948, the strength of the Negro constituency was crucial for the democratic victory: they held the balance of power in 16 states, with 278 electoral votes, against only 127 controlled by the south (Bloom 1987, 76; McAdam 1982, 81).

Negroes also challenged the so-called democratic values the United States promoted at home and abroad. Adversary nations, such as Japan during World War II and the Soviet Union during the Cold War (1947–1991), picked up the contradiction between U.S. foreign policy and its record or racial oppression at home. A critical example of that was the treatment that Negro soldiers received during and after the Civil War and the two World Wars: not only were they relegated to subhuman segregated lodgings, but many were terrorized and lynched (Baker 2016); President Truman was said to have been deeply moved by such graphic accounts. In 1946, Negro veterans clamored for the right to vote on a march to the Birmingham, Alabama, courthouse. "They were turned away," notes Bloom (1987, 78), "but their demonstration helped to unite black pressure on Truman. He responded by establishing the President's Committee on Civil Rights," under consultation with the NAACP, the first U.S. president to do so. In October of the following year, the committee issued "to Secure These Rights," a report which "identified race discrimination in virtually every area of American life—education, employment, voting, military service, and so on—and its recommendations charted the course of the civil rights movement for the next 20 years" (Today in Civil Liberty History). Because Congress ignored his recommendation for a civil rights legislation, President Truman desegregated the armed forces by signing Executive Order 9981 and also desegregated federal employment on July 26, 1948. The grandson of slave owners, who in private referred to people of African and Asian descent in derogatory terms and whose election had delighted southern politicians (Brown, DeNeen 2018), ended up being the one president who sought to decrease White supremacy decades before the gains of the civil rights movement in the 1960s.

Truman's successor was Dwight David "Ike" Eisenhower (1953–1961), an army general who had served in World War II and who had run on the Republican Party. Unlike Truman, Eisenhower, a staunch supporter of states' rights, had no penchant for civil rights. In the words of Roy Wilkins (1982, 222), by then the executive director of the NAACP,

> Dwight Eisenhower was doing as little as he could to help us. [He] was a fine general and a good, decent man, but if he had fought World War II the way he fought for civil rights, we would all be speaking German today.

It was in Eisenhower's tenure, however, that a major Supreme Court decision reverted legal racial segregation: *Brown v. Brown of Education* (of Topeka), the 1954 ruling that made the "separate but equal" doctrine unconstitutional and stipulated school racial integration in the country. Actually, Brown was the culmination of a series of cases brought on by Charles Hamilton Houston (1895–1950), a prominent lawyer who, as a segregated soldier in World War I, vowed to fight for Negroes' civil rights if he came out of the war alive. For decades, he attacked the *Plessy v. Ferguson* 1896 decision by successfully challenging its postulates in a number of cases involving school facilities, teachers' salaries, and Negro university students. Even though he died before 1954, his legacy was present in Thurgood Marshall (1908–1993), one of his Howard University law students, who was the chief attorney for Brown. The chief Supreme Court justice at the time was Earl Warren, who had been appointed by President Eisenhower the year before. Justice Warren concluded, "In the field of public education, the doctrine of 'separate but equal' has no place. Separate educational facilities are inherently unequal." President Eisenhower would later declare "that his appointment was 'the biggest damned-fool mistake I ever made'" (Biography.com 2014). Justice Warren would go on to preside over other landmark cases, such as *Reynolds v. Sims* (1964), which read that current census data must determine the boundaries of legislative districts; *Miranda v. Arizona* (1966), which stipulated the "Miranda rights" of a suspect (i.e., "to remain silent" and to have legal representation); and *Loving v. Virginia* (1967), which deemed anti-miscegenation laws unconstitutional (Biography .com 2014). Loving was a significant civil rights gain, for it not only rested the right to choose a mate on the individual instead of on the state, but also expunged the eugenist idea that racial intermarriage would lead to the "mongrelization" of the population.

In the south, concerned that the Brown ruling might catapult a "Second Reconstruction" and reasoning that "discouraging black registration would impede integration," the White leadership organized a massive resistance to social change, evidenced by the foundation of the White Citizens' Council in Mississippi in 1954, which soon spread through most of the region. Using old tactics such as economic coercion, intimidation, but also careful to differentiate themselves from Klan members, the Citizens—members of the older, traditional, agrarian upper class, together with judges and the police—achieved considerable success in delaying racial integration. The White south challenged federal orders of desegregation until the infamous Little Rock bombing in 1957. As late as 1968, George Wallace, former governor of Alabama, ran a presidential campaign whose motto was "Segregation Forever!"

Indeed, the judicial death of legal segregation in 1954 did not guarantee its de facto end, as the Court failed to specify the length of time to which the phrase "with all deliberate speed" referred. Negroes continued to be discriminated against, so they continued to push back. The Montgomery Bus Boycott (1954), during which they refused to ride buses until they were allowed to sit wherever they wanted without being forced to give up their seats to Whites, brought nationwide attention to the racist abuses in the south. Pressure in the form of demonstrations, marches, and sit-ins, organized both by young southerners and, later, college-age northerners, as well as by the Southern Christian Leadership Council (SCLC), pointed to the prominent role of religion on Negroes' social organization and the growing involvement of the baby-boomer generation in changing the country (Chalmers 2013). The movement followed a stance of nonviolence as it demanded full racial integration in the country. As the movement became more radical, however, and after the 1963 March on Washington; the display of police brutality in the Birmingham, Alabama, demonstration in May of the same year; and two years of debates about the "Omnibus Civil Rights Bill" in the Senate, President Lyndon B. Johnson (1963–1968) signed the Civil Rights Act on July 2, 1964, with Dr. Martin Luther King Jr. the head of the SCLC, A. Philip Randolph, Roy Wilkins, and others looking on. The intention of the act was to carry out the process toward racial integration initiated by the

1954 judiciary decision, but left stagnant. With 11 titles, the Civil Rights Act of 1964 covered voting rights, discrimination in public areas and in jobs, and school desegregation. The act instituted affirmative action policies; Dr. King called it "a second Emancipation Proclamation" (King Jr. 1964). The following year, with strong public opinion support (American Institute for Public Opinion 1965), President Johnson (1963–1968) signed the Voting Rights Act. In 1968, in the aftermath of Dr. King's assassination, Johnson passed the Civil Rights Act, of which the Fair Housing Law is part (Kivisto 1995, 318; Lipsitz 2006, 28).

All those gains of the civil rights movement brought hope that White supremacy in the United States might finally end. However, both acts have been ultimately unable to enforce Blacks' right to live wherever they please and work at fully integrated jobs, as the burden of proof often falls on the victims of discrimination. Regarding the weakness of the Fair Housing Act, Lipsitz (2006, 29) is categorical:

> During the 1970s, fewer than 30 percent of the complaints filed with HUD [Department of Housing and Urban Development] led to mediation; close to 50 percent of those remained in noncompliance. A study conducted in 1980 demonstrated that only slightly more than one-third of the complaints to HUD led to voluntary consent agreements. Half of those were settled in favor of the party accused of discrimination. As of 1980, only five victims of discrimination had received damages in excess of $3,500. By 1986, the antidiscrimination mechanisms established in the 1968 law had led to decisions in only about four hundred fair-housing cases. Subsequent changes have strengthened aspects of the law's enforcement and punitive mechanisms significantly, but even today, most experts estimate more than two million cases of housing discrimination occur every year without legal action being taken against them.

As late as the dawn of the second decade of the twenty-first century, obstacles to the full integration of Blacks in mainstream society still persist. The fact that Blacks—more than any other group—continue to find it difficult to occupy all spaces in the United States shows that the "American apartheid" (Massey and Denton 1993) has yet to be eradicated.

BECOMING "HONORARY WHITES": ASIAN AMERICANS AND WHITE LATINOS

Because the greatest divide in the United States is between Black and White, it is fair to assume that, once Blacks voice their demands, other oppressed groups soon follow. Such was the case of the civil rights movement, which preceded the second wave of the feminist movement and the gay rights movement. In fact, although affirmative action policies first targeted racial discrimination against Blacks, it expanded to include discrimination based on sex in 1967 and, in 1971, discrimination against Latinos (Anderson, Terry 2004).

The once despised people of Chinese, Japanese, and Filipino descent also benefited from the relative opening of society toward non-Whites. In 1943, the Chinese Exclusion Act was lifted. Continuing after World War II, "racial liberalism," that is, "the growing belief in political and intellectual circles that the country's racial diversity could be most ably managed through the assimilation and integration of nonwhites" (Wu, Ellen 2016, 62–63), paved the way for a change in the perception of the Chinese and the Japanese, with the goal of promoting their integration and giving legitimacy to the United States as the leader of the "free world." Although they continued to be seen as non-White, they became acceptable non-Whites: in 1966, as urban riots erupted through the nation, a University of California sociologist by the name of William Petersen referred to Japanese Americans as a "success story" and a "model minority" in a *New York Times Magazine* article. Wang (2016) notes that Petersen's praise of Japanese Americans' "cultural values, strong work ethic, family structure, and genetics" sharply contrasted with Daniel Patrick Moynihan's depiction of the family as the root of all the social problems that Negroes experienced at the time, a much-cited report that had come out the year before. She also points out that Petersen's praise ignored the fact that the Immigration Act of 1965 favored the entry of Asian professionals. Extended to other Asians, the model minority stereotype ignores intergroup disparities in educational attainment and income, but it contributes to the maintenance of a racial hierarchy with Whites at the top and Blacks at the bottom; Asian Americans became "a racial group distinct from the white majority, but lauded as well assimilated, upwardly mobile, politically non-threatening, and *definitely not-black*" (Wu, Ellen 2016, 61; emphasis in original).

To regard Asian Americans as politically inoffensive is no less of a stereotype than regarding Asian women as subservient. According to Espiritu (1992), the Black Power movement of the 1960s, a more radical wing of the civil rights movement, inspired those whose ancestors had been called "Orientals" and "yellow" to action. By the 1960s, most of them were native-born and English-speaking, which broke down language barriers both with one another and with mainstream society. Like many other baby boomers, they also pursued higher education in large numbers; on campuses, they organized and developed an Asian American ethnicity, which Espiritu calls "the development of a pan-Asian consciousness and constituency." The all-encompassing term "Asian American" was favored because it incorporated Filipinos, who see themselves and are seen by Far Eastern Asians as "Brown Asians." With the reopening of the U.S. borders in 1965, immigration from Asia increased once again and became more diversified, with the entry of people from the previous countries, but also of Southeast Asia starting in the 1970s.

In general, Asian Americans have indeed experienced significant economic prosperity in the United States. Since the 1980s, they have had higher college completion rates and median family income than any other racial-ethnic group in the country (Blank 2001; U.S. Census Bureau 2019; Tran, Lee, and Huang 2019). Another sign of social acceptance is the fact that, when Whites marry interracially, they are most likely to marry Asian Americans (Fryer Jr. 2009; Steinbugler 2016).

Likewise, "Latino" is an umbrella term that encompasses a diverse population with diverse histories of entry into the United States. As I have already discussed, Mexican Americans, the largest group, became part of the country when the United States annexed one-third of the Mexican territory in the mid-nineteenth century. Since 1965, Mexicans have constituted the largest immigrant group to this country. Puerto Ricans have been U.S. citizens since the early twentieth century, which allows them to come and go freely between the island and the mainland, except when the federal government has decided either to prevent or to curtail their migration, such as in the 1970s. Both Mexican Americans and Puerto Ricans have been discriminated against for usually having darker skin. In border states, such as California, Arizona, and Texas, Mexican Americans have been singled out as "illegal aliens" regardless of their citizenship status.

Cuban Americans, the third largest Latino group, immigrated to the United States in large numbers after the Cuban Revolution in 1959. Because they were fleeing a "communist" country, they were granted political refugee status and economic aid from the federal government. Added by the fact that most in that first wave had been middle-class professionals in Cuba and tended to be lighter-skinned as well, they achieved social and economic success relatively fast. In comparison, Cuban Americans have the highest educational attainment, on a par with White Americans, while Puerto Ricans have the lowest (Noe-Bustamante, Flores, and Shah 2019; Reyes 2017).

Despite the emphasis on White purity since 1896, the way the United States has looked at Latinos has been far from clear-cut. For instance, in the 1930 census, "Mexican" was a "race." However, 20 years later, the census counted them as "White." In the 1980 census, they were counted as "Hispanic." In the 2000 census, a number of Latinos classified themselves as "some other race," but in 2010, a growing number classified themselves as "White" (Cohn 2014). Given the histories of the former Spanish, Portuguese, and French colonies in the Americas, in addition to the immigratory waves to the region, Latinos may be of any race, but in the United States they have often been treated as an interstitial "race" between Whites and Blacks. Colorism, that is, the idea that light skin is more prestigious than dark skin, is a function both of White supremacy in this country and of racism in Latin America. Therefore, it so happens that in their own countries of origin many Latinos are classified as White or some gradation closer to White; upon arrival in the United States, they may reject racial classifications altogether, they may opt for "some other race," or they may classify themselves as White because that was their original racial classification. On the other hand, less White Latinos (i.e., those who may have been classified as *trigueño(a)*, *moreno(a)*, or even *negro(a)* in their countries of origin) may opt for the labels Latino or Hispanic upon setting residence in the United States in order to ascend in the racial hierarchy in opposition to African Americans. In any event, the White majority at once treats Latinos as if they were a race and also differentiates among them by color. Evidence of that is the fact that the lightest-skinned Latinos live closer to European Americans and intermarry with them at considerable rates, whereas their darkest-skinned counterparts live closer to African Americans and are more subjected to racial discrimination (Fu 2007; Gonzalez-Barrera 2019).

The contrast between light-skinned and dark-skinned Latinos and Asian Americans of Far Eastern descent and those of Southeast Asian descent (among other groups) in addition to the growth of a multiracial population resulting from an increase in interracial marriages led Gans to predict in 1999 that a new racial order was being formed in the United States based on a Black versus non-Black dichotomy, "with a third, 'residual,' category for the groups that do not, or do not yet, fit into the basic dualism." Later, Bonilla-Silva (2004, 224) postulated that the United States was undergoing a transformation in its racial hierarchy, moving away from a racial dichotomy and toward a "tri-racial system with 'Whites' at the top, an intermediary group of 'honorary Whites'—similar to the coloreds in South Africa during formal apartheid, and a nonwhite group or the 'collective black' at the bottom." Economically successful Asian Americans and White Latinos would compose the "honorary whites," whereas light-skinned multiracial individuals would join the "Whites." This new system would encompass both color and socioeconomic status, much like it is in Latin America, so that Filipinos, a darker-skinned Asian group, might be placed at the "collective black," but at the highest position given their professional success. Despite the higher educational qualifications of African immigrants (Logan 2009), Bonilla-Silva still places them toward the bottom of the "collective black," together with "dark-skinned and poor Latinos." That shows that White supremacy and colorism are likely to persist. The United States may indeed become more like Brazil, where "money whitens," but only so much.

WHITENESS: FROM POST-RACIAL
TO WHITE NATIONALISM

The civil rights movement led to political gains to African Americans, women, Latinos, American Indians, Asians, and LGBTQIA+ persons (Chalmers 2013). To review, the *Brown v. Board of Education* 1954 Supreme Court decision made legal racial segregation unconstitutional and paved the way for school integration; the Civil Rights Act of 1964 made discrimination in employment, education, and public facilities illegal and instituted affirmative action policies; the Voting Rights Act of 1965 enfranchised African Americans throughout the land; the *Loving v. Virginia* 1967 Supreme Court decision made interracial marriages legal; and the Fair Housing Act of 1968 targeted housing racial discrimination. As for gender rights, the Civil Rights Act of 1964 allowed women to sue employers for gender discrimination and the *Roe v. Wade* Supreme Court decision, in 1973, legalized abortion. Homosexual behavior ceased to be a crime in 2003, same-sex marriages were allowed in 2015, and same-sex adoptions, a year later. After decades of affirmative action programs, women and African Americans have made significant strides in higher education and the professions (Sokoloff 1992); the Black middle class has also grown, from less than 5 percent in the 1950s (Frazier 1957) to about a third of all African Americans today (Oliver and Shapiro 1995).

Even with all those gains, it took until 2008 for an African American man, Barack Obama, to be elected president, and then reelected four years later. Those unprecedented events changed history and made many believe the United States had become "colorblind" and "postracial," as sociologists have noted (Gallagher 2009). That was far from reality, however. Attacks on African Americans, from calling the First Lady, Michelle Obama, "an ape in heels" (in Allen 2016) to recurrent murders of men, women, and children by civilians and the police throughout the country highlighted the equivocation of such a thought. Quite possibly, the discourse was a deliberate effort to hasten the dismantling of affirmative action programs: minorities had had enough "help"; if a Black man had been elected to the most powerful position in the world, it was time Blacks were treated "like everybody else." It is also possible that some, such as the young Whites Gallagher (2009) interviewed, thought Blacks in general and minorities in particular had gone so far that "white people's rights" were being "forgotten."

I believe that helps explain the election of Donald Trump. By questioning the citizenship of Obama and of U.S. citizens of Mexican descent; by calling Mexican immigrants "criminals" (therefore, undesirable); by ignoring the Hart-Celler Act of 1965, which reopened U.S. borders; by vilifying his opponent—a White woman—as "crooked"; and by promising to bring back jobs historically associated with the White working class, Trump conjured a racism, a nativism, and a populism that had been quite successful at closing the country nearly 100 years earlier. Once again, it was the triumph of race (and the male gender) over class interests. As historian James Horton reasoned about presidential candidate Andrew Jackson's appeal to the White masses in the late 1820s,

> When Jackson speaks out in a kind a of populist way, speaking for the little guy, speaking out against privilege, his little guy, his citizen is increasingly a white, male citizen. As America is becoming more democratic for white males, it is becoming increasingly more race based. (*Race: The Power of an Illusion, Episode 2*)

While the language may be different in the twenty-first century, the roots of the ideas still manage to flourish.

NOTES

1. Although World War II had started in 1939, the United States began fighting in it only after the Japanese attack on Pearl Harbor, on December 7, 1941. Likewise, the Vietnam War started in 1955, but the United States sent its first troops 10 years later.

2. In eighteenth-century colonial North America, married women had the legal status of *"feme covert*, which prohibited them from owning property, establishing businesses, signing contracts, or in other ways managing personal affairs or supporting themselves. Once divorced, women returned to the status of *feme sole*, which allowed them to conduct personal business and seek a livelihood" (Riley 1991, 20).

3. Given that women have yet to be paid equally to men in comparable occupations, it could be argued that they are still treated as inferior to men.

4. "Among the cowboys who went up the trails from Texas during the years following the Civil War, more than five thousand Negroes played a part and did a job— doing no more and no less than cowboys of other races and nationalities" (Durham and Jones 1965, 3).

5. For a historically accurate fictionalized narrative of the Gold Rush in San Francisco and the treatment of former Mexican citizens, Negroes, and Chinese immigrants, see Allende (1999).

6. The reverse can also be true. Evidence that prejudice continued to fuel the practice of lumping different nationalities together with disastrous results was the murder of Vincent Chin, a 27-year-old Chinese American, in a city near Detroit in 1982. As Chin enjoyed his bachelor's party, he was beaten to death by two Crysler employees, who mistook him for Japanese, whom they blamed for its decline. The two murderers, Ronald Ebens and Michael Nitz, were convicted of manslaughter, "sentenced to three years of probation and fined $3,000. . . . Mr. Chin was buried on the day he was to have been married" (Wu 2012).

7. For a synthesis of the case that led to the 1896 Supreme Court decision, its consequences, and a comparison with racial classification in Brazil, see Daniel (2006) and Penha-Lopes (2017).

8. A. Philip Randolph was then the mastermind of a march on Washington, which would end up taking place 22 years later. By then toward the end of his life, Randolph introduced and gave the floor to a young Dr. Martin Luther King Jr. who delivered his classic "I Have a Dream."

Chapter 2

Whiteness and the Idea of Nation in Brazil

If the United States presents itself as the land of opportunity, Brazil presents itself as a racial democracy. Just as that image of the United States is too simplistic, so is the Brazilian image. As countries dependent on African-based slavery for centuries, both the United States and Brazil have dealt with racial diversity and inequality from early on. In the case of Brazil, however, racial inequality has appeared to be less clear-cut. For starters, unlike the United States, Brazil has had seven Constitutions since its independence from Portugal in 1822, not all of which prescribed laws concerning race relations. Moreover, Brazil relied on a slavery system that covered a much larger territory and lasted much longer than in the United States. Indeed, not only was Brazil the last country in the Americas to abolish slavery, in 1888, but it is also the country with the largest population of African descent. With the proclamation of the republic a year after Abolition, the Brazilian elite felt the need to react to the pseudoscientific theories of the late nineteenth century to the early twentieth century that predicted the demise of any country with a large non-White population due to its "racial inferiority." Ever since then, Brazil has grappled with the dilemma of longing to "dilute" its African "blood" while knowing full well that even its so-called White population is, for the most part, miscegenated, which makes the country not White in the eyes of the United States and European nations. Therefore,

in Brazil, "White" was not formed by the exclusive ethnic mixture of European peoples, as it occurred in the United States with the "ethnic pot"; on the contrary, we count as "White" those mestizos and light-skinned mulattoes who can exhibit the dominant symbols of Europeanness: Christianity and education. (Guimarães, Antonio Sérgio 1999, 47)

53

Finally, the longer years as a European colony and reliance on slavery created an authoritarian structure based on a racial and economic hierarchy that persists despite the insistence of the country in portraying itself as "cordial," inclusive, and "tolerant" (Schwarcz 2019; Holanda 1936; Souza, Jessé 2018).

TERRA BRASILIS: EUROPEAN COLONIALISM AND THE MAKING OF BRAZIL

It is impossible to think of Brazil as a nation without considering the race question. In effect, after the Portuguese first landed in the South American territory in 1500, they took Africans in subsequent voyages in the mid-sixteenth century with the specific purpose of working as slaves. Portugal instituted African slavery on the land it had taken as its colony well before the first enslaved African arrived in the North American colonies in 1619. In time, Brazil became the final destination of the largest contingent of enslaved Africans up until the late nineteenth century.

Despite the belief that slavery in Brazil was benevolent in comparison with the North American version (e.g., Freyre 1933; Tannenbaum 1947; Moynihan 1965), there are plenty of accounts of the physical cruelty to which slaves were submitted, such as severe beatings and lacerations that were covered with salt, bonding, rapes, and amputations, but also the psychological punishments, such as public beatings and the separation of families by sales. In other words, rather than benevolent, the system was maintained by force.

Another fallacy attributed to slavery in Brazil is that the enslaved population was docile and passive. It is thus important to mention the considerable number of slave insurrections. Escapes were also commonplace; like in other areas in the Americas, fugitive slaves established *quilombos*, self-governing areas that flourished throughout the land. The largest of them was Palmares, governed by Zumbi, in the present-day state of Alagoas. Palmares was finally conquered and Zumbi was assassinated by Portuguese troops when Portugal regained control of Brazil from the Dutch in 1654, after 30 years. That shows that relations among enslaved, overseers, and owners were fraught with tension and the fear of rebellion.

The vast indigenous population—counted as about six million in the sixteenth century—was also legally enslaved in Brazil, be it to work in the primitive exploration of the Atlantic Forest, or as the result of their losing "just wars," that is, attacks by the colonizers to usurp their land, or by acquisition of those who lost wars with other indigenous groups. Until the seventeenth century, the enslavement of indigenous peoples was legal in Brazil, even though they had the status of "subjects of the Crown" (*súditos da coroa*). Moreover, many natives perished due to the introduction of European diseases in their midst, a practice that would continue well into the twentieth century. Schwarcz (2019, 163) qualifies the systematic disappearance of the indigenous population as "genocide." For instance, the Tamoio, the main group that occupied the city of Rio de Janeiro, were obliterated in a war with the Portuguese in the mid-sixteenth century. Having landed in that southeast area early in that century, the Portuguese all but abandoned it, only to see it overtaken by the French, who planned on establishing "Antarctic France" there. In the process of reconquering the territory, the Portuguese killed all the Tamoio, who had sided with the French.

Other agents of attacks against the indigenous population of Brazil were *bandeirantes*, literally those who carry flags, thus called after "the indigenous practice of raising a flag as gesture of war" (Silva, Sandro 2018, 64). During the colonial period (1530–1815), *bandeirantes* were slave traders and frontiersmen, who went into the Brazilian hinterland, thus invading indigenous territory. Romanticized as *fidalgos* (i.e., well-to-do White men) with adventurous spirits centuries later, they were actually landless and often of mixed-race. Hence their interest in improving their social status by the capture of natives to be sold as slaves and by exploring mines, as news of the discovery of gold and precious stones spread.

Bandeirantes were not settlers like the frontiers people in the United States. Often by foot, they explored the territories in groups composed of Paulistas (i.e., those born in the present-day state of São Paulo), Portuguese, Mamelucos (i.e., Brazilians of White and indigenous ancestry), slaves of African descent, priests, and even natives; Paulistas held the highest status among them. As a whole, they were very violent toward the indigenous population (Silva, Sandro 2018, 64; Schwarcz 2019, 163–164).

Although the enslavement of natives continued, it was not widespread as the enslavement of Africans and their descendants, in part because indigenous peoples were more knowledgeable of the territory and more successful at fleeing into the hinterland, but also because Portugal was a major player in the African slave trade. The colonial exploration of Brazil was based on a slavery system that maintained itself both by the importation of Africans and by their reproduction in Brazilian territory. Manumission was possible, but not easily obtained because it was costly and, by definition, slaves were not remunerated.

THE *INCONFIDENTES*: RACE AND
INDEPENDENCE ASPIRATIONS

As a colony, Brazil generated tremendous wealth for the Portuguese Crown, with its natural resources such as coastal wood, and later, gold and precious minerals, but also with its crops of sugarcane, and subsequently, cotton and coffee. While the Portuguese had first landed in the present-day state of Bahia, located in the northeast, they expanded their reach all the way to the south, with major profit from the southeastern area, which includes Rio de Janeiro, São Paulo, and Minas Gerais.

In the seventeenth century, *bandeirantes* found gold, emeralds, diamonds, and other stones in an area that, for that reason, was named "Minas Gerais" (i.e., general mines); that discovery led to the growth of that mountainous region, away from the coast, resulting from the migration of a significant population and the development of a number of towns (Costa 2011). Gold mining was so bountiful that, between 1740 and 1780, Portugal appropriated about 40 tons of gold per year. Much of that gold ended up covering the walls of Catholic churches in the metropolis, but, also in the colony, churches were built which showed opulence in their interiors and in the images of saints. The towns of Vila Rica (literally, "wealthy village"), which was later renamed Ouro Preto (i.e., "black gold"), São João del Rey, Diamantina, and Congonhas do Campo became the center of the Brazilian baroque.

Besides the appropriation of gold, Portugal charged taxes on the extraction, at the rate of 20 percent of the total extraction. The blatant economic exploitation of the colony led to discontent among the residents. By the late eighteenth century, an insurgence against Portugal emerged in the province of Minas Gerais. In 1788 to 1789, a group composed of members of the Brazilian colonial elite (i.e., mineowners, army officers, members of the clergy, and writers), all residents of Vila Rica, plotted to declare independence from Portugal and establish a republic encompassing Minas Gerais and Rio de Janeiro, the latter, the capital of the colony and the closest connection to a port (Luisa April 20, 2018); they were labeled the *inconfidentes* (i.e., the disloyal), and their movement, the *Inconfidência Mineira* or *Conjuração Mineira* (i.e., the Conspiration from Minas Gerais). Inspiration for their ideas came from the French Enlightenment and, more specifically, the American Revolution. Great admirers of Thomas Jefferson that they were, their proposal was freedom from Portugal, while maintaining the economic system of slavery, on which the region was heavily dependent. According to Carvalho (2020),

> Slave labor in the mining region was not restricted to gold extraction, as slaves performed diverse functions, such as activities related to transportation, (street) trade, and the construction of bridges, streets, and buildings. Mining was regarded as the most painful and heaviest jobs enslaved Africans performed in Brazil.

On the other hand, slaves who worked in the mines were afforded relatively more autonomy than those who worked in the fields, given the threat of accusation to the Crown of a mineowner who failed to report the accurate amount of extraction and payment of taxes (Costa 2011, 181).

Historical research shows that many of the *inconfidentes* were slave owners who relied on the African slave trade to acquire their possessions (Rodrigues and Freire 2018, 562); all were White men in the Brazilian context. Reported by Joaquim Silvério dos Reis, a Portuguese army officer and mineowner who had learned of their plot and told on them in exchange for the pardoning of his debt, they were arrested in 1789 and subsequently banished to exile. However, their most visible member had a different fate: Joaquim José da Silva Xavier, an army sublieutenant who also worked as a dentist, hence his nickname *Tiradentes* (i.e., one who removes teeth), was tried and sentenced to death by hanging as a traitor. That took place in a public square in Rio de Janeiro, the capital of Brazil, on April 21, 1792. Afterward, his body was quartered and taken to Vila Rica; the house where he had lived was subsequently destroyed, "the soil was salted so that nothing ever grew there again, and the authorities declared all of his descendants infamous" (*Só História*). Historians have concluded that such a harsh fate may have had to do with the fact that Tiradentes had the lowest status of the group and was not as well-connected (Bernardo 2018). Lauded as "the Martyr of Independence" almost a century later, Tiradentes is always portrayed with long hair and a long beard, even though that would have been forbidden to a prisoner in late eighteenth-century Brazil (*Só História*); his appearance in paintings quite resembles that of Jesus Christ, which, I believe, augments his mystique. The flag the *inconfidentes* designed—a white sheet with a red triangle in the middle, around which is inscribed the Latin phrase *Libertas Quae Sera Tamen* (in English, "freedom even if late")—was later adopted as the flag of the state of Minas Gerais. With the proclamation of the republic in 1889, Tiradentes was deemed a hero and April 21 was declared a national holiday; Tiradentes is the only figure in Brazilian history whose death is honored as such (Luisa April 20, 2018).

Much more encompassing, yet much less known, was the *Inconfidência Baiana* (i.e., the Conspiration from Bahia), which took place in the capital city of Salvador in 1798, so-called in allusion to the Minas Insurrection nine years earlier. However, race- and class-wise, the movement in Bahia was unique in that it was conceived by "poor men and Black men" (Araújo 2004). Unlike their counterparts from Minas Gerais, not only did they not own slaves, they advocated abolition; that fact alone makes them closer to the ideals of the French Revolution than of the American Revolution. The Bahia insurrection also counted with *brancos da terra*, that is, Brazilian-born Whites, whose status was lower than that of European-born Whites. Araújo (2004) notes that because most Brazilian Whites were relegated to bureaucratic positions, they ended up being "in open conflict with Portuguese-born

Whites," which prompted them to fight for independence in 1823. There were also class divisions among poor Brazilian Whites: they were barred from entry into a number of occupations reserved for the very wealthy, who could afford to send their sons to be educated in Europe, and for European Whites. In sum, poor Brazilian Whites were only above Blacks, be they free or enslaved.

Salvador was a major port of entry for the African slave trade. Therefore, it had a large population of African-born slaves. According to Araújo (2004), they occupied the lowest rung of society and aimed at recreating Africa in Brazilian soil. In turn, Brazilian-born Blacks wished to open up work opportunities for themselves beyond manual labor.

In colonial Bahia, Blacks and poor Whites often joined the army, where living conditions were subpar. In addition, the stigma of race prevented Blacks from being promoted, whereas poor Whites were subordinated to the Portuguese. Araújo (2004) concludes that their collective discontent led to the articulation of the revolt.

On August 12, 1798, copies of a manifesto against the subjugation to Portugal and against slavery appeared about the city of Salvador. The authors were members of the *Partido da Liberdade* (Freedom Party), which counted with 676 members altogether. They were a racially diverse group that included officers, soldiers, merchants, and clergymen. Among their goals were the abolition of slavery, autonomy from Portugal, defense of private property, and the opening of the Port of Salvador to foreign powers, especially France. Below are excerpts from their manifesto, in which the ideals of the French Revolution are clearly in evidence:

> The people want that all military members, militias, and ordinances; White, Brown, and Black men run for the popular freedom. . . . Each soldier is a citizen, especially Brown and Black men who live scorned and abandoned. All will be equal, there will be no difference; there will be only liberty, equality, and fraternity. (in Araújo 2004)

Thirty-three members were arrested, the majority of whom were slaves, followed by tailors, soldiers, and professionals. However, only four were sentenced to death: two soldiers—Luís Gonzaga das Virgens e Veiga, who was accused of plotting to overturn the Portuguese rule, and Lucas Dantas do Amorim Torres—and two tailors—João de Deus do Nascimento and Manuel Faustino dos Santos. Because of the latter, the insurgency is also called the Tailors' Revolt. All four were *mulatos* (i.e., Brown or mixed-race). They were hanged, beheaded, and quartered; their body parts were strewn over Salvador. Araújo (2004) concludes that their proposal to abolish slavery scared the discontented who sympathized with the *inconfidentes mineiros*, for fear that Salvador would undergo a revolution like the one that was taking place in Haiti about the same time, a slave revolt that resulted in the abolition of slavery and Haiti's independence from France. In the end, fears of racial equality trumped the desire for social equality, and the non-White would-be revolutionaries ended up paying the heaviest price:

> After all, what did those men from 1798 do? They did no revolution, nor revolt, nor sedition, as no arms were used. They formulated proposals and sought alliances to collectively overcome the crisis in the city. They propagated their ideas. They engaged in politics, and for that they were cruelly repressed. In fact, tailors and soldiers were hanged and quartered because they represented the audacity of men of color to get into terrain that was beyond their control, that is, city government. Their humiliation was the blow directed at all the city population of color, free and enslaved, to break their pride, their desire for change, their desire for equality. Despite the repression, those men from 1798 remained in people's memory as the first Black politicians in Bahia. (Araújo 2004)

AN EMPIRE IS BORN: BRAZILIAN INDEPENDENCE

In the early years of the nineteenth century, Portugal counted on its vast colony in South America to escape from the threat of subjugation to France. In 1806, Napoleon closed the European ports to England and negotiated a treaty with Spain which would allow him to invade Portugal. The following year, the Portuguese Royal Family composed of the king, Dom João VI; his wife, Dona Carlota Joaquina—who history claims openly plotted in favor of her native Spain—and their four children; the oldest son, Pedro (1798–1834), was nine years old. They arrived in Salvador, the previous capital of the colony, in January 1808, when the king opened the ports to "friendly nations." Two months later, they arrived in Rio de Janeiro, where they set up court. According to Brazilian historians, the move was significant in that it implemented in the colony a bureaucratic and, to a certain extent, an economic structure that made Brazil function more as a sovereignty than as a colony. In 1816, the king decreed Brazil a United Kingdom to Portugal and Algarve, thus ending, at least in theory, the status of Brazil as a colony of Portugal. Now the center of the Portuguese kingdom, Rio de Janeiro had its port open and saw a flourishing of the arts which would continue to deem it the cultural capital of Brazil well into the late twentieth century. Dom João VI built libraries and theaters, the Botanic Garden, the Firefighters' Corps, and factories. Moreover, the transference of the court to Brazil led to the development of an educational system that allowed the formation of professionals there rather than only in Europe (Schwarcz 2019, 12).

The death of Dom João's mother, Dona Maria I, in 1816 made necessary his return to Portugal to assume the throne. However, although he was crowned two years later, he postponed his return until 1821, when he in vain tried to send his son Pedro in his stead. Pedro remained in Rio as the regent of Brazil, where he was involved in plans to make Brazil independent from Portugal, with the supposed knowledge of the king; separatist movements had started in the northeast of Brazil, for example, leading to the formation of the Brazilian army, whose members supported the sovereignty of Brazil. On September 7, 1822, on a return trip from São Paulo, Dom Pedro was informed by a letter from his wife, Dona Leopoldina (1797–1826), who was acting as regent and was also sympathetic to the idea of independence from Portugal, that his presence was required back in Europe. He then turned to his troop, told them all ties to Portugal were severed, and swore to give Brazil independence (Lustosa 2006). Pedro became Pedro I, emperor of Brazil; Portugal would recognize the new nation in 1825. For Schwarcz (2019, 13), "political independence in 1822 did not bring many institutional innovations, but it consolidated a clear goal, namely, to structure and justify a new nation, actually . . . very peculiar in the American context: a monarchy surrounded by republics."

Dom Pedro I was the emperor of a "constitutional monarchy," that is, a government based not on divine right such as a kingdom but on "a tie between political power and society" (Oliveira, Eduardo 2005). The product of a constitutional assembly that met in 1823, the first Brazilian Constitution was written in 1824. Its most unique aspect was the stipulation of the Moderating Power (*Poder Moderador*), a fourth power rested solely in the hands of the emperor which granted him authority over the legislative, the judiciary, and the executive powers. The Moderating Power could be applied in "exceptional" situations that threatened the very existence of the state and society, rather than an absolutist power (Oliveira, Eduardo 2005). In the late nineteenth century, Benjamin Constant, founder of the Military Club and one of the articulators of the coup that established the republic in Brazil in 1889, defined it as "the key to all political organization." In more recent times, Celso Mello, the jurist with the longest tenure in the Brazilian Supreme Court as of 2021, regards the 1824 Constitution as "a very important constitutional document, especially because it expressed, at that particular historical moment, an instance of sovereign affirmation of the Brazilian state" (Jus Vigilantibus 2008).

While the 1824 Constitution prescribed the rulings of the new nation, it is important to emphasize the limitations on the idea of nation, that is, who belonged as a citizen. Although the first article of the Constitution reads that "the empire of Brazil is the political association of all Brazilian citizens" who "form a free and independent Nation" (Constituição Política do Império do Brasil March 25, 1824), not all inhabitants had full rights. Paragraph 1 of Article 6 of Section II defines as citizens "those born in Brazil, either free children of slave women [*ingênuos*] or freed, even if the father is a foreigner"; five more paragraphs define Brazilian citizenship, none of which includes slaves, regardless of their place of birth. According to legal scholar Hédio Silva Júnior, the law kept them in a liminal status between a "person" and a "thing," that is, not fully human. Thus, a slave, "if accused, was considered a person. If a victim, he was taken as a thing, or, in the best case scenario, livestock" (in Baraviera 2005, 2–3). Given that the majority of the Black population in Brazil in the nineteenth century was enslaved, of course most Blacks were not citizens. As for the indigenous population, nowhere in the Constitution is it mentioned, which then denies it citizenship.

As I discussed in the previous chapter, a sure mark of citizenship is the right to vote. Chapter 6 of Section IV of the Constitution ("On the Legislative Power") is entitled "On Elections." Voting for legislators was indirect; citizens would vote locally for provincial representatives, who would then vote for senators and members of the General Assembly. Article 92 determined that "single men, younger than 25 years of age, married men younger than 21, the clergy, servants, and those who owned less than 100,000 liquid réis in real estate, industry, commerce, or employment"[1] were not eligible to vote. Again, considering the opportunities available to former slaves, it is safe to assume that the 1824 Constitution excluded most of them from voting. It also excluded the poor, regardless of race. In sum, full citizen rights were afforded to the wealthy and, as in any kingdom, to the nobility, expanded by the emperor's diligence in conceding titles to those who granted him favors, so much so that the practice was prescribed in the Constitution itself (Schwarcz 2019, 75).[2]

Amid a succession crisis in Portugal and his decreased approval in Brazil after the loss of present-day Uruguay in 1828, Pedro I abdicated the Brazilian throne and returned to Portugal in 1831, leaving his five-year-old son Pedro as the regent. Evidently, at such a young age, Pedro was the regent only in name; instead, a triumvirate governed the country. The leader of the three was José Bonifácio de Andrada e Silva (1763–1838), who had had such a prominent role in Brazil's quest for independence in 1822 that he was named "The Patriarch of Independence."[3] Andrada e Silva, a learned man and politician with prominent positions in Pedro I's reign, tutored the future emperor for two years, which would help explain his vast scholarly interests as an adult.

Pedro II ruled from 1841 to 1889. According to Schwarcz (2019, 76–77), he continued his father's practice of granting titles of nobility: if the father had granted 119 titles, the son would end up granting over a thousand of them, usually to landowners and professionals. The significance of that practice was the creation and maintenance of an elite intimately tied to the monarch, "the

Rio de Janeiro court" (Schwarcz 2019, 77). Even though Brazil abruptly ceased to be a monarchy in 1889, remnants of that practice are visible in the names of streets in the older Rio de Janeiro neighborhoods where the titled elite used to live, such as Laranjeiras, Flamengo, and Botafogo, all of which have an abundance of streets named after viscounts, marquises, counts, and barons.

Blond, blue-eyed Pedro II is often portrayed as an older man with a serene expression. He is remembered as deeply nationalistic and fond of science and the arts. Brazilians are proud of his friendship with inventors such as Alexander Graham Bell, his interest in botany and architecture, and his proficiency as a polyglot. He was also a patron who sponsored both White and Black artists and scientists. Still, Schwarcz (2019, 164) notes that, although the emperor stimulated the study of indigenous languages, he also promoted the "romantic indigenism," which, in literature and painting, portrayed the natives as "good" when they succumbed to the wishes of Europeans, colonizers, and Whites and as "bad" or "savages" when they defended their land. In that respect, then, his thinking resembled that of Thomas Jefferson in the early part of the century; the taking of indigenous territory went on during Pedro II's reign.

Likewise, the slavery system in Brazil persisted almost through the entirety of the nineteenth century, remaining the largest in the Americas. An abolitionist movement, however, forged ahead which was fueled by economic and moral reasons. Expanding industrialization in Western Europe and in Brazil pushed for the demise of an economic system that kept millions of workers without acquisitive power. Morally, slavery was deemed inhuman and un-Christian. Under pressure from England, which had abolished the international slave trade in 1806, Brazil passed the Feijó-Barbacena Law of 1831, which outlawed the entry of new enslaved Africans in Brazilian territory. In 1850, the Eusébio de Queirós Law abolished the slave trade. In the late 1860s, an interracial abolitionist movement emerged in Brazil, garnering journalists, such as José do Patrocínio (1853–1905); politicians, such as Joaquim Nabuco (1849–1910); novelists, such as Artur Azevedo (1855–1908); professionals, such as André Rebouças (1838–1898) and Luís Gama (1830–1882); and poets, such as Castro Alves (1847–1871) (Alonso 2015). The Paraguayan War (1864–1870), however, delayed measures toward abolition. The war concerned the attack by Brazil, Argentina, and Uruguay, the "Triple Alliance," on Paraguay over land disputes and access to water ways. Brazil relied on a considerable number of soldiers who were poor or who had been slaves and were either freed in order to enlist in the army (something that the emperor himself did) or were forced to fight instead of their owners. They were called *voluntários da pátria* (i.e., volunteers of the nation), an irony in view of their lack of input in that situation (Toral 1995).

Abolition in Brazil was piecemeal. Having suffered pressure from abolitionist organizations from the United States and France (Alonso 2015), when the emperor addressed the Legislative Assembly in 1867, he called on measures to end slavery gradually (Bezerra n.d. a). On September 28, 1871, Princess Isabel, the 25-year-old daughter of the emperor who was acting as the regent while he was in Europe, signed the law proposed by José Maria Silva Paranhos, Viscount of Rio Branco (Frazão December 17, 2019).[4] Commonly known as the Free Womb Law, it freed the children born of enslaved women henceforth. It continued,

> The so-called minor children will be under the authority of the owners of their mothers, who will be obligated to raise them until they reach the age of eight years. Once the slave's child reaches that age, the owner of his mother will have the option of receiving 600,000 réis for compensation from the State, or of making use of the services of the minor until he reaches 21 years of age. (in Bezerra n.d. a)

In practice, how "free" was a child whose mother was enslaved? How feasible was that freedom, if a minor could not fend for himself or herself? Furthermore, who was to guarantee that the mother's owner would not continue to treat her children in the same fashion as before, given that the law demanded that he pay for their upkeep?

A similar argument could be made about the next law, which concerned older slaves. In 1884, Senator Manuel Pinto de Sousa Dantas (1831–1894), an abolitionist, introduced the bill which would free slaves who had reached 60 years of age without compensation for the slave owners, but with the absorption of former slaves into farming colonies, much as it would take place with European and Japanese immigrants a few years later. On September 28 of the following year, the Saraiva-Cotegipe Law, better known as the Sexagenarian Law, was passed, but only with two crucial modifications: under pressure from coffee plantation owners, Senators José Antônio Saraiva (1823–1893) and the Baron of Cotegipe (1815–1889), anti-abolitionists, changed the law so that former slaves would have to work for free for 3 years or until they reached the age of 65 years, thus compensating their former owners for the loss of private property (Bezerra n.d. b). In addition, no land would be offered to the former slaves.

Given the slaves' quality of life, the probability that most would survive past age 60 was low. After all, enslaved Brazilians suffered from overall neglect, including poor diets, inadequate clothing, exposure to diseases, and, of course, physical abuse. According to historical data from the late nineteenth century, the longevity of the Brazilian slave was lower than 20 years, that is, about 8 years lower than that of Brazilians in general. In comparison, the longevity of slaves from the United States at mid-century was 35.5 years, which led historian Luiz Nogueira (2011) to conclude that, in Brazil, "life conditions, in the 19th century, were bad for all and much worse for the slaves." Therefore, for all intents and purposes, the Sexagenarian Law, like the Free Womb Law, was heavily biased toward the slave owners and of little benefit for the slaves.

Unrestricted abolition would only be sanctioned on May 13, 1888, with Law no. 3353, better known as the Golden Law (*Lei Áurea*). That was the result of the efforts of the abolitionists, who managed to garner enough support to their cause that theirs is regarded as the first truly national social movement in Brazil (Alonso 2015). Like the Free Womb Law 17 years earlier, the Golden Law was also signed by Princess Isabel, who again was the regent while the emperor was in Milan, Italy. The terms of the law that put an end to almost 400 years of the slavery system are quite succinct:

> The Regent Imperial Princess, in the name of His Majesty the Emperor, Pedro II, makes it known to all subjects of the Empire that the General Assembly decreed and she has approved the following law:
>> Article 1: Slavery in Brazil is declared extinct since the date of this law.
>> Article 2: Contrary dispositions are revoked.
> Therefore, she demands that all authorities, to whom knowledge and execution of the aforementioned Law belong, enforce it, see to it that it is enforced, and keep it entirely as it is. (in Presidência da República)

As a result of having signed the law that freed about 700,000 enslaved persons, Princess Isabel entered history as "The Redemptor." That, however, masks all the groundwork behind it. Alonso (2015) convincingly argues that the express character of the law was a compromise between the abolitionists, who wanted the state to provide viable working conditions for the former slaves in addition to their emancipation, and the proslavery side, who not only were against abolition, but also wanted the state to compensate the former owners for their economic loss; that impasse came close to provoking a civil war (Alonso 2014). Indeed, the Golden Law made no provisions for the insertion of former slaves into the free job market.

In the centennial of Abolition, a reinterpretation of it led to a dismissal of the idea that it had been mostly a gracious act from the part of the princess (Alonso 2014). More and more contested, its significance was questioned; instead, November 20, in large part as a result of pressure from the Black movement in Brazil, the date of Zumbi's death, was promoted as more significant for the struggle for equality of the descendants of enslaved Brazilians. On November 10, 2011, Law no. 12519 instituted November 20 as Black Conscience Day, a national holiday. Although not unanimously accepted,

Zumbi Day has gained increasingly more enthusiasts, while May 13, which was never a holiday, has lost prestige. By 2020, May 13 was being called "National Denouncement of Racism Day" and also "Inauguration of Racism Day" (Honorato May 13, 2020), meaning that abolition did not guarantee former slaves and their descendants full rights to move freely and to ascend socially.

While I strongly agree that Brazilian Blacks—especially those with dark skin—continue to be relegated to a second-class socioeconomic status, I also believe that the rejection of May 13 dismisses the efforts of social actors who were much more numerous than the princess regent and presumes an understanding of the slaves' feelings when abolition was announced. Furthermore, it makes little sense to be against a date that ended the slavery system but not be critical of the day that celebrates the "Martyr of Independence" whose platform included the maintenance of that system. Finally, in the Afro-Brazilian syncretic religion of Umbanda, which combines elements from Catholicism, African, and indigenous religions, May 13 is celebrated as the *Dia dos Pretos Velhos* (literally, Old Blacks' Day), that is, the occasion when the souls of old slaves return and speak to the living. Portrayed as gentle entities who speak Creole Portuguese, smoke wooden pipes, and drink coffee, they give advice to the living while incorporated in practitioners of Umbanda. Doing away with May 13 altogether might eventually eliminate this rich cultural manifestation as well.

Abolition helped put an end to the monarchy (Vieira 2012), as the former slave owners (many of whom were members of the nobility by the emperor's granting of titles) felt it had betrayed their economic interests. By the same token, the former slaves were also left destitute, given that the abolitionist wish for agrarian reform did not materialize. Landless, vagrant, pushed over by the arrival of European immigrants, they were left to their own devices. A little over a year later, on November 15, Marshal Deodoro da Fonseca, who had been a monarchist until close to that date, proclaimed the country a republic with a coup d'état in Rio de Janeiro. The royal family was exiled and relocated to France, where Dom Pedro II died in 1891 and Princess Isabel in 1921.

THE REPUBLIC OF THE UNITED STATES OF BRAZIL AND THE RACE QUESTION

As I have mentioned elsewhere (2017), Republican Brazil was fashioned after the United States, to the point where its original name was "Republic of the United States of Brazil." Identification with the American country from the north included the desire for a Whiter population, given that, as we saw in the previous chapter of this book, by the end of the nineteenth century, so-called scientific theories postulated that non-White, including mixed-race, populations were genetically inferior. Unlike the United States, Brazil had to grapple with a much larger and widespread African-descended population. In 1890, the total population of Brazil was 14,333,915; of those, 6,302,198 were White, 2,097,426 were Black, and 5,934,291 were Brown (*pardos*, in the current language). In other words, Whites were in the minority as compared with the non-White population (IBGE 2020).

As a consequence, Brazilian officials of the First or Old Republic (1889–1930) promoted the entry of millions of European and Japanese immigrants, first to work in the agricultural fields formerly cultivated by slaves, and, later, in urban factories. According to official records,

> The immigratory fluxes in the First Republic were the most expressive in the period that goes from the 19th to the 20th centuries: between 1889 and 1930, more than 3.5 million foreigners arrived in the country, which corresponds to 65 percent of the total number of immigrés between 1822 and 1960. (Cpdoc n.d.)

Even though about 50 percent of them were sojourners, there was the hope that the newcomers would help "dilute" Brazilian "blood," which was, for the most part, African.

By the turn of the century, it was obvious that Brazilians of African descent had not only built the country with free manual labor, but had also stuck the foundation of Brazilian culture, be it in literature, music, architecture, engineering, or sculpture. In order to mask that, the government made sure to lighten the portraits of successful Afro-Brazilians. One glaring example is Machado de Assis (1839–1908), widely regarded as the most prominent Brazilian writer and the founder of the Brazilian Academy of Letters, who, until late into the twentieth century, was portrayed as almost White. Another example is Mário de Andrade (1893–1945), one of the propellers of the modernist movement in Brazil, whose "Negroid" traces were modified in his photographs.

This eugenist concern was officially expressed, even if not overtly. In 1891, a new Constitution was written to replace the monarchic regime. In an obvious difference from it, the Republican Constitution established the principle of equality, explicitly eliminating the recognition of nobility. However, as Baraviera (2005, 3–4) notes, "There is no concern over racial equality; quite the contrary. In the first two items of the second paragraph of Article 70, beggars and the illiterate, conditions of the great majority of the newly freed, are excluded from political rights." In practice, former slaves had few chances of a decent insertion into the polity and the job market. Under meager options, the rural population continued working in the fields; those who migrated to cities or who already lived there found employment in menial occupations, such as domestic servants, and resorted to living in subpar tenement houses and, later, up in the hills, in makeshift shanties that gave rise to favelas that persist to this day and continue to lack basic infrastructure such as sanitation.

As for the indigenous population, their situation in the First Republic was no better than during the years of the empire. According to Schwarcz (2019, 167–168), the only difference was that they were even more displaced and exterminated in the name of territorial integration. As an example, she cites the genocide of the Kaingang in 1905, who defended their land against the construction of a railroad. The argument was that they were violent savages who stood in the way of "civilization," an idea that persists over a century later. The 1891 Constitution enforced an 1854 law which allowed for indigenous land to be regarded as "vacant land" and transferred to the states (Azanha 2005). It was not until 1988 that their right to the land was finally recognized; it is, however, constantly challenged, much like the right of *quilombolas* to occupy their settlements.

Although the capital of Brazil in the Old Republic remained in Rio de Janeiro, power was concentrated in two states: São Paulo and Minas Gerais; the former generated wealth with industrialization and coffee plantations, whereas the latter relied on cattle. It was so common for presidents to be elected who came from either state that the oligarchical regime was called "the *café au lait* republic." Meanwhile, revolts erupted throughout the country, in protest against rampant economic and social inequality. For instance, the northeast of Brazil, plagued by long-term droughts and exploitative local governments, was the stage for a number of them, such as the *Canudos* Revolt in the state of Bahia (1893–1897), the *Cangaço* (1870–1940), and the Whip Revolt (*Revolta da Chibata*, 1910).

Canudos was a community founded by Antônio Conselheiro (1830–1897), a preacher, with the goal of living equally and peacefully in the semiarid region. The landowners demanded that the army destroy it for fear it might grow and threaten their own hegemony. Conselheiro was deemed a madman and his community massacred after years of confrontation. The *Cangaço* was a type of militia organized by members of the impoverished, disenfranchised population of the northeast against the power of landowners. It was fought against and finally obliterated by the police.

In a way, both *Canudos* and the *Cangaço* were reactions against social relations that granted practically all economic and political power to landowners. One example was the way elections were conducted: local chiefs had a way of controlling elections by keeping voters under surveillance in a shed where "they received a substantial meal, leaving only when it was time to deposit their vote—which they received in a sealed envelope—directly in the ballot box" (Schwarcz 2019, 54).

Schwarcz (2019, 53) argues that such a way of controlling election results was but one way slavery has colored every aspect of Brazilian social life even after Abolition. Another legacy of slavery was the behavior that led to the Whip Revolt, a rebellion that took place in Rio de Janeiro. A group of 240 sailors was led by João Cândido Felisberto (1880–1969) against the harsh treatment that dark-skinned personnel received in the navy: they were routinely punished by whip, just as in slavery times; had lower salaries and had poor nutrition. The revolt was successful in ending that abuse, although the participants were ostracized. João Cândido, who had gotten the nickname *O Almirante Negro* (the Black Admiral), was expelled from the navy (Arquivo Público do Estado de São Paulo November 18, 2014; Presidentes do Brasil; Pronotícia May 17, 2016).

Black Brazilians also raised their voices against racial discrimination in other areas. Since the beginning of the twentieth century, there emerged organizations that aimed at unifying the population around the issue of their social condition. At a time when Afro-Brazilian culture was attacked, most of them were civic groups aimed at entertainment and social welfare. There were also a number of newspapers, which, together, came to be known as the "Brazilian Black press." One of them, entitled *Clarim d'Alvorada*, stood out as having a clearly political goal (Oliveira, Laiana 2002, 54). For the most part, however, they suffered from the low acquisitive power of their target readership, which led to the demise of most of the publications. The city of São Paulo housed many of them, including the Palmares Civic Center (*Centro Cívico Palmares*). Antônio Carlos, a former army sergeant, founded it in 1926 after having joined the efforts of revolutionary leader Luís Carlos Prestes (1898–1990) two years earlier, which led him to devise a way to bring together Blacks who lived throughout Brazil. In addition to a newspaper, the center created schools and libraries, and objected to the barring of Blacks from certain occupations. The center would end its activities in 1929 amid internal political disputes (Oliveira, Laiana 2002, 48–53).

In sum, once the country instituted a republic, it had to deal with the race question as former slaves and their descendants were now free individuals with legal rights. However, old issues of social inequality remained, including practices that were common during slavery, as the wish for a White majority made the insertion of non-White Brazilians into the larger society difficult. Given that the republic of Brazil was fashioned after the U.S. republic, that reality should not come as a surprise.

THE VARGAS ERA AND THE RACE QUESTION (1930–1945)

The Old Republic came to an end in 1930, a consequence of the rupture of the political alliance between São Paulo and Minas Gerais, and the subsequent association of the latter with the state of Rio Grande do Sul. According to Perissinotto (1994, 224), the reason behind the rupture of the old allies had been disagreement over the economic interests São Paulo had on coffee exportation, whereas Minas Gerais was more focused on expanding the domestic market. Because it also favored the internal market,

> Rio Grande do Sul saw the split between the two great states as the great opportunity to come out of political ostracism, to bar the radicalization of the defense of the export sector, and to end the economic abandon that production for the internal market was facing. . . . It is no wonder that the platform of the Liberal Alliance reflected the interests of the dominant classes not associated with the coffee nucleus.

The "Revolution of 1930" was an armed coup d'état orchestrated by the economic elites of Minas Gerais, Rio Grande do Sul, and the northeastern state of Paraíba, led by Getúlio Dornelles Vargas (1882–1954), a landowner and military man from Rio Grande do Sul. The coup deposed the president, Washington Luís (1869–1957), and ousted his successor, Júlio Prestes (1882–1946). That initiated the "Vargas Era," with the Provisional Government (1930–34). Two years later, the São Paulo elite reacted to Vargas's government with the Constitutionalist Revolution, which demanded that Vargas rule be based on a constitution. São Paulo threatened to secede from the republic, and the movement eventually involved a contingent beyond the elite:

> The imbalance between the ruling and the constitutionalist forces was big. The federal government had military power, and the rebels counted only with civil mobilization. The *Paulista* troops fought practically alone against the rest of the country. The armament and food were provided by the state itself, which later gathered the support of Mato Grosso. Close to 135,000 men joined the fight, which lasted three months and left almost 900 soldiers dead on the *Paulista* side—nearly double the loss of the Brazilian Expeditionary Force during World War II. Although the movement had been born out of demands by the *Paulista* elite, it had ample popular participation. (Bigelli July 7, 2014)

Black Brazilians, both men and women, also participated in the revolution, going so far as to organize their own troops, which came to be known as *Os Pérolas Negras* ("the black pearls). Although academia for decades ignored the Black presence, more recent work has recognized São Paulo Blacks' "tradition of anti-racist struggle" (Domingues 2003). For the purposes of this book, the relevance of the coup of 1930 and the Revolution of 1932 is the extent to which they led to a reconsideration of the role of race for the new regime. Indeed, it was then that the Brazilian elite grappled with the race dilemma of the country under a new light. As I wrote elsewhere,

> This "peaceful absorption" is part and parcel of the ideology of racial democracy, made famous by the writing of *Masters and Slaves*, by Gilberto Freyre, first published in 1933, with which Brazil is identified to this day. Unlike the Dominican Republic decades later, which declared all Dominicans were White, racial democracy assumes that Brazilians are the product of three "races": the Whites (Portuguese), the native "Indians," and the *negros* (Africans). For Freyre, . . . this mixture constituted the uniqueness of the Brazilian "national character"; "deterioration" became "genesis" in his discourse. In sum, according to Freyre, miscegenation was both positive and unavoidable; I remember seeing him on national television in the 1970s, during the military dictatorship, predicting that Brazil would be a "country of *mulatos*" in 50 years' time. (Penha-Lopes 2017, 20)

Not only did the new regime consider a novel way of thinking about the deep racial inferiority feeling that the Brazilian elite felt, it also brought forth a new constitution, thus initiating the Constitutional Government (1934–1937) in Vargas's long presidential tenure. Compared with the two previous constitutions, the 1934 Constitution was more comprehensive in regard to civil rights, in that it granted suffrage to women, instituted the secret ballot, and guaranteed the indigenous population's land rights (Jus Vigilantibus; Schwarcz 2019, 171). It also refers specifically to "race," a first for Brazilian constitutions (Baraviera 2005, 3, 4). Article 113 reads, "All are equal before the law. There will be no privileges, nor distinctions, due to birth, sex, race, one's professions or those of one's parents, social class, wealth, religious creed, or political ideas" (in Baraviera 2005, 3). Although that passage makes the Constitution sound egalitarian, it is actually quite contradictory, in that, in other paragraphs, it emphasizes the same eugenic aspirations that had first surfaced in the United States at the turn of the century. Article 121, sixth paragraph, reads, "The entry of immigrants to the national territory will suffer the necessary restrictions to guarantee the ethnic integration and the physical and civil capacity of the immigrant." Article 138 is even more explicit: "It is the duty of the Union, the states, and the municipalities, in the terms of the respective laws, to stimulate eugenic education" (in Baraviera 2005, 3–4). In sum, notwithstanding the ideology of racial democracy and the writing of a new constitution that seemed to support that ideology, the republic in the 1930s was not that different from the Old Republic as far as race relations were concerned.

That is not to say that racism in Brazil went unchecked. The concern over racial inequality that had given birth to the Black press and to a number of organizations in the Old Republic increased in the Vargas Era, with the foundation of the Brazilian Black Front (*Frente Negra Brasileira* [FNB]) in São Paulo in 1931 by former members of the Palmares Center and of *Clarim d'Alvorada*, for a total of 20 individuals who were seen as representatives of the Paulista "Black elite." Laiana de Oliveira (2002, 57) defines "elite" in this case to mean those "most of whom were literate, undergoing a process of awareness of the problems Blacks had after abolition, and, finally, were interested in discussing those problems and transmitting them to the largest number of people, seeking answers and solutions."[5] It published a newspaper, *A Voz da Raça* (The Voice of the Race), and it expanded to other states (Oliveira, Laiana de 2002, 59). In the 1970s, AbdiasNascimento (1914–2011), who went on to found the Experimental Black Theater (*Teatro Experimental do Negro*—TEN) and made a lifelong struggle of the denouncement of the lower status of Afro-descendants, especially the darker-skinned, thus reflected on the importance of the organization:

> My first experiences of combat were with the *Frente Negra Brasileira*. Some of the FNB directors had been trying to articulate a movement since the 1920s. Yes, there was a plan to host the Black Youth Congress (*Congresso da Mocidade Negra*), in 1928, in São Paulo, but it never materialized. Only in 1938 did five young Black men and I organize the First Afro-Campineiro Congress.[6] In 1950, the *Teatro Experimental do Negro* sponsored the First Brazilian Black Congress, in Rio de Janeiro.
>
> The persons and the ideas were from earlier, but it was in the beginning of the 1930s that the movement was institutionalized as the *Frente Negra Brasileira*. Among its founders were Arlindo Veiga dos Santos and José Correia Leite; as a mass movement, it was the most important organization that Blacks enjoyed soon after the abolition of slavery in 1888.
>
> The Front protested against racial and color discrimination in public places . . . under the perspective of integrating Blacks in national society. That way, the FNB combatted the hotel, bars, barbers, clubs, the police, etc. that vetoed the entry of Blacks, which much resembled the civil rights movement of North American Blacks. (in *Geledés*, September 16, 2011)

Laiana de Oliveira (2002, 61–64) argues that the main goal of the FNB was to raise the self-esteem of Brazilian Blacks, who were constantly passed over on the job market, which favored immigrants, especially in São Paulo. For that, its newspaper published articles emphasizing the contributions of Afro-Brazilians to the development of the country and even asserting that people of African descent were a superior race. She also provides evidence that the organization encouraged Blacks to be above moral reproach in order to decrease discrimination against them, specifically citing "vices of the race" such as alcoholism, prostitution, and even "frenzied samba" as justifications for discriminatory behavior against them. In that respect, I would argue, the FNB quite resembled Booker T. Washington's approach to handling racism. In *Up from Slavery* (1901), his autobiography, he insisted that American Negroes must improve themselves by first mastering menial occupations before they aimed at higher statuses and more acceptance by the larger society. As is well-documented, that approach made Washington clash with Du Bois, who advocated for Negroes to take advantage of every opportunity to achieve upward mobility, despite the many impediments society placed in their path. Finally, Laiana de Oliveira notes that the FNB tended to consider incidents of racism as exceptions rather than proof that Brazil was a racist country, a description that it attributed specifically to the United States. Instead, the Black Front was proud of the mixed heritage of the country, created out of the encounter of the Portuguese with the indigenous and the African. Put together, those attitudes approximated the FNB more to the ideology of racial democracy than to a break with the way Brazil saw itself as a nation.

Over the years, the Brazilian Black Front expanded its interests beyond a preoccupation with Blacks' morals to venture into politics, for example, by participating in the discussions about the elaboration of the 1934 Constitution. By 1936, with national representation, it had become a political party, whose platform was quite in accordance with President Vargas's staunch nationalism (Oliveira, Laiana de 2002, 80–81). However, the party was short-lived. Abdias Nascimento recalled,

> [The Front] was a vanguard with the goal of preparing the Negro to take on a political and economic position in the representation of the Brazilian people before Congress. And the movement spread from São Paulo to other states with a significant Black population: Bahia, Pernambuco, Rio Grande do Sul, Rio de Janeiro, Minas Gerais, Maranhão. . . . "The so-called New State (*Estado Novo*), or Getúlio Vargas' dictatorship, installed in 1937, closed the FNB together with all political parties in existence then." (in *Geledés*, September 16, 2011)

The year 1937 marks the beginning of Vargas's dictatorial government, named the New State (1937–1945). Fruit of a coup d'état by Vargas himself, the New State fit in the international climate at the time, with the growing influence of authoritarianism in Europe, such as the rise of Nazi-fascism in Germany and Italy, and the dictatorships in Portugal and Spain. It also fit with Vargas's plan to increase his power at least since 1935, when the Communist Conspiracy (*Intentona Comunista*), led by Luís Carlos Prestes, attempted an uprising in various Brazilian cities. It is said that Vargas had a document forged, the Cohen Plan, which mapped a "communist" invasion by the Soviet

Union (Fernandes, Cláudio n.d.). That gave him the subterfuge to install a dictatorial regime in Brazil.

A new constitution came forth, nicknamed "Polish" (*A Polaca*) because it was inspired by the 1925 Polish Constitution of Marshal Pilsudski's government; he was regarded as a hero in the war against the Bolshevik invasion of 1920. The 1937 Constitution concentrated all power in the executive branch of government, in that it determined the elimination of the legislative and the curtailing of the judiciary. Moreover, all the media were subjected to censorship, the right to strike was taken away, and "political crimes" were punishable by death (Jus Vigilantibus; Todamateria.com.br).

Although the 1937 Constitution maintains indigenous land rights, it omits the term "race," something Baraviera (2005, 3–4) labels a "curious retrocession." On the other hand, I believe that makes sense in a dictatorial regime, especially one with such a nationalist stance as Vargas's. After all, to this date in Brazil, bringing up the issue of racial inequality may be regarded as an attempt to incite "racial hatred" and, thus, to divide the country; both the Brazilian Black Front in the 1930s and the current Brazilian Black Movement have been accused of such. Moreover, dictatorships rest on the requirement that a country stay united around certain ideas; dissent may lead to exile and even death. The New State emphasized industrialization under governmental control and the nationalization of foreign companies (Todamateria.com.br).

Even though the New State was dictatorial and repressive, Vargas is still remembered by many as a "father" of the people. In large part, that is due to his concern with the establishment of laws that protected workers. Between 1930 and 1943, Vargas presided over the "Consolidation of Labor Laws" (*Consolidação das Leis Trabalhistas*), which included the eight-hour day, regulation of overtime, maternity leave, and paid vacations (Direitos Brasil). As Schwarcz (2019) points out, authoritarianism is appreciated in Brazil.

POPULISM AND RACE (1945–1964)

With the end of World War II, Brazil underwent a process of re-democratization; the fact that Brazil had fought in the war on the Allies' side despite Vargas's authoritarianism and increasing domestic manifestations against his dictatorial regime made that transition more feasible, "in 'a proper environment of peace and order,'" in his own words (FGV CPDOC 2020). Under pressure, Vargas scheduled presidential elections for December 1945 and for governors for the next year. In October of the same year, he was deposed by the military and, in January 1946, Eurico Dutra, who had won the elections, was sworn in as the new president (FGV CPDOC 2020). Yet Vargas would continue his political career as a senator from his home state of Rio Grande do Sul; as such, he briefly participated in the Constituent Assembly (Moreira 2020).

The 1946 Constitution differentiates itself from the previous ones for mentioning racial prejudice and making it illegal. According to Bertulio (1989), that was due to the efforts by Black Brazilians for the government to recognize the existence of racism in the country. With re-democratization, organizations that fought for racism to be recognized as a social problem in Brazil reemerged. Examples are the Union of Men of Color (*União dos Homens de Cor* [UHC]), founded by João Cabral Alves in Porto Alegre in 1943, and the Black Experimental Theater (TEN), founded by Abdias Nascimento the following year. UHC's goal was "to elevate the economic and intellectual level of persons of color in the entire national territory in order to make them apt to enter the country's social and administrative life, in all activity sectors." In a few years' time, UHC indeed spread to several Brazilian states. In turn, TEN started out as an all-Black cultural organization, but it became more politically engaged over the years, including fostering pan-African connections (Domingues 2007). In fact, during the Negro National Convention (*Convenção Nacional do Negro*) in São Paulo in 1945, "Abdias Nascimento, who presided over that important conclave, requested that the manifesto addressed to the Nation include an item proposing punishment against discrimination to the Brazilian penal code" (in Grin and Maio 2013, 36).

Despite making racial prejudice illegal, the 1946 Constitution does not establish ways to combat it in practice. Bertulio (1989) notes, "Jurists, legal scholars, or political scientists are unaware of the fact. In the repressive sphere of the state, however, racist manifestations are frequent." In other words, racial discrimination went on despite the efforts of Black organizations to denounce it and its recognition by the Constitution. It would be necessary for a racist incident involving a Negro woman artist from the United States to occur for the Brazilian authorities to recognize the presence of racism in their midst and give some semblance of interest in addressing it.

The incident concerned a U.S. Negro artist, Katherine Dunham, who was prevented from staying at Serrador Hotel in São Paulo in 1950. The repercussion abroad was noteworthy (Acervo *O Globo*), enough to question the validity of the ideology of racial democracy that Brazil so vehemently projected onto the world. So many years later, it is interesting to note that Dunham's light skin would clearly categorize her as "Negro" in her home country, since the United States did not recognize the obvious product of miscegenation as a separate category in 1950, but, in Brazil, where racial mixture was purportedly celebrated, she could have been seen as *mulata* or even as *morena* (i.e., brunette).[7] That the hotel personnel ignored that widespread way of looking at race stands out. Furthermore, it is significant that it did take a foreign Black person to highlight a racist practice to which, to be sure, many Brazilian

Blacks had been submitted before and have been since. That would be an example of what Jessé Souza (2018) has called "the Brazilian subcitizenship" (*subcidadania brasileira*), namely, the tendency of the Brazilian elite to see itself as inferior to Europe and the United States. According to the author, that results from their belief in conservative culturalism, which claims that European and U.S. cultures are more rational and impersonal (which makes them superior and modern), whereas Brazilian culture is more emotional and personal (which makes them retrograde, and thus, inferior). Under that logic, a Black person from the United States would be superior and more deserving of rights than a Black person from Brazil.

A year after the Dunham incident, the Afonso Arinos Law (Law no. 1390) was approved in Congress. For the first time in its history, Brazil recognized the existence of racial discrimination and made it illegal. Grin and Maio (2013) offer an alternative argument for the passing of the law: rather than a consequence of the international scandal discrimination against Dunham had caused, Law no. 1390 was an attempt to suppress the growing demands by Black activists for state recognition of racism in Brazil, which had been quite evident during the elaboration of the 1946 Constitution. The 1950s were also when the UNESCO sponsored studies about race relations in Brazil under the assumption that its racial democracy could be replicated elsewhere so as to avoid the type of racism and ethnic discrimination that had characterized World War II. Those studies ended up showing that racial prejudice and discrimination were common in Brazil and prevented the descendants of former slaves to achieve social, economic, and political equality. In sum, both among Black activists and social scientists, voices rose that pointed to the farce of racial democracy. Afonso Arinos proposed a law that saw racism as a moral problem and acted preventively. Reactions among Black activists varied, with TEN considering it as support of the effort to embark on "a second Abolition," whereas FNB saw it as easy to violate (in Grin and Maio 2013, 36–37). The law also sought to prevent the fight against racism in Brazil from turning into a racial war. As Grin and Maio (2013, 43–44, 45) conclude,

> Soon after the speech, the amendment to Arinos' project is presented, elaborated by socialist congressman Hermes Lima . . . , which suggested "the prohibition of the formation of 'Black fronts' or of any modality of association with political goals based on color." Lima's amendment mirrored the preoccupation Afonso Arinos and Gilberto Freyre shared that the project, by shedding light on the existence of racism in Brazil, would lead to perverse results regarding the strengthening of associations, organizations which potentially stimulated a "reverse racism." Once again, the anticipatory character of the project was present.
>   . . . For [Arinos], it was a matter of "rescuing" the genuine atmosphere of racial harmony present in the trajectory of race relations in Brazil since

Abolition. The law, in those terms, should be directed to the guarantee, under penalty of law, of an environment impervious to exogenous values of a racist type. (Grin and Maio 2013, 43–44)

By the time of the approval of the Afonso Arinos Law, Getúlio Vargas had been again elected president, with an expressive victory in October 1950. He would remain in power until 1954, when, amid threats against his government, he committed suicide. He was followed by Juscelino Kubitschek (1956–1961), Jânio Quadros (January 31–August 25, 1961), and João Goulart (1961–1964). Kubitschek's tenure was concerned with economic development and the transferring of the capital of the country to Brasília. In addition to resigning after a few months, Quadros is famous for having appointed the first Black Brazilian diplomat, Raimundo Sousa Dantas (1923–2002), who served in Ghana amid great rejection by the members of the Brazilian diplomatic corps, almost all of whom were White men from well-to-do families. Goulart's tenure (1961–1964) was interrupted by a military coup d'état that instituted a dictatorship for 21 years.

THE MILITARY DICTATORSHIP AND RACE (1964–1985)

In the Cold War climate, under the justification that Goulart's government was sympathetic to communism, the military took over power on March 31, 1964, sending Goulart to exile in Uruguay and placing Marshal Humberto de Alencar Castelo Branco (1897–1967) as the first president. Throughout the 21 years they remained in power, the military referred to the abrupt change as "the 1964 Revolution." Since then, that term has been rejected. The military regime in Brazil was but one of the many such regimes in Latin America. Declassified documents in the early twenty-first century show that all of them were sponsored by the United States, which feared that the entire region might fall under Soviet control after the Cuban Revolution of 1959, the so-called "domino effect." The documents also confirm the extent of interference by the Central Intelligence Agency, responsible for training the Latin American officers of the dictatorships in repression techniques, including torture.

Evidently, such a regime would rely on a new, repressive constitution. As Supreme Justice Celso de Mello notes, "The constitutional process was violated and power was usurped. We had to face situations of absolute disregard for the public liberties regime. In 1967, we had a new Carta" (in Jus Vigilantibus). The 1967 marks the new name of the country: from Republic of the United States of Brazil, the official name from 1891 to 1937, to United States of Brazil since 1937, and, finally, to Federative Republic of Brazil (Struck 2017).

A reading of the entire document points to contradictions. For starters, although the first paragraph of the first article of the new constitution reads, "Every power emanates from the people and in its name it is exercised," it is followed by a much less democratic tone, with an emphasis on national security, mention of the possibility of war, and on "censorship of public entertainment." Chapter IV lists individual rights, which include "the inviolability of the rights to life, liberty, safety, and property," the freedom of thought and speech, of association, the right to come and go. In sum, "No one will be forced to do or not do something unless by virtue of the law" (Article 150, paragraph 2). Yet the next chapter, entitled "On the State of Siege," deals solely with censorship. The president is granted the right to take on the following "coercive" actions:

> a) the obligation to reside in a determined location; b) detention in buildings not destined to common criminals; c) home search and seizure; d) suspension of freedom of meeting and associating; e) censorship of mail, the press, telecommunications, and public entertainment. (Presidência da República 1967)

There were plenty of examples of that along the 21 years of the regime. Television programs and films, for example, were always preceded by a certificate of censorship that stipulated the minimum age of those allowed to watch them. Especially after 1968, when President Artur da Costa e Silva (1899–1969) signed Institutional Act no. 5, all individual rights were suspended, habeas corpus was denied, politicians were stripped of their power, those deemed as enemies of the state were exiled, Congress was closed, and a number of dissidents disappeared.

Another glaring contradiction of the 1967 Constitution concerns race. Unlike the previous constitution, it is explicit about racial equality. Following the Afonso Arinos Law, it deems racism illegal: "All are equal before the law, without distinction of sex, race, work, religious creed, and political convictions. Racial prejudice will be punished by law" (Article 150, paragraph 1). Yet, in a regime that focused on national security and censorship, discussions about racial prejudice or discrimination could be and was often censored as a threat to national security. In fact, after the dictatorship turned even more repressive in 1968, questioning racial harmony was regarded as subversive. The Constitutional Amendment of 1969 added institutional acts to the 1967 Constitution, making it even more repressive, but maintained the text about race. It was as if claiming that racism was illegal was a deterrent to bringing it up at all; from then on, "publication of news about the Black movement and racial discrimination" were prohibited (Garaeis July 13, 2012). A number of social scientists and activists who studied the issue left the country. One of them was Abdias Nascimento.

After he was prevented from speaking at the University of São Paulo and seeing his name on more and more lists of personae non gratae, Nascimento decided to accept an invitation from the Fairfield Foundation and move to New York City. Reflecting on his exile, Nascimento said, "My stay in the U.S. gave me the ground and the territory to fly high every which way. I was called to every city in the U.S., but, above all, to Africa" (in Contins 2005).

Not until the mid- to late 1970s, during General Ernesto Geisel's government (1974–1979), did serious discussions about racial inequality come to the fore, with the gradual ease of restrictions in a process known as *abertura política* (political opening). Exiled scholars and activists returned and the voices that called racial democracy a myth became louder as speaking in public about the existence of racism was no longer considered a crime against the nation. In 1975, the Institute for the Research of Black Cultures (Instituto para a Pesquisa de Culturas Negras) was founded in Rio de Janeiro. In 1978, members of the Black movement demonstrated in São Paulo, the largest city in Brazil, against racial discrimination.

Another indication of the opening process was the legalization of political parties beyond the only two that were allowed during the dictatorship, the National Renovation Alliance (*Aliança Renovadora Nacional*) and the Brazilian Democratic Movement (*Movimento Democrático Brasileiro* [MDB]). In 1981 to 1982, returning political exile Leonel Brizola, a former Vargas ally and governor of Rio Grande do Sul, founded the Democratic Workers' Party (*Partido Democrático Trabalhista*). Abdias Nascimento took on a prominent role in it, acting as secretary of the state of Rio de Janeiro, and being elected to the National Congress in 1982. He saw his tenure there "exclusively for the Black cause," an unprecedented feat. He edited the six-volume *Combat of Racism* (*Combate ao Racismo*) in which he proposed several affirmative action measures: job quotas for Blacks and for women (20 percent for each category); college scholarships for Blacks; ways to guarantee the entry of Blacks into the foreign service; curricular change on all educational levels, such as the teaching of African history cultures in grade school; and making racism a crime (Contins 2004). Nascimento proposed those measures as "reparation for the history of Blacks in Brazil." With the end of the military dictatorship in 1985, with General João Baptista Figueiredo (1979–1985), racial activism grew even more.

THE NEW REPUBLIC AND RACE (1985 TO PRESENT)

Even before the last military dictator left the presidency of Brazil, the country embarked head-on on a national campaign toward democracy. Not only were there a series of strikes since the late 1970s, but there was also a movement, *"Diretas Já"* (direct right now), which garnered support from the larger public, students, artists, and politicians. The massive campaign, regarded as one of the largest in Brazilian history, centered around the approval for a constitutional amendment, authored by congressman Dante de Oliveira (1952–2006), that would authorize direct presidential elections in the same year. On April 10, 1984, over one million people gathered at See Square, in São Paulo, their faces painted in green and yellow, two of the colors of the Brazilian flag; Rio de Janeiro was also the stage for a similar demonstration and other cities followed suit. However, the Amendment was defeated in Congress 15 days later for lack of a quorum. Tancredo Neves (1910–1985), a civilian with a long career of opposition to the military regime, was indirectly elected by the Electoral College on January 15, 1985. Neves fell ill the next day and died of diverticulitis on April 21, a date many considered symbolic, as it coincides with the national holiday in honor of Tiradentes. His vice president, José Sarney (dates1985–1990), was inaugurated as president in 1986 and stayed in power until 1989 (Biografias; Silva, Vinicius). That was the beginning of the "New Republic."

In accordance with the post-dictatorship climate, Sarney's motto for his tenure was *Brasil: Tudo pelo Social* ("Brazil: All for Society"). It was during his years as president that the country adopted yet another constitution. The constituent congress met between 1987 and 1988, congregating congressmen and groups with diverse interests, such as wealthy landowners, and those concerned with decreasing social and racial inequality in Brazil, such as Black activists. The pressure that had started before the end of the dictatorship for Brazil to acknowledge that racial democracy was but a myth and its debt to the descendants of slaves grew stronger during the constituent. Though President Sarney had suggested the establishment of the Black Council of Compensatory Action (Conselho Negro de Ação Compensatória) in the first year of his tenure but never really followed through (Telles 2003), he did institute the Palmares Cultural Foundation (Fundação Cultural Palmares) in 1988, whose goal was to aid in Afro-Brazilians' full participation in society. In turn, members of the Black movement and other antiracists kept their agenda alive. For instance, Carlos Alberto Oliveira, known as Caó (1941–2018), an activist who had been arrested during the dictatorship and later became a politician, was responsible for overturning the Afonso Arinos Law with Law no. 7.437/1985, which came to be known as Caó Law. The significance of that law was that it labeled racism a crime. As Jean Wyllys, a Brazilian congressman, recalls,

In the Constituent, he was responsible for including in the Magna Carta of 1988 the subparagraph in Article 5th that made the practice of racism an imprescriptible felony. Later, Caó was the author of Law 7.716/1989, which regulated the constitutional text that established the penalty of prison for the crime of race or color prejudice and discrimination. (Bittencourt February 4, 2018)

It is in that context that the Constitution of 1988 becomes the first to recognize racial inequality and attempt to decrease it, long a demand by members of the Black movement (Silvério 2004). Specifically, Title I, "On Fundamental Principles," lists as its goals "to eradicate poverty and marginalization and to reduce social and regional inequalities"; "to promote the well-being of all, without prejudices based on origin, race, sex, color, age, and any other form of discrimination"; and "repudiation of terrorism and racism." Title II, "On Fundamental Rights and Guarantees," reinforces those ideas in Chapter II, which concerns "social rights," by prohibiting any form of wage discrimination (Presidência da República 1988). Chapter III, "On Nationality," facilitates the naturalization of those "from Portuguese-speaking countries." The innovation of that clause is the inclusion of Africans whose countries are former Portuguese colonies, most of whom are Black. Moreover, the current constitution recognizes the "multiracial character of the Brazilian population" (Baraviera 2005, 6), as it introduces the teaching and learning of Afro-Brazilian history and culture as well as the contributions of the indigenous population and the immigrants who also formed Brazil. Finally, in addition to continuing to acknowledge indigenous rights, this constitution protects *quilombolas*' right to land unlike any of the previous ones. In other words, the 1988 Constitution buried the eugenic tone of previous constitutions (Baraviera 2005), finally making the idea of equality, present in all others, actually workable. Further recognition of the struggle of the Afro-Brazilian population was the institution of November 20 as Black Conscience Day in November 2003, so chosen because it was the day of Zumbi dos Palmares's murder in 1695. In 2011, the date became a national holiday.

However, racial-ethnic equality continues to be elusive; a thirst for land threatens indigenous and *quilombola* territories and their very lives. In 1967, the Costa e Silva government had created the Indigenous National Foundation (*Fundação Nacional do Índio—Funai*) to oversee indigenous' rights on the federal level, under the purview of the Ministry of Justice (Schwarcz 2019, 169), but that has not guaranteed their constitutional rights. As of 2019, there were over 300 indigenous groups who spoke 274 languages constantly under attack due to the desire from the larger society to explore their land for capitalist gains, such as mining, large-scale agriculture, deforestation, and even the construction of hydroelectric plants, despite the fact that they are an obsolete source of energy. As a result, between 2015 and 2017, nearly 250 indigenous persons were murdered (Schwarcz 2019, 169), often with impunity.

Likewise, the 1988 Constitution recognizes 3,200 *quilombola* communities; in 2003, an act ratified ownership by the residents. Yet, "until 2018, less than 7 percent of those lands were recognized as belonging to quilombo remnants or were regularized" (Schwarcz 2019, 173). Furthermore, as we will see in chapter 5 of this book, their removal was a campaign promise of Bolsonaro, in clear violation of the Constitution.

In the 1990s, ongoing pressure on the federal government to acknowledge racial inequality and to consider measures to combat it resulted in the implementation of affirmative action policies, the most prominent of which were university quotas for Afro-descendants and public school students, first in the states of Rio de Janeiro and Bahia, in 2003, later spreading to the entire country. In 2012, after 13 years of discussions in Congress and the Senate, President Dilma Rousseff signed the program into federal law (Penha-Lopes 2017).

From the start, a debate ensued about the need and even legitimacy of the program. According to its opponents, miscegenation makes it impossible to determine who is Black in Brazil; therefore, the quotas are but an imitation of a U.S. problem. They also claimed that there is no racism in Brazil and that reserving a portion of slots for Blacks at state and federal universities is illegitimate. Another argument against quotas was that they are antimeritocratic because university admission in Brazil is solely based on entrance exams. Defendants of the program counterargued that Brazil has a debt with the descendants of slaves, that darker-skinned Brazilians have been and continue to be victims of racial exclusion, and that quotas would increase the proportion of Blacks with university degrees, which would lead to better chances of experiencing upward mobility.

Studies have shown (see Penha-Lopes 2017) that the adoption of university quotas has generated the largest contingent of college graduates among Afro-descendants to date and that many of them have found success, rather than stigma, on the job market. That has led to the growth of a Black middle class in Brazil, but also of the White middle class, as they are able to take advantage of university quotas for public school students, regardless of race.

Regarding the working class, the occupation of domestic worker was finally regulated in 2015, after much groundwork by the Union of Domestic Workers. The informality of that occupation had long been a legacy of slavery. In Brazil, it has been historically common for families to take in impoverished girls and young women, usually Black, who become responsible for housework and childcare; they are called *empregadas* (literally, "employed," but whose equivalent in English is "maid") or *criadas* (literally, "raised," that is, impoverished girls who are raised by better-off families in order to serve as their maids). It is also common for them to live with the family who employs them, usually sleeping in tiny quarters with no ventilation. Because the occupation was informal, maids might not be regularly paid, or paid very little. They may also be regarded as "a member of the family," though they might be forbidden from sitting at table with the family, let alone benefit from an inheritance. Put together, those characteristics made Brazilian maids reminiscent of house slaves. The 2015 legislation sought to change that by establishing paid vacations, maternity leave, and contributions toward retirement (Brêtas June 2, 2020, 9). Because of the high concentration of Black and Brown women in that occupation, its regulation can be seen as a change toward improving the socioeconomic conditions of Brazilians of African descent; evidence shows that a number of university quota students are either children or grandchildren of domestic workers (Penha-Lopes 2017).

Another change we observe since the implementation of affirmative action in Brazil is the fact that more Brazilians than ever have come to recognize themselves as African descendants. At the same time, that is only a partial victory, given that most Brazilians of any race do not reach university level, and that the stigma of darker skin persists, from being called "monkeys" to being murder victims, including at the hands of the police. As I will show in later chapters, the election of Jair Bolsonaro—which followed the impeachment of President Dilma Rousseff in 2016—boosted opposition to the quota policies in particular and to social programs in general due to their strong association with the Workers' Party and in line with his posture toward racism in Brazil. Telling evidence to that argument was his appointment of Sérgio Camargo to be president of the Palmares Foundation in November of 2019. A journalist and self-proclaimed *negro de direita* (i.e., a right-wing Black man), who is in line with Bolsonaro's platform, Camargo immediately created controversy by negating the existence of racism in Brazil, affirming that Brazilian slavery was "beneficial for the descendants [of enslaved] Africans," and by dismissing November 20 as a "shameful" holiday (*Folha de S. Paulo* November 27, 2019). On April 30, 2020, Camargo was recorded calling Zumbi "a son of a bitch who enslaved Blacks," referring to the Black movement as an *escória maldita* ("wretched slag"), and disrespecting Afro-Brazilian religions (*Meia Hora* June 4, 2020, 9).

In sum, behind Brazil's façade of racial democracy, there lies a history of racism, social inequality, and authoritarianism. Brazil is the country that kills the largest number of Blacks and LGBTQIA+ persons in the world; as part of Latin America, it has one of the highest rates of violence against women as well (*The Dialogue* October 15, 2018). Under that view, the election of Jair Bolsonaro for president was neither a surprise nor an aberration. Rather, it was a reflection of national values that resurfaced after a brief period of re-democratization. Therefore, the full inclusion of minorities in the definition of what it means to be Brazilian is at serious risk.

NOTES

1. *Réis* were the Brazilian currency up until 1833.

2. Pedro I was infamous for his many extramarital affairs, the longest of which with Domitila de Castro do Canto e Melo (1797–1867), a married woman from an elite family from São Paulo. Three years into a relationship that lasted seven years (1822–1829) and produced five children, Dom Pedro first appointed her lady-in-waiting of Leopoldina, his wife, much to the empress' chagrin. A few months later, he decreed her Viscountess of Santos, "for services rendered to the Empress." In 1826, he elevated her to the title of Marquise of Santos. He ended up granting titles of nobility to her whole family. Dom Pedro also had one child with Maria Benedita de Castro Canto e Melo, Domitila's sister, whom he titled Baroness of Sorocaba (Frazão November 1, 2019; Rezzutti October 28, 2014).

3. A statue of José Bonifácio stands on Avenue of the Americas, also known as Sixth Avenue, in New York City, as part of a row of prominent political figures from the continent.

4. In the North Zone of the city of Rio de Janeiro, there is a neighborhood named "Vila Isabel" (i.e., Isabel's Village), so-called in honor of Princess Isabel. The main avenue of the neighborhood is called September 28 Boulevard, after the Law of the Free Womb.

5. Oliveira's conception of "elite" more closely resembles Frazier's use of the term "Black bourgeoisie" (1957), meaning American Negroes who, in the 1950s, were literate and gainfully employed, usually in service occupations in governmental agencies. It is less similar to Du Bois's "the talented tenth" (1903), by which he meant the proportion of U.S. Negroes who, like him, were highly educated professionals with an awareness of racial inequality who should lead the uneducated masses toward pushing for better living conditions.

6. "Campineiro" is the noun indicative of or from Campinas, a city in the state of São Paulo.

7. For a discussion of the social construction of race in Brazil, see Penha-Lopes (2017), especially Chapter 3, "University Quotas and Racial Identity."

Chapter 3

"Make America Great Again"
Donald Trump's Presidential Campaign

Starting with John Adams (1735–1826), the second president of the United States, 25 out 45 presidents have been lawyers. Four of them, including John Adams himself, and Barack Obama, the forty-fourth president, graduated from Harvard University; another four went to Columbia University, Yale University, Duke University, and the University of Virginia (Reference.com; Beran February 15, 2016). Even more common has been for presidents to have held some political post; only six never served in Congress, the Senate, a state government, or the House of Representatives (Murse January 16, 2020).

Presidential candidate Donald Trump is one of the exceptions. Having started a career in real estate in the early 1970s, he gained prominence in the early 1980s as a successful businessman, and became a television host in the first decade of the twenty-first century before he announced his candidacy.

AN UNCONVENTIONAL CANDIDATE

Donald J. Trump was born in Queens, a New York City borough, on June 14, 1946, in a family formed out of the Great Immigration (1880–1924). His paternal grandfather, Friedrich Drumpf, was an adolescent when he arrived in the United States in 1885 from Germany. While the immigration bureaucrats changed his last name to "Trumpf" upon arrival, he himself would change it to "Trump" when he became a naturalized U.S. citizen in 1892 and was settled in Washington State. A barber in Germany, Friedrich Trump made money as a builder, a restaurant owner, and even as the owner of a bordello. When it came time for marriage, Trump went back to his native country for a bride; he married Elizabeth Christ in 1905, the same year when they moved to Queens and their son Frederick, Donald's father, was born. There, Friedrich

Trump did very well in real estate right when Queens became more accessible to Manhattan with the construction of the Long Island Rail Road. After his death in 1918, the family experienced some downward mobility due to the 1920 to 1921 recession, but the orphan worked in construction until he rose to real estate developer together with his mother. Frederick (Fred) married Donald's mother, Mary Anne MacLeod, in 1936; she was a Scottish immigrant who also came to the United States as an adolescent. The Trumps lived a comfortable life, made possible by Fred's success in real estate (D'Antonio 2016, 20–23).

Although one's place of birth is a matter of public record, Donald Trump has denied his German ancestry, as had his father; both men claimed to be Swedish. According to John Walker, a cousin of Donald Trump, and Gwenda Blair, author of a biography of the Trumps, Fred Trump acted that way for financial reasons: to avoid conflict with Jewish customers and to escape "anti-German sentiment after World War II" (Khan November 30, 2017). In fact, Fred Trump's business had profited from the incentive that the Federal Housing Administration had given to homeownership with the New Deal, in the 1930s, and then with the GI Bill, in the postwar period. "By 1940," writes D'Antonio (2016, 31), "he was hailed as one of Brooklyn's biggest builders in a report noting that his crews were bulldozing the last patch of forest in that borough." Given that New York City comported nearly two million Jews in 1940 (Jewish Virtual World 1998–2020), who were in a position to purchase homes, Fred Trump was bound to meet many of them. Interestingly enough, he is remembered as having been "very German" for the way he treated his children, that is, always expecting them to "be a killer" (D'Antonio 2016, 39; 43). As for Donald Trump, while he called himself "a proud German-American" (Khan November 30, 2017), he has also somehow affirmed his ties to Swedish roots, such as during an interview for the *New York Times* in 1976, when he claimed "that though he was often mistaken for Jewish, he was actually Swedish" (D'Antonio 2016, 115).

After having gone to a private school in Queens, young Donald was sent to the New York Military Academy in an effort to curb his "rebellious" nature. There he was noticed for his desire "to be first, in everything, and he wanted people to know he was first" and also for his athletic prowess (D'Antonio 2016, 43). The fourth of five children, Donald Trump showed a keen interest in his father's business from early on. Upon graduation, he enrolled at Fordham University, in the Bronx, while continuing to live with his parents in Queens and learning about real estate from his father. In 1966, he left Fordham for the University of Pennsylvania, thus satisfying his father's wish that he would go to an Ivy League school. There he enrolled in the Wharton School of Finance and Commerce, majoring in real estate. He graduated two years later, purportedly at the top of his class, but that cannot be verified because the university does not keep official rankings; however, he would claim that recurrently. By then, Fred Trump "had thousands of apartments in buildings he owned and operated." That allowed him to generate wealth from rent, even if, by the late 1960s, urban unrest and White flight slowed real estate developments (D'Antonio 2016, 47–48; 51; 65–68).

As a member of the early years of the baby-boomer cohort (1943–1960), Trump joined the largest ever college population in the history of the country (Chalmers 2013). Unlike so many baby boomers, however, he was not known to join in student protests, experiment with drugs, or even drink. On the other hand, like many college students at the time, he was able to avoid the draft to the Vietnam War. Once he graduated in 1968, he was lucky to be dismissed due to "heel spurs on both feet" (in D'Antonio 2016, 70). He continued to work with his father.

In the early 1970s, Fred Trump's rental practices got him in trouble with the federal government. As I noted in chapter 1 of this book, one of the gains of the civil rights movement was the Fair Housing Law, which was a provision of the Civil Rights Act of 1968. Most buildings Fred Trump owned were located in Brooklyn and Queens, also the areas with the largest Black populations in the city. Starting in 1970, a middle-class Black flight from Brooklyn increased the Black population in Queens (Black Demographics 2020), though Brooklyn still retained twice as many Blacks (25 percent) as Queens (13 percent). Therefore, it would be expected that Trump's Black tenants amounted to more than 4 percent, the actual figure. That prompted the Open Housing Center of the Urban League to file a complaint against Trump Management Company, which by then was presided over by Donald Trump, on the grounds of racial housing discrimination. At that time, that was "one of the biggest federal housing discrimination suits ever brought" (Lusher February 16, 2017). The Trumps countersued, alleging a US$100 million loss over the claims of the federal government; by then, they owned 14,000 to 16,000 units (D'Antonio 2016, 79). They denied the practice of racial discrimination, but admitted that their business "excluded welfare recipients" because they were a financial liability (D'Antonio 2016, 79–82). Siding with the government were Trump employees who testified that Fred Trump himself had told them "not to rent to blacks." An employee continued, "He also wanted me to get rid of blacks that were in the building by telling them cheap housing was available for them [elsewhere] at only $500 down payment, which Trump would offer to pay himself." Those statements were made public by a substantive Federal Bureau of Investigation dossier declassified in 2017, that is, when Donald Trump was already serving as the 45th president of the United States (Lusher February 16, 2017). They settled the case, with Donald Trump claiming a victory of sorts by stating, in *The Art of the Deal* (1987), that "in the end the government couldn't prove its case,

and we ended up making a minor settlement without admitting any guilt."
However, according to Lusher (February 16, 2017),

> The Justice Department claimed victory, calling the consent decree "one of the
> most far-reaching ever negotiated." It explicitly barred the Trumps from "dis-
> criminating against any person in the terms, conditions, or privileges of sale or
> rental of a dwelling." It also ordered the Trumps to "thoroughly acquaint them-
> selves personally on a detailed basis" with the Fair Housing Act. And it required
> them to place adverts telling ethnic minorities they had an equal opportunity to
> seek housing at Trump properties. Some newspaper headlines from the time
> appeared to reflect the view of a Justice Department victory. The *New York
> Amsterdam News* ran with: "Minorities win housing suit."

The accusation of racial discrimination against Fred Trump in 1973 may
have brought back his arrest, on Memorial Day in 1927, at a Ku Klux Klan
demonstration in Jamaica, Queens. While newspaper accounts at the time
reported the demonstration to be a nativist rally against attacks "by Roman
Catholic police of New York City" (Bump February 29, 2016), there was by
then enough history of terrorism perpetrated by the Klan against all who did
not fit into the White Anglo-Saxon Protestant category, especially people of
African descent. Even if the newspapers do not specify the reason for Fred
Trump's arrest, it is curious that he would be accused of racial exclusion so
many decades later at a time when society was paying more attention to discrimination than in years past.

According to D'Antonio (2016, 83), the 1973 lawsuit showed how Donald
Trump, who was only 27 years old at the time, would operate henceforth:
"always on the offensive." Influential in the cultivation of that style was Roy
Cohn, their defense attorney. Donald Trump had befriended Cohn, Senator
Joseph McCarthy's former assistant, when he went to live in Manhattan after
graduating from college and started frequenting exclusive nightclubs. The
son of a New York judge, Cohn graduated from Columbia University Law
School at the age of 20. At only 24 years of age, he starred in Ethel and Julius
Rosenberg's trial, in which his unscrupulous ways of getting testimony led to
their conviction as spies and to a death sentence. The fact that he was Jewish
favored his employment with Senator McCarthy, in that many of those he
accused of communism were Jewish; the understanding was that the investigations could not be labeled anti-Semitic for that reason (Russo Jr., March
10, 2019). Known for his cutthroat ways, which included blackmail, Cohn
has been described as an anti-Semitic Jew, a scammer, and a homophobic
gay man (D'Antonio 2016, 78). An example of his scams was his role in
the mayoral victory of Abe Beame, a Brooklyn Democrat with ties with the
Trumps, by leaking damaging information about his opponent. Beame would

later be instrumental for Donald Trump to secure the development of Penn Central, near the Hell's Kitchen neighborhood in Midtown Manhattan, which is how young Trump started to take Manhattan, so to speak (D'Antonio 2016, 84–85; 90). Evidence of Cohn's homophobia was his habit of "taking his boyfriends to meetings where the right to homosexuality was denounced" (Russo Jr., March 10, 2019). He died of AIDS in 1986, even though he denied he was infected until the very end; shortly before his death, he was disbarred. Curiously, Roy Cohn's anti-communism has been identified as Olavo de Carvalho's role model (Russo Jr., March 10, 2019). As I show in chapter 5, Olavo de Carvalho is considered Jair Bolsonaro's "guru" and main articulator of his presidential campaign.

Donald Trump's friendship with Roy Cohn and his coming on his own in real estate at the young age of 27 happened in the 1970s, which Tom Wolfe labeled "the 'Me' Decade" in an essay that made the cover page of *New York Magazine* on August 23, 1976. After the focus on families in the 1950s and the concern with social change in the 1960s, the focus of the 1970s was on subjectivities and individuality: an interest in self-help, but also in standing out amid the crowd. A few years later, Christopher Lasch would call it *The Culture of Narcissism* (1979). Writing more recently, Kakutani (2018, 63) concluded, "With this embrace of subjectivity came the diminution of objective truth: the celebration of opinion over knowledge, feelings over facts—a development that both reflected and helped foster the rise of Trump."

The rise of Trump in real estate, in the 1970s, began when he took advantage of the dismal state of New York City—with high crime and poverty rates, all but bankrupt—to acquire lots at more attractive prices. As mentioned earlier, the first was Penn Central, on which he profited over US$1 million, but did not get to fulfill his wish to call the finished development after his father, since the city of New York opted to call it "Javits Center" (D'Antonio 2016, 96). After that, he acquired and tore down hotels, always with tax incentives. Trump's young age, business acumen, and self-promotion put him on the path of celebrity.

Toward the end of the decade, in April 1977, Donald Trump married a woman who fit his preference for blonde models and who would also work with him. Ivana Zelníčková (also known as Ivana Winklmayr) was a former athlete said to be an Olympian in the Czechoslovakian ski team, though such claim could not be verified; she had also had a modeling career in Canada. They moved into Olympic Tower, a Fifth Avenue building, and proceeded to have two sons and a daughter, all of whom, but especially his daughter, Ivanka, would play roles in his business and, later, in his presidency (D'Antonio 2016, 119, 124).

In 1979, Trump unveiled Trump Tower, a 58-story-high mixture of "a casino blended with a bank" due to the decor of the atrium which he claims is 10 stories high (Kakutani 2018, 81). The exterior and the atrium signaled opulence, what with the marble and the high-end stores, and the apartments were expensive enough (the selling price of some reached the US$1 million mark). True to the "diminution of objective truth," Trump sought to raise the glamour of his property by claiming that the Prince and Princess of Wales were thinking of buying an apartment there, though Buckingham Palace never confirmed that (D'Antonio 2016, 129; 139). The building became a tourist attraction along with other skyscrapers on Fifth Avenue.

Trump became a household name of sorts in the 1980s, when he established himself as a savvy and successful businessman. In 1982, he was granted a gaming license, which allowed him to get into the development of casinos. The first one, Harrah's at Trump Plaza, opened two years later; his wife was responsible for its decor (D'Antonio 2016, 160; 162). In 1983, he was featured on *Lifestyles of the Rich and Famous*, a new television program that showcased "celebrities" and their wealth. He was also profiled in the *New York Times* Sunday magazine and even made the cover of *GQ* magazine, as a poster boy of "success." In 1986, *Playgirl* magazine elected him "sexy." Though Trump was more and more visible, D'Antonio (2016, 152) notes that Graydon Carter, the editor of *Spy* who would later edit *Vanity Fair*, "was probably the first to suggest . . . that a lot of people just don't like Donald Trump very much."

The 1980s were the Reagan years (1981–1989), a time of social conservatism and state divestment from social programs. President Ronald Reagan (1911–2004), the former Hollywood B-actor and governor of California, was fond of "trickle-down economics," the idea that businesses should get all kinds of incentives and perquisites for, if they were successful, their riches would "trickle down" to the rest of society. In the 1980s, there was also a push for "family values," a longing for the "good old times" (i.e., the 1950s), and condemnation of the "excesses" of the 1960s and 1970s. Those were opulent years, exemplified by the return of big weddings and conspicuous consumption. The media displayed those trends both on film and on television. The film *Wall Street* (1987) depicts the world of the cutthroat New York stock market, with its huge deals and insider trading, whereas *Trading Places* (1983) dealt with the same themes, but with clever humor. On television, the prime-time soap opera *Dynasty* (1981–1989) spanned the entire decade centered around two wealthy families constantly at war. In addition to the plots, the series became famous for its over-the-top figurines by designer-to-the-stars Bob Mackie, in which sequins and extremely broad shoulder pads for women were prominent.

Donald Trump fit right into that world. His real estate developments were notorious for their extravagant decor both inside and out; gold details were everywhere. Trump Tower, for example, was a glass monument with the name TRUMP perched up for all to see: quite a leap from his buildings in Queens. His own living quarters in the tower followed that style, one that appealed more to the nouveau riche than to the patrician families of Old New York society. As Pye (1993, 354–355) put it,

> More boorishly, Donald Trump's Louis XVI barstools, his marble dining table for seventy-five, his bedroom painted, he said, "with the quality of the Sistine Chapel" are exercises in promotion as well as excess. In Queens the Trumps rent middle-income housing to ordinary Joes, but in Manhattan they sell hotel rooms and apartments to people who need proof that they have chosen right. The more ink the Trumps required the more they were models of richness and success, the more certain people wanted to live in Trump Tower, where there is a dearth of captains of industry and powerbrokers, but a number of California absentees including the TV talk-show host Johnny Carson, and a certain notorious Madam. You could see the Trumps' social existence, even their claims of billionaire status before the fall, as the promotional expenses of the more sober investors—in the case of Trump Tower, the Equitable Life Insurance Company—could not overprice the property on their own.

Pye refers to Trump's modus operandi, that is, his reliance on wealthy partnerships for his acquisitions. That was so for the Plaza Hotel, which he acquired in 1988; a football team; and several casinos over the years. In addition, he invested his profits from one development to acquire loans for his next projects. That was the crux of *The Art of the Deal* (1987), his best-selling first book, which Tony Schwartz ghostwrote: Trump was able to get powerful investors for his deals despite the fact that so many of them—casinos, hotels, an airline, the football team—did not pan out. The image that he cultivated and promoted was that of "the man who has everything," as Barbara Walters declared on her television show *20/20* on the same day his book came out (D'Antonio 2016, 183–184; 200).

By the time Trump published his first book, his marriage was falling apart. Having met Marla Maples, a model, in 1985, he started a relationship with her that led to a showdown between Maples and Ivana Trump on the Colorado slopes at Christmas in 1989. Like his business deals, his marriage woes and subsequent divorce two years later were headlines in every major newspaper, in magazine, and on television. Maples's interview on *Primetime Live* (1992) was "the biggest ever audience for the program" (D'Antonio 2016, 215), which showed that Trump was able to generate a celebrity status for the women in his life as well. They would be married in late 1993, after the birth of their daughter, Tiffany. David Dinkins, the first African American mayor of New York City, officiated the civil ceremony; the reception, during which he later claimed he was "bored," was at the Plaza Hotel (D'Antonio 2016,

226). They divorced in 1997. The following year, he met Melania Knauss, a model from Slovenia, who would become his third wife in 2005 and give birth to their son, Barron, in 2006; authors (D'Antonio 2016, Kikutani 2018) have noted that "Baron" was the fictitious last name Trump would employ to promote his books and business deals anonymously.

The fact that Donald Trump is a thrice-married man with a documented history of adultery adds to the list of unconventional characteristics of him as a presidential candidate. As I will discuss later, those characteristics made a difference for a portion of the electorate who holds on to Puritanical values, but not enough to prevent his victory in 2016.

A CANDIDATE IS BORN: TRUMP'S PRESIDENTIAL CAMPAIGN

Before Donald J. Trump became the official Republican Party presidential candidate on July 19, 2016, he had tested the political waters. After the publication of his 1987 book, Trump made a series of public appearances during which he expressed his opinion on themes that would stand out in his 2016 candidacy. For instance, he gave a speech in New Hampshire about the loss of economic power the United States was suffering on the international arena, evidenced by its being bullied in trade deals and paying for the defense of other countries. In addition, he was a guest of *The Phil Donahue Show*, which led to a congratulatory note from former president Richard Nixon (1969–1974), urging him to run for president someday. Even more noteworthy were his actions in 1999, when he joined the Reform Party and announced his plans to be a presidential candidate the following year. Interestingly enough, he claimed he could garner voters who were put off by the Republican Party having gone to the far right and named African American television host Oprah Winfrey as his "ideal running mate" because "she's popular, she's brilliant, she's a wonderful woman." Moreover, in opposition to President Bill Clinton (1993–2000), who had reneged on his promise in his first presidential campaign to allow gays and lesbians to serve in the military, instead instituting the "Don't ask, don't tell" policy, Trump favored an open policy. Finally, very much unlike his way of thinking in 2016, he proposed higher taxes for the very wealthy and the establishment of a comprehensive health care system, "with subsidies for the poor" (D'Antonio 2016, 182–183; 185; 200).

Although Trump boasted that he would be a great candidate because he was so wealthy and well-known, he withdrew from the race in February 2000, alleging that the Reform Party was "a mess." The Reform Party, of Ross Perot fame, retorted that all Trump ever wanted was to promote his business and his books (by then, Trump had published four). Citing Neil

Postman's classic 1985 thesis about the all-encompassing effect of television on politics, religion, and education, D'Antonio (2016, 256) places Trump's campaign in the realm of entertainment, of giving people what they want, that is, endless amusement. Evidence of Trump's lack of seriousness, according to him, was his choice of the Reform Party. In 2012, he again announced his candidacy, only to drop out of the race once more (Allen and Parnes 2017, 50). This time, he would be running out of the Republican Party, but his low acceptance rate convinced him to withdraw from the race, though he deemed the country "a once great nation divided" and "a disaster" (D'Antonio 2016, 294–295). It is telling that, 16 years later, Trump would win the Republican Party nomination.

When Donald Trump announced his candidacy in 2015, he emphasized his career as a successful businessman as a major asset, even if, by a number of accounts and his own admission of a fondness for hyperbole, his success was often exaggerated.[1] In case there were those who were oblivious to his celebrity businessman status, they got a dose of it from *The Apprentice*, a reality TV show conceived by Mark Burnett of *Survivor* fame, that ran from 2004 to 2015 on NBC; Trump got to keep half of the profits as the host (D'Antonio 2016, 263). To his spectators, Trump appeared as a cutthroat boss who did not hesitate to eliminate the contestants who failed to live up to his expectations. "YOU'RE FIRED!," his catchphrase, was embraced by fans of his show. And there were many: according to D'Antonio (2016, 12; 265), "A genuine hit, *The Apprentice* was a top-ten program in its first season." If 20 million people watched the premiere, "almost 30 million viewers [watched] . . . the final night of its run." That led to two stints—on April 3, 2004 and November 7, 2015—as host of *Saturday Night Live*, the comedy show that has aired on NBC for over 40 years. On both occasions, skits centered on Trump's self-promotion as the greatest at everything he does, although his second time was marred by demonstrations against his negative remarks about Mexicans (Associated Press November 4, 2015). Between television appearances and Twitter, "many implored him to seek the presidency" (D'Antonio 2016, 4). He also hosted *The Celebrity Apprentice* (2008–2017), also created by Mark Burnett. The show brought back Omarosa Manigault-Stallworth, who had reached celebrity status as a stereotypical "angry Black woman" who got fired on the first season (D'Antonio 2016, 267).

Collins (1990) argues that the double oppression of race and gender has afforded Black women only four archetypes through which they are judged: the "mammy," a benevolent, often overweight, and asexual Black woman who is nurturing, an obvious remnant of slavery times; the "Jezebel," an oversexualized woman who is not wife material; the "bitch," an angry Black woman who emasculates men; and the "welfare queen," a Black woman who has several children in order to be eligible for financial aid from the

government. In the next chapter, we will see that Trump invited Manigault-
Stallworth to be a member of his cabinet once he was elected president,
a cabinet that stood out for its dearth of non-White members. The fact
that the only Black woman member was one who played on a stereotype
did not go unnoticed. *The Celebrity Apprentice* also counted on the three
Trump adult children. Once Trump announced his presidential candidacy,
he stepped down as host of *The Apprentice*. He was replaced by Arnold
Schwarzenegger, the Austrian-born Hollywood actor and former governor of
California, who was also one of the executive producers of the show (NBC
.com).

Trump and Burnett exported the premise of the TV businessman. *The
Apprentice* has a franchise in Brazil, titled *O Aprendiz*, which was first broadcast in November 2004 on TV Record, the station owned by the Universal
Church of the Kingdom of God (*Igreja Universal do Reino de Deus*), a neo-
Pentecostal church with branches all over the world. The host was Roberto
Justus, a successful Brazilian businessman who is also famous for his marriages to blonde women who are many years his juniors. Justus was replaced
between 2009 and 2013 by João Agripino da Costa Doria Jr., himself a
businessman from the city of São Paulo, who would be elected governor of
the state of São Paulo in 2018. In that same year, the reality show began to be
broadcast by TV Bandeirantes (*Exame* October 10, 2010).

Trump was accompanied by his wife when he announced his candidacy
from Trump Tower on June 16, 2015. He focused on the fact that he had
never been a politician, unlike most of the other candidates. The idea was that
he would use his purportedly successful business skills to run the country if
elected, which would be good for it. Out of 19 Republican Party candidates,
Trump and Ben Carson, a neurosurgeon, were the only ones who had never
held political offices; among the nine Democratic candidates, only Lawrence
Lessig was not a politician (CNN Politics June 2016). That the U.S. elector-
ate might be ready for unconventional presidential candidates because it was
tired of politics as usual (Sago, Markus, and Joffe-Block February 28, 2016;
Beason July 14, 2016) was reflected in the fact that Ben Carson, the only
African American contender, came close to Trump for polled prospective
Republican voters, on September 9, 2015, that is, right before the second
Republican debate: Trump had the lead at 27 percent; Carson had 23 percent.
Jeb Bush, the son and brother of two former U.S. presidents and former gov-
ernor of Florida (1999–2007), placed well below at only 6 percent (Peoples
September 15, 2015). Trump would dismiss Bush as "a nervous wreck" and
"very, very unstable at this moment" during a telephone interview he gave to
Fox News, the channel that endorsed him, in early 2016 (YouTube February
8, 2016). Bush withdrew from the presidential race less than two weeks after
that, appalled with "the angry mood of the country that helped Trump log

wins" (*Time* Staff February 20, 2016). Soon after, on March 4, Ben Carson followed suit (Jackson and Kelly March 4, 2016).

Interestingly enough, the mainstream media viewed Trump's candidacy as a joke. The June 17, 2015 cover of the *New York Daily News*, for instance, blasted, "Trump throws rubber nose in GOP ring." Beneath it, it read in large font, "CLOWN RUNS FOR PREZ." A picture of Donald Trump adulterated by a clown nose and mouth sat beside the banner, which directed the reader to Trump's "circus speech" on pages 4 and 5.

Only there was nothing funny about Trump's speech. In this order, Trump attacked the other Republican candidates for sweating too much, the country for losing economic ground, Latin America for sending criminals, Middle Easterners for "Islamic terrorism," U.S. involvement in Iraq, a slow domestic economy, politicians, Obama's health care program, and Obama's behavior as "a bad negotiator," and China as a trading partner. And then Trump went on to boast about his success as a real estate developer and to promise to fix the economy, the educational system and the U.S. airports, and to protect veterans. He concluded thus, "Sadly, the American dream is dead. But if I get elected president I will bring it back bigger and better and stronger than ever before, and we will make America great again. Thank you. Thank you very much" (*Time* Staff June 16, 2015). In sum, Trump presented himself as the country's savior and focused on an extreme chauvinism that invoked xenophobia, with hints of racism, all bathed in hyperbole and self-aggrandizing, such as when he claimed a crowd of "thousands" awaited him, while Alana Wise, a Reuters reporter present, counted "dozens" who, it turned out, had been paid to be there (Gabbat June 14, 2019).

Trump's 45-minute speech "struck an emotional chord with downtrodden working-class white men" (Allen and Parnes 2017, 49). Reflecting on Trump's New Orleans appearance on the eve of the Louisiana primary the following year, Hochschild (2018, 225) employs the same adjective to describe the Republican presidential candidate's effect on his followers' attitudes by calling him "an 'emotions candidate.'" The evidence she presents is compelling: the way he includes the audience when he tells them about his clinching the Republican nomination, how he implies that other countries are robbing the United States, how he implies his career as a "greedy" businessman will come in handy when he runs the country, and how he alludes to resorting to violence in order to silence protestors (whom he calls "disruptors") if need be. Moreover, in a city that was nearly 60 percent Black in 2019 (U.S. Census Bureau), the few Blacks in attendance were "Black Lives Matter" protestors and those working in security or selling T-shirts. Based on her fieldwork in the area, Hochschild characterizes the audience as Whites who have been feeling "culturally marginalized" and economically unstable due to the social, economic, and political changes that have been taking place for over three decades. She concludes,

> More than any other presidential candidate in decades, Trump focuses on elic-iting and praising emotional responses from his fans rather than on detailed policy prescriptions. His speeches—evoking dominance, bravado, clarity, national pride, and personal uplift—inspire an emotional transformation. Then he *points to* that transformation. "We have passion," he told the Louisiana gath-ering. "We're not silent anymore; we're the loud, noisy majority." He derides his rivals in both parties for their inability to inspire enthusiasm. "They lack energy." Not only does Trump evoke emotion, he makes an object of it, present-ing it back to his fans as a sign of collective success. (Hochschild 2018, 225; emphasis in original.)

Further sociological data have found support for that argument. The "racialization of U.S. politics" (LeCount 2018, 1), that is, the tendency for Whites to vote according to "racial resentment" even when controlling for socioeconomic status, age, education, and region, has been noted since 1986. Whites have felt that Blacks are undeserving of what they get because they do not try hard enough to do well (LeCount 2018, 2). Although Trump did not mention African Americans in his speech, he did focus on foreign nation-als who are not White. Therefore, he might be implicitly playing on racial resentment. And that rhetoric, I add, brought Trump very close to Andrew Jackson, his favorite president, a populist who appealed to landless Whites in the nineteenth century, as I related in chapter 1 of this book.

Observers came out of that event thinking it quite impossible that Trump's campaign would succeed (Gabbat June 14, 2019). However, in June of 2016, a poll showed that, although Trump would lose to Hillary Clinton, the Democratic candidate, if the election took place then, "some 64 percent of those respondents who believe the country needs a new direction favor him" (Danner 2016).

"SAVIOR"

Armed with the images of outsiders, both Trump and, as I show in chap-ter 5, Jair Bolsonaro presented themselves as the most apt candidates to "save" their countries, a discourse that appealed to the many voters who had become disenchanted with traditional politicians, who are, according to Trump, "all talk, no action." Each insisted that only he was capable of taking his country back to a glorious past. In Trump's case, that glory would appear as a "restoration" of the economy by bringing jobs back to the United States and regaining world leadership, though the execution of those promises were left vague (*Chicago Tribune* November 11, 2016). Trump's slogan, "Make America Great Again" (MAGA, for short), was printed in red baseball caps that he and his followers proudly wore. Trump vowed to revitalize the automobile industry (On the Issues), generate coal mining jobs (Tabuchi 2017), and take from Mexico jobs that should be back on U.S. soil.

From the moment Trump announced his candidacy, he displayed his disappointment over the supposed inability of the United States to compete with Japan on the automobile market. During his speech in Trump Tower, he shouted,

> When did we beat Japan at anything? They send their cars over by the millions, and what do we do? When was the last time you saw a Chevrolet in Tokyo? It doesn't exist, folks. They beat us all the time.

By singling out the Japanese car production, Trump stirred negative sentiments that had been around at least since the 1980s, when U.S.-built cars started to lose ground to Japanese imports even in U.S. territory. The decline of the U.S. automobile industry, once sovereign, led to the economic depression of cities such as Detroit, Illinois, and Flint, Michigan, from which they have yet to recover. As I mentioned in chapter 1, anti-Japanese prejudice grew, which led to the 1982 murder of a Chinese American man whose ethnicity was mistaken as Japanese. Trump vowed to impose taxes on car imports and was very critical of automobile companies that moved to Mexico to lower production costs, such as Ford and General Motors. Therefore, he condemned President Obama for having bailed out automobile companies so as to avoid bankruptcy and the subsequent loss of jobs. At a rally on November 7, 2016, President Obama mentioned Trump's criticism of his decision, suggesting instead that the companies move to states with a nonunionized labor force. By mentioning that, President Obama wished to shake Trump's strong appeal among working-class Midwesterners (Zanona November 7, 2016).

Trump also spoke about China. On the one hand, he was displeased with the way China conducted business because, according to him, it lowered its currency rate so as to deem any transaction unfair:

> Right now, think of this: We owe China $1.3 trillion. We owe Japan more than that. So they come in, they take our jobs, they take our money, and then they loan us back the money, and we pay them in interest, and then the dollar goes up so their deal's even better. How stupid are our leaders? How stupid are these politicians to allow this to happen? How stupid are they? (*Time* Staff June 16, 2015)

On the other hand, Trump proclaimed his "love" for China because the Chinese purchase his real estate units. The problem for him seems to be China's ascension on the global market, which threatens to overtake the role the United States has played.

Experts have argued that the promises Trump made to Appalachian coal miners to generate more jobs for them were unfulfillable because those jobs "no longer exist" (Tabuchi 2017). Even if Trump managed to reverse Obama's environmental concerns, there would be little return, for those jobs have been replaced by automation; moreover, the low price of natural gas makes coal too expensive. As for bringing factory jobs back from Mexico to the United States, for decades sociological research has shown that workers from developing nations earn much less than U.S. workers, which makes them more attractive to capital. Moreover, postindustrialization has made factory work "disappear" from U.S. soil (Wilson 1996). As Trump would hear from Gary Cohn, the president of Goldman Sachs who served as director of the National Economic Council in his first year as president, the bulk of the U.S. economy in the twenty-first century was in service (which includes sophisticated technology), not in manufacturing, so that the federal government was better off being innovative in generating jobs rather than holding on to a picture which no longer exists (Woodward 2018, 59–60). After having repeatedly shown to Trump data on job turnover from the Bureau of Labor, Cohn told him, "See, the biggest leavers of jobs—people leaving voluntarily—was from manufacturing." Noticing Trump's difficulty in understanding that, Cohn insisted, "People don't want to stand in front of a 2,000 degree blast furnace. People don't want to go into coal mines and get black lung. For the same dollars or equal dollars, they're going to choose something else" (Woodward 2018, 138).

RACIAL TENSION

The association of Trump's name with racial tension precedes his presidential campaign by decades. In April of 1989, he took out a full page in four newspapers demanding the return of the death penalty, so that the "Central Park Five" could be sentenced to it. They were five New York City African American and Latino teenagers between the ages of 14 and 16 who were arrested for the rape of a White woman jogger in Central Park. Under duress, they confessed to the act. In his newspaper manifesto, Donald Trump called them "wild criminals." During their trial in 1990, members of the Guardian Angels, the unarmed anti-crime group, carried signs which called for the accused to be "put away" and to be given "hard time."[2] All of them were convicted without DNA evidence that linked them to the attack.

Four of them were convicted to 5 to 10 years; one had already served 14 years in prison when a man confessed to the crime. Only then were they exonerated. Filmmaker Ava DuVernay portrayed their tragedy on a 2019 Netflix series, *When They See Us*. Meanwhile, Donald Trump continued to state that they were guilty (D'Antonio 2016, 192–ff, 328; Sperling May 17, 2019).

Also in 1989, Trump was a guest on the *Today* show, the long-running NBC morning program whose anchor was Bryant Gumbel. Trump told Gumbel, who is Black, that well-educated Blacks were at an advantage over their White counterparts "in terms of the job market. I've said on one occasion, even about myself, if I were starting off today, I would love to be a well-educated black because I believe they have an actual advantage" (in D'Antonio 2016, 193). Trump was not alone in that viewpoint. In fact, that is often one of the justifications those who are against affirmative action programs raise to defend their elimination. As early as 1975, Glazer argued that affirmative action was a case of reverse discrimination because it penalized the groups excluded from it. As I mentioned in chapter 1, the idea that affirmative action discriminated against White men became quite popular in President Reagan's tenure. Implicitly or explicitly, affirmative action was viewed as antimeritocratic, so that Blacks who took advantage of it in order to get a college education were usurping a slot from "deserving" (because they were supposedly better prepared) Whites. In the early 1980s, the belief that affirmative action was unfair was strong among Whites (Kluegel and Smith 1983). Nationally representative data from the late 1980s showed that Whites continued to resist policies specifically directed at Blacks (Bobo and Kluegel 1993). Even though White women have been the greatest beneficiaries of affirmative action (Sokoloff 1992), the overall view is that Blacks—especially the college graduates—have done so well under it that is no longer necessary. However, that belief is far from correct. Longitudinal data indicate that a college education does not guarantee Blacks equitable wages to Whites; as of 2015, at every educational level, Whites earned more than Blacks. Moreover, they show that the racial wage gap decreased in the 1979, only to increase in 1989 (Wilson and Rodgers III September 20, 2016).

Although Trump was incorrect, his statement about the advantage of educated Blacks ingratiated him with working-class White men, the ones who most felt left behind by affirmative action. D'Antonio (2016, 244) applies Thomas Frank's term, "market populism," to suggest that Trump's remarks about race were his way of "pander[ing] to the prejudices that arise out of fear." Market populism attributes the existence of social problems to the actions of government and intellectuals. By talking in a language that working-class and poor Whites could understand, a member of the economic elite such as Trump could appear to be aligning himself with the downtrodden. If left unchecked, this alliance of race regardless of class could breed support for White supremacy.

Trump would generate racial tension again in 1993. A casino owner by then, he took issue with the federal law that allows American Indians to operate casinos without paying taxes. According to Trump, the law discriminated against non-Indians (D'Antonio 2016, 229–230). In other words, he ignored the fact that American Indians have much fewer opportunities for socioeconomic achievement than the rest of the U.S. population; they lag behind all other groups in terms of health, education, and wealth (National Congress of American Indians June 1, 2020). Once again, Trump interpreted minority racial status through the lens of self-interest. This time, however, he stopped short of saying that he would love to be a member of an indigenous group.

Trump is also famous for correlating anti-Black racism with Islamophobia. Well before he announced his presidential campaign in 2015, he had joined a campaign to discredit Barack Obama's presidency with claims that he was not a U.S. citizen. Called "birtherism," the rumors had started in 2004, when Andrew Martin, a lawyer, issued "a statement claiming Obama was not a Christian but 'a Muslim who has concealed his religion'" (D'Antonio 2016, 284). Martin's claim seems to have been motivated by mental illness. Described as "a fringe politician from Illinois," the "serial Illinois political candidate" (Cheney September 16, 2016), and "a perennial losing candidate for office" who "once registered to campaign under the banner of the Congressional Campaign to Exterminate Jew Power in America," Martin had been prevented from advocating in the state where Obama had built his political career by a judgment of "paranoia" and lack of "self-restraint" by the Supreme Court, amid other charges (D'Antonio 2016, 284). In 2008, that is, the year of Obama's first election, Trump stirred those rumors again. According to newspaper accounts, "Three years later, Trump began pushing the issue in television interviews as he was considering whether to run for president in 2012" (Megerian September 16, 2016). For instance, on *The View*, the talk show anchored by Barbara Walters, Whoopi Goldberg, and others, Trump asked on March 23, 2011, "Why doesn't he show his birth certificate?" Trump said, "I wish he would because I think it's a terrible pall that's hanging over him. . . . There's something on that birth certificate that he doesn't like" (Cheney September 16, 2016). Despite releases of Obama's short and long birth certificate forms, Trump insinuated that Obama had been born in Kenya, like his father, or was perhaps "a Muslim," perhaps in hopes of capitalizing on the Islamophobia that has increased in the United States since the attacks on September 11, 2001. During his speech to announce his candidacy in June 2015, Trump speculated that Islamic countries were "probably" sending "not the right people" to the United States. Later on the campaign trail, Trump emphasized that there was "something within Islam which hates

Christians" and considered closing the U.S. borders to them (Hochschild 2018, 226). Only in September 2016, that is, two months short of his presidential victory, did Trump finally acknowledge Obama's U.S. citizenship. However, he continued to stir the pot of controversy by blaming his opponent, Hillary Clinton, for having spread the "birthering" rumors (Megerian September 16, 2016), even though Clinton had disregarded the rumors and refused to act upon them (Cheney September 16, 2016). Eventually, Trump accused both Obama and Hillary Clinton of weakness for not going against "radical Islamic terrorism" (Allen and Parnes 217, 246).

The xenophobia that Trump displayed in regard to China and Japan as economic traders was even more pronounced toward Mexico, which he claimed makes fun of the "stupidity" of the United States, surpasses it economically, and is not a friend. Trump further offended Mexican citizens and Mexican Americans when he famously referred to them as criminals, including drug dealers and "rapists":

> When Mexico sends its people, they're not sending their best. They're not sending you. They're not sending you. They're sending people that have lots of problems, and they're bringing those problems with us. They're bringing drugs. They're bringing crime. They're rapists. And some, I assume, are good people. But I speak to border guards and they tell us what we're getting. And it only makes common sense. It only makes common sense. They're sending us not the right people. (Gamboa June 16, 2015)

In August 2015, before he had Jorge Ramos, a Mexican American reporter, removed from his press conference under the shout "Go back to Univision," Trump blamed the Mexican government for intentionally exporting "the bad ones" (Edelman August 31, 2016). That was his justification for building a wall on the Mexico-U.S. border, for which he insisted the Mexican government would pay. Mexican president Enrique Peña Nieto not only criticized Trump's idea, but countered that Mexico would not finance his plan and equated Trump with Hitler and Mussolini to boot, a comparison shared by Vicente Fox and Felipe Calderón, both former presidents of Mexico (Reuters March 7, 2016).

Eventually, Trump extended his insults to U.S. citizens of Mexican ancestry by complaining about partiality on a judgment concerning one of his developments. Trump had founded Trump University in 2005, with promises of delivering the best business education. In 2010, Eric Schneiderman, the attorney general of New York, sued Trump University for fraud; the plaintiffs alleged that they never got internships or opportunities to network with powerful people. Trump counterargued that the suit was a result of President Obama going after him to avenge the birtherism claims (D'Antonio 2016,

281–283). He also complained that Gonzalo Curiel, the federal judge assigned to the case against Trump University, was biased against him because "he's a Mexican." Judge Curiel is an Indiana native (Edelman August 31, 2016).

Trump once claimed that he is "the least racist person" (in D'Antonio 2016, 292). Yet, on close observation, all peoples he finds fault with to the point of denying them entry into the United States happen to be non-White. While the targeted groups may have changed from the beginning of the twentieth century, the tone of Trump's attacks against them is similar to the nativist sentiments that were then in vogue.

MISOGYNY

Trump's presidential campaign was marked by many accusations of sexual abuse against him, all by White women. The most explosive of them all, however, came from Trump himself. A month before Election Day, on October 7, 2016, a videotape emerged in which Donald Trump dialogued with television interviewer Billy Bush about touching women without their consent. Published by *The Washington Post* on its website, the tape had been recorded in 2005, when Trump made an appearance on the gossip NBC show *Access Hollywood* to talk about his guest appearance on *Days of Our Lives*, a soap opera on the same television channel. The material in question had never been broadcast.

The tape starts with a bus on a television lot. Trump and Bush are on the bus, but only their voices are heard. Trump mentions an unnamed woman whom he had tried to woo even though she was married; he describes her beauty in vulgar terms. He admits that, might as he try, he was unsuccessful. Then, Bush seems to spot the actress who will work with Trump; enthusiastically and rudely, Bush comments on her beauty. Trump responds thus,

> Yeah that's her with the gold. I better use some Tic Tacs just in case I start kissing her. You know I'm automatically attracted to beautiful . . . I just start kissing them. It's like a magnet. Just kiss. I don't even wait. And when you're a star they let you do it. You can do anything.

Bush obsequiously agrees with Trump, saying, "Whatever you want." And then Trump utters the words by which the videotape is henceforth known: "*Grab them by the pussy.* You can do anything" (BBC October 9, 2016; emphasis mine). Throughout, Billy Bush, who is a nephew of former president George H. W. Bush (1924–2018), pandered to Trump's behavior by laughing and cheering him on. As they approach the unnamed actress, the two married men flirt with her. For instance, Bush suggests that she hug Trump, who adds that "Melania said this was okay," and proceeds to ask her who of the two she would choose for a date; at first, she takes "the fifth" and then relents by saying she would take both of them.

The repercussion of the videotape was immediate and widespread. A number of prominent Republicans, including Condoleezza Rice, who had been secretary of state under President George W. Bush (2001–2009), disavowed Trump (Allen and Parnes 2017, 341). Three women from different generations came forth to denounce Trump's behavior toward them. One of the women, a flight attendant in the 1970s, stated that Trump "groped and kissed her on a flight" (Shear December 11, 2017). Another, a former Miss Venezuela (1995) and Miss Universe (1996), complained that she suffered from eating disorders after Trump, the owner of the Miss Universe pageant, called her "Miss Piggy" and "Miss Housekeeping"; he was also critical of her weight on Howard Stern's radio show (Reilly May 23, 2016). At first, Trump denied any wrongdoing both in regard to the *Access Hollywood* tape and the women's allegation of sexual misconduct. However, soon after, due to pressure from the Republican Party, he "issued a semiapology for the video" (Allen and Parnes 2017, 343), though "he vehemently denied the allegations of misconduct and harassment by the other women" (Shear December 11, 2017). Billy Bush was fired from NBC, even though he too apologized for his behavior. Fewer than two years later, his wife divorced him (Fernandez July 13, 2018).

The accusations against Trump followed a lifelong list of complaints. Nearly 70 women have accused him of sexual harassment and assault going as far back as his youth, which has made some authors refer to him as a "sexual predator" (Levine and El-Faizy 2019). Trump has denied the reports, claiming in 2018 that they were all false accusations; in some cases, he even claimed he had never met the women who accused him. Moreover, while Stormy Daniels, a performer on adult films, came forth before the elections about having had an affair with Trump during his latest marriage and alleged she was paid for her services by Michael Cohen, Trump's attorney, several other women told of liaisons with Trump and sexual assaults (Taylor August 25, 2018). The manner in which he ended his first marriage, as I have mentioned earlier, was also brought up as evidence of his adulterous behavior.

To be sure, Trump was not the first presidential candidate to be dodged by charges of illicit affairs. President John F. Kennedy is notorious for many such rumors. Democratic presidential contender Gary Hart withdrew from the 1988 race when pictures emerged of a woman who was not his wife sitting on his lap on a yacht in Bimini. President Bill Clinton underwent impeachment hearings after he lied about having had an affair with a White House intern. The novelty about Trump's situation had to do with how members of his own party considered replacing him as a presidential candidate and also how the accusations surfaced right when the Me Too movement was exposing the sexually predatory behavior of so many prominent men. Started by Tarana Burke, an African American woman, in 2006, the goal of "Me Too" was "to help survivors of sexual violence, particularly Black women and girls, and other young women of color from low wealth communities, find pathways to healing" (Me Too 2018). In 2017, Alyssa Milano, a former television child star, encouraged women who had been assaulted or molested to speak up about it on social media by writing "me too." From then on, the phrase "#Metoo" took on an international dimension. Out of it the movement "Time's Up" sprung, focusing on sexual harassment in the film and television industries. By 2018, a number of male actors and producers saw their careers crumble—one even went to jail—as a result of the attention brought to the issue (Hutchinson October 8, 2018). For all of that, it was expected that Trump's candidacy would suffer. Yet "after he was pummeled for days, a *Washington Post-ABC News* poll revealed that only 13 percent of Republicans and 38 percent of independents said they were less likely to vote for Trump because of the *Access Hollywood* video" (Allen and Parnes 2017, 343). A month later, the irrelevance of the tape for his campaign was confirmed by his election.

In addition to accusations of sexual harassment, before the infamous videotape, Trump was already known for his habit of measuring women by their physical appearance. For instance, in 2011, during Trump's aborted presidential campaign, Gail Collins, a *New York Times* columnist, referred to him as "a financially embattled thousandaire." While *Vanity Fair* praised Collins "for making wall-to-wall Trump coverage not only bearable but enjoyable" (Weiner April 20, 2011), Trump "sent [her] a copy of her column with her photo circled and the message 'The Face of a Dog!' scrawled beside it" (D'Antonio 2016, 10).

Trump has notoriously attached pejorative nicknames to his antagonists. For instance, because Senator Elizabeth Warren of Massachusetts had claimed American Indian ancestry in 2012, only to admit later that was unfounded, Trump referred to her as "Pocahontas" throughout his campaign (Howard May 16, 2016), at once insulting American Indians, Warren, and women in general.

Even more disturbing has been the way Trump has treated his older daughter, Ivanka Trump, in public. A Wharton School graduate like her father, Ivanka had had a modeling career like her mother, but was a successful businesswoman with a prominent position in her father's businesses when he announced his presidential candidacy. Yet he tends to emphasize her looks over her brain. In 2004, during one of his several appearances as a guest on *The Howard Stern Show*, Trump did not object when the host referred to his daughter's "piece of ass" and her voluptuousness. In fact, Trump agreed:

"She's always been voluptuous." Crystal Jones, one of the anchors of *The View*, asked Trump in 2006, "I'm afraid to ask this question, but what would you do if *Playboy* put Ivanka on the cover?" Ivanka Trump interjected, "This is going to be an interesting answer." Trump replied, "It would be really disappointing—not really. I don't think Ivanka would do that inside the magazine, even though she does have a very nice figure. I've said if Ivanka wasn't my daughter, perhaps I'd be dating her." When father and daughter were guests of *The Wendy Williams Show* in 2013, talk show host Wendy Williams asked them what they had in common. Ivanka paused briefly before answering, "Either real estate or golf." Trump infamously replied, "Well, I was gonna say 'sex,' but I can't relate that to her." Finally, it fell to Ivanka to introduce her father in the 2016 Republican National Convention. After her speech, which focused on how Trump's businesses had more women than men executives and protected motherhood, Trump went on the stage, kissed her on the cheeks, and then patted her on her hips. That caused a stir in the news (Lewis July 21, 2016; Nicky Swift June 23, 2018).

In view of the sexist way Trump has allegedly treated women, including his own daughter, it should be expected that he would treat a woman opponent likewise. Thus, behind the anti-corruption discourse he directed at his Democratic opponent, Hillary Clinton, was a particular way of insulting her that attacked her womanhood. Trump repeatedly referred to her as "Crooked Hillary" (Geier 2016), a term he first uttered in April 2016, thus capitalizing on the view of her as "untrustworthy" after her alleged irregular use of an official email account, and retiring "incompetent Hillary," his earlier nickname for her. In June of that year, Trump retweeted a meme in which Clinton's face was next to a Star of David on which the charge "Most Corrupt Candidate Ever!" was written, all over a background of 100 dollar bills; the meme, which he later deleted, was first posted on "8chan's/pol/—an Internet message board for the alt-right, a digital movement of neo-Nazis, anti-Semites and white supremacists newly emboldened by the success of Trump's rhetoric—as early as June 22, over a week before Trump's team tweeted it" (Smith 2016). Never mind that Trump's allegedly favorite child, Ivanka Trump, had converted to Judaism before marrying Jared Kushner in 2009 and giving birth to their three children.

On August 16, 2016, less than two months after the meme had come out, two controversial figures joined Trump's campaign: Kellyanne Conway and Steve Bannon. She was hired as campaign manager and he, as chief campaign manager. Trump related that he had brought them in because "They are extremely capable, highly qualified people who love to win and know how to win" (Keneally January 5, 2018).

Conway was born in New Jersey in 1967. After graduating from college with a political science degree, she founded her own pollster firm, the polling company, inc./WomanTrend, and built a career "advising Republicans on how to appeal to female voters"; prior to working for Trump, Conway had also consulted for major corporations (Married Biography June 17, 2020). Conway's ability to mold political issues so that women identify with them paid off: when she joined Trump's campaign, Hillary Clinton was 13 percentage points ahead of him; as we will see in the next chapter, Trump won among women by 12 percentage points on Election Day (Bunker August 25, 2016; Tyson and Maniam November 9, 2016).

Born in Virginia in 1953, Bannon was the executive director of *Breitbart News*, the conservative internet publication founded by Andrew Breitbart (1969–2012), who is credited as having revolutionized right-wing social media. Under his tutelage, *Breitbart News* had promoted the ideas of the Tea Party (Rahn August 19, 2016). After Breitbart's death, the publication is thought to have become even more conservative under Bannon's leadership, by promoting antiabortion and anti-contraceptive views, defending tougher immigrant laws (especially against Muslims), and "trying to discredit the Black Lives Matter movement." Some of the publication's headlines refer to gays and women in homophobic and misogynist terms and, according to executive editor Alex Marlowe, the publication paid particular attention to Hillary Clinton. Prior to *Breitbart*, Bannon had produced films about conservative women, such as Sarah Palin and Margaret Thatcher (York November 16, 2016). Trump found commonalities with Bannon's style that would come in handy:

> Bannon's Breitbart distinguished itself from the rest of the conservative media in two significant ways this cycle. The first was becoming a mouthpiece for Trump while other, older conservative periodicals were declaring war on him. The second was through their embrace of the alt-right, which mainstream conservatives tend to abhor. (Rahn August 19, 2016)

One characteristic of the alt-right media that distinguishes them from mainstream conservative media is the lack of concern for "respectability" (Rahn August 19, 2016). In practice, the impact of the news may be more important than its accuracy. If we add that to Trump's already mentioned penchant for hyperbole, we can see how useful Bannon's tactics were for his campaign. Just a month after Bannon came aboard, during an interview on the Fox News channel, Trump referred to CNN, the acronym for "Channel News Network," as "Clinton News Network," because, according to him,

> it is so biased it's ridiculous, and they're very dishonest, very dishonest people, so I called them out and I'm very proud of it. And now I see the [media's] poll numbers are at an all time low, and frankly I think I had something to do with that, but I'm very proud of it. (Takala September 18, 2016)

He also claimed most reporters were "disgustingly dishonest." Given Trump's association with a reporter who not only did not pay much attention to accuracy, but also ran his campaign, it seems obvious that Trump dismissed any news that did not favor him as "fake news." Based on an analysis of Trump's tweets from his campaign to his presidential inauguration, Ross and Rivers (2018) argue that Trump recurrently practiced "discursive deflection," that is, he disseminated misinformation about his election opponent, the sitting president, and other topics, while accusing mainstream media of misinforming the public. In so doing, he "can actually be cast as a serial distributor of mis- and disinformation when his own agenda and goals are best served by doing so" (2). As I show in the next chapter, both Conway and Bannon would have prominent White House positions once Trump was elected.

THE EVANGELICAL CONNECTION

Donald Trump was brought up in a mainstream Protestant household: his father was Lutheran and his mother was Presbyterian; the family attended Presbyterian churches in Queens and Manhattan. Yet, Trump's campaign had a wide appeal among Evangelicals, whose voting behavior on November 8, 2016 was significant for his victory.

The definition of the term "Evangelicals" varies both among laypeople and scholars. The word arose in eighteenth-century Protestantism and signifies a break with Catholicism in that it "emphasized a personal relationship with God, the practice of being born again, and a call to spread God's message worldwide" (Casanova June 15, 2018). Evangelicals also believe in the "second coming," that is, Jesus's return to Earth. Being born again is how Evangelicals refer to conversion. Since the 1980s, the spread of God's message, or proselytism, got a boost from so-called televangelism, broadcast services of megachurches. Since the 1990s, White Evangelicals and White Catholics have come together over conservative issues, such as the protection of heterosexual marriage and attempts at eliminating abortion laws. Although "today, the word is used to describe the religious right, or in some cases, all Christians, or even the conservative masses" (Casanova June 15, 2018), not all Evangelicals are politically conservative, nor do they all espouse the same interpretation of the Bible. Therefore, for the purpose of this book, Evangelicals refer to a socially diverse religious group affiliated with certain Protestant denominations. Although they vary according to race, education, generation, and religious affiliation, what unites them is a common ethos (Smidt 2013).

In her ethnographic study of a White, working-class, and conservative town in Louisiana, Hochschild (2018) encountered a population that centered their lives around Evangelical churches and based their worldview on Biblical passages that asserted the right of human beings to rule over the Earth, even if that led to the destruction of the environment because that would only hasten Jesus' return. Thus, economic activities such as mining, for example, which have been proven detrimental both to humans and to the land, are not as damaging as left-leaning environmental advocates claim, given the end result. Hochschild (2018, 124–125; emphasis in original) cites a gospel singer, the wife of a preacher, who elaborates,

> "The earth will groan," she tells me, "and earthquakes, tornadoes, floods, rain, blizzards, strife will occur, and the earth *is* groaning." Drawing from the books of Revelation and Daniel, Madonna believes that within the next thousand years, gravity will release the feet of believers as they ascend to Heaven, while non-believers will remain on an earth that will become "as Hell" (Revelation 20:4–20; Daniel 9:23–27). After the rapture, the world will end for a time before Christ creates it anew and begins a new thousand-year period of peace, Madonna explains.

Although there are signs of environmental protection among Evangelicals, nationally representative data from 2010 found that two-fifths of the U.S. population "believe the Second Coming 'probably' or 'definitely' will happen by the year 2050" (Hochschild 2018, 125). That a sizeable minority of the U.S. population agrees with the majority of Evangelicals brings the latter closer to mainstream society and also helps explain Trump's courting of them as a significant voting actor. After all, "the National Association of Evangelicals is a voice for its 30,000,000 members, who make up a quarter of the American electorate, and a leading organization of the religious right with a political voice" (Hochschild 2018, 123). Moreover, White Evangelicals are also worth courting, in that they comprise "one-fifth of all registered voters and about one-third of all voters who identify with or lean toward the GOP" (Bailey November 9, 2016). That, however, does not mean that there was a consensus among Evangelicals regarding Trump. The fact that he is in his third marriage, has been accused of adultery, and owns casinos—all examples of sinful behavior for Evangelicals—weigh against Trump. On the other hand, Trump had in his favor the hope that he would nominate a Supreme Court judge who might help revert *Roe v. Wade* (1973), that is, the Supreme Court decision that legalized abortion. Ultimately, that was worth more than the fact that Hillary Clinton "is a churchgoing United Methodist who taught Sunday school and, as a senator, attended weekly prayer breakfasts"; that was not enough to offset the intense dislike that 70 percent of Evangelicals felt toward her due to her feminism (Bailey November 9, 2016).

Another force that ran against Clinton in the eyes of Evangelicals was her association with the "liberal media," such as CNN, as I mentioned above. In turn, Trump's appeal to Evangelicals is heavily tied to the conservative media, particularly the Fox News Channel, but also including Rush Limbaugh (1951–2021) and other radio, television, and internet right-wing personalities. Among Hochschild's Louisiana respondents, for instance, Fox News is so important that some regard their anchors as fictive kin. With such a deep emotional tie to the messengers, it is understandable why Louisiana residents would see Fox News as more neutral than CNN, even though its approach caters to "white middle- and working-class people" (Hochschild 2018, 127). Furthermore, they resented the "liberal commentators," whom they felt saw them as inferior. That was yet another reason Evangelicals were attracted by Donald Trump's populism and repelled by Hillary Clinton's intellectualism: to them, Trump sounded as if he were talking with them, whereas Clinton seemed to be talking down to them.

JEWS AND ISRAEL

At a little over 2 percent of the total U.S. population, American Jews are a small minority of the electorate. However, they are worth noting due to their voting patterns: except for 1920, when 43 percent of them voted for the Republican candidate, 38 percent voted for the Socialist candidate, and only 19 percent voted for the Democratic candidate, American Jews have consistently voted Democrat at least since 1916. In three elections, their support reached 90 percent: in 1940 and 1944, when they voted for Franklin D. Roosevelt, and in 1964, when they helped to elect Lyndon B. Johnson. More recently, most of them voted for Barack Obama, the Democratic presidential candidate, in 2008 (78 percent) and again in 2012 (69 percent) (Jewish Virtual Library 1998–2020). Comedian Sarah Silverman famously incited Jewish elders to vote for Obama or risk not being visited by their grandchildren any longer.

Besides an identification with the Democratic Party, American Jews are committed to the well-being of Israel. As I have shown (Penha-Lopes 2010), American Jews became confident about supporting Israel in the late 1960s, when most were native-born, anti-Semitism had decreased and Israel had won the Six-day War in the Middle East (1967). In fact, as recently as 2013, nationally representative data

> showed that 76% of Jews (identified by religion) said they were at least some-
> what emotionally attached to Israel. In addition, almost half said that caring
> about Israel is an essential part of being Jewish (with most of the rest saying it is

important although not essential) and nearly half reported that they had personally traveled to Israel. (Newport August 27, 2019)

Given such a voting pattern and commitment, American Jews presented a
challenge to Donald Trump, who tried to attract Jewish voters by claiming
to be more committed to Israel than his opponent, Hillary Clinton. During
a speech at the American Israel Public Affairs Committees in Washington,
DC, on March 21, 2016, Clinton accused Trump of wavering his support to
Israel in its dispute with Palestinians by being "neutral on Monday, pro-Israel
on Tuesday, and who knows what else on Wednesday because everything is
negotiable! Well, my friends, Israel's security is non-negotiable" (Kreutz and
Dukakis March 21, 2016). In response to Clinton's assertion, Trump declared
to CNN reporter Wolf Blitzer on the same day that he agreed with Clinton
about Israel's security, and added

> I am very pro-Israel, I've always been pro-Israel, I have many awards from
> Israel, many awards. I've contributed a lot of money to Israel. There's nobody
> more pro-Israel than me. We have to protect Israel. Israel is so important to us.
> (CNN March 21, 2016)

He also mentioned that Clinton had taken the United States to a dangerous
situation in the Middle East, thus reinforcing his claim, two months earlier,
that Clinton had "created ISIS" (i.e., the Islamic State in Iraq and Syria, a
terrorist organization) together with President Obama when she served as his
secretary of state (LoBianco and Landers January 3, 2016).

Both Clinton and Trump may have been too simplistic in their profes-
sion of alliance with Israel. Americans in general are supportive of Israel;
60 percent of them favor Israeli over Palestinian concerns. The more religious, however, are even more supportive, as over 70 percent of them are
pro-Israel, compared with less than 50 percent of the less religious. That
correlation, however, is even stronger when political affiliation enters the
picture, in that Republicans who practice their religion assiduously are
much more likely to support Israel than are their Democratic counterparts.
Based on his analysis of longitudinal Gallup data between 2001 and 2014,
Newport (March 19, 2019) concludes that "Republicans thus remain more
positive than Democrats about Israel in part because they are more religious, given that religious people are themselves the most positive about
Israel."

Trump misses the nuances in American Jewish and in Israeli thinking that
make him believe all Jews must or should think alike. Although a numerical
minority, U.S. Jews are vocal about social issues and are politically engaged,
in part due to their high educational levels well above the national average.

For instance, well into Trump's tenure as president, in 2019, a national poll revealed that "U.S. Jews are more likely than Christians to say Trump favors the Israelis too much." Nearly 60 percent of Christians (and more than 70 percent of Evangelicals), but fewer than half of Jews think that President Trump is impartial toward the two Middle Eastern issues. Race also plays a factor in those attitudes, in that African Americans Christians are more likely to feel the same way about Israeli and Palestinians. Equally interesting is the finding that, regardless of religious affiliation or race, people in the United States distinguish governments from peoples, so that they are much more sympathetic toward Israelis and Palestinians than to their governments (Smith May 6, 2019).

Likewise, there is considerable variation in Israelis' self-identification and, consequently, their political attitudes. According to data from 2014 to 2015, almost half of Israelis identify as Hilonim, or secular. A number of them are atheist and, much like American Jews, see being Jewish more as a cultural than a religious identity; they are also supportive of Israel. At the other end of the spectrum are the Haredim, that is, the ultra-Orthodox, who number 9 percent of the Israeli population and who, for religious reasons, are the least supportive of a state of Israel. At 29 percent, the Masortim (or traditional) stand between the ultra-orthodox and the mostly secular Jews. The Datiim comprise 13 percent of the total population. Also religious, they are known as "modern Orthodox Jews" in that they are more likely to participate in secular life, such as serving in the army and traveling, than the Haredim; politically, they lean toward the right and support Israeli occupation of the West Bank (Starr and Masci March 8, 2016).

In sum, in both countries the Jewish community is divided. In the United States, many Jews object to Trump's far-right associations, which they consider too close to Nazism; in an opinion piece from August 2019, Michelle Goldberg, an author and columnist for *The Nation* and the *New York Times*, wrote, "Mazel Tov, Trump: You've Revived the Jewish Left." The diversity of standpoints characteristic of U.S. and Israeli Jews reinforces the argument that Trump's support of Israel may have more to do with his courting of White Evangelicals, who have an affinity for it because they believe it is the land where Jesus came from and to which he will return. For instance, Trump made a campaign promise to relocate the U.S. embassy from Tel Aviv to Jerusalem, a controversial plan given the contentious nature of the city for all it represents for Judaism, Christianity, and Islam, but one highly favored by Evangelicals (Newport March 19, 2019).

In sum, Donald Trump displayed blatant racism at a time when the United States was believed to be "postracial" by attacking people of African descent here and abroad, Mexicans, and Muslims. Reflecting on his successful campaign, Allen and Parnes (2017, 51) wrote,

Trump took advantage of the increasing power of the Tea Party by appealing to the mistrust of government ingrained in lower-income, less-educated voters. He ran on nostalgia, adopting a campaign slogan—"Make America Great Again"—ripped off from Ronald Reagan, and traced the decline of the country to the mid-1960s. Though he didn't mention the Johnson era's Civil Rights Act, Voting Rights Act, or public subsidies for housing and health care, Trump's dog whistle was just the right pitch to attract the support of white supremacists and nearly all-white crowds of thousands at his campaign rallies.

Donald Trump based his presidential campaign discourse on ideas that feed on the fear of a significant proportion of the population to lose ground to minorities, women, and foreigners. Behind his allegation that Obama and Mexican Americans are not really American is the old view that only Whites could be citizens. As I show in the next chapter, those ideas resonated amid a large enough portion of the U.S. population that guaranteed his election. On one hand, Trump was an unconventional candidate in that he was not a career politician; on the other, he was conventional in that he emphasized ideas that were part and parcel of U.S. history, but which seemed to have been dormant for most of the twenty-first century.

NOTES

1. D'Antonio (2016, 186) quotes Trump in *The Art of the Deal* (1987) thus, "A little hyperbole never hurts. I call it truthful hyperbole. It's an innocent form of exaggeration and a very effective form of promotion."

2. The Guardian Angels were founded by Curtis Sliwa in New York City in 1979. Dressed in red pants and berets and white T-shirts, they patrolled the city unarmed. Since then, the organization has established chapters in other cities in the United States and in over 10 countries (guardianangels.org).

Chapter 4

Donald Trump's Presidential Victory

Between October and November 2016, both Hillary Clinton, the Democratic candidate, and Donald Trump faced challenges to their campaigns. John Podesta, Clinton's campaign manager, saw Wikileaks expose his email account, while Trump was accused of abusing women in addition to requesting that Russia interfere in the elections against Clinton. Ultimately, the Podesta email debacle proved to be the most damning because it was associated with Hillary Clinton's use of her personal account to conduct governmental business earlier in the year, which reinforced the accusations that she was "crooked." Not only did Bernie Sanders, Clinton's former Democratic candidate contender, insist that she was the peon of corporations, but Trump also played it to his favor by noting again and again that she was untrustworthy. Although Clinton tried to call attention to Russia's interference on the U.S. elections during the candidates' final debates, mentioning that Trump had personally appealed to a foreign power to discredit her, Trump deflected that by claiming that there was no proof of such interference (Allen and Parnes 2017, 347).

Clinton's reputation was further questioned mere days before the election, when James Comey, the director of the Federal Bureau of Investigation, announced that he would reopen his investigation of Clinton's accounts. This time, the focus was on the improper use of Huma Abedin's account. Abedin was vice-chair of Hillary Clinton's campaign; her husband, Anthony Weiner, had used her account to send sexually explicit pictures of himself (Allen and Parnes 2017, 355–356). As I mentioned in the previous chapter, Russian interference and the *Access Hollywood* video fell by the way side in comparison. Allen and Parnes (2017, 366) report that Comey's announcement negatively affected Clinton by leading undecided Republican voters to flock to Trump and some Democrats to give up on the election altogether for fear that she would be investigated throughout her tenure if she won the election. Comey declared on November 6, 2016 that his investigation cleared Clinton and she was touted as the winner by a number of news media reports. She was ahead on the polls and would go on to win the popular vote two days later, but she lost crucial delegates, leading to her defeat on the Electoral College. This chapter examines Donald Trump's victory, a result that many academics and journalists had not anticipated.

Donald Trump never wavered in his campaign style of blaming non-White immigrants for whatever woes prevented the United States from being "great again." As late as November 6, 2016, he singled out Somali refugees, who, as African, dark-skinned, and Muslim, embody a number of stereotypes Trump favors. The state of Minnesota stands out as the home of two-fifths (69,000 persons) of the total Somali population in the United States as of 2019 (Brown July 23, 2019); as of 2017, close to 80 percent of them lived in the twin cities of Minneapolis–St. Paul (Minnesota Compass 2020). Minneapolis is recognized as a refugee-friendly city, which has made it extremely attractive to Somalis, who have been fleeing a civiwar since the 1990s. It is no wonder that Trump would choose a campaign stop there to attack Somalis, telling those present that

> they had "suffered enough" as a result of "filthy refugee vetting" that had allowed an influx of Somalis into their state. He promised that if he became president, refugees would not be admitted "without the support of the community where they are being placed." (Chiu October 12, 2019)

What Trump did not mention was the role refugees and other immigrants have played in the revitalization of the Minneapolis population, which grew 11 percent between 2000 and 2018, but which had fallen from a high of 521,718 in 1950 to 368,284 in 1990 (biggestuscities.com 2020). However, in a campaign that counted on racial fears, foreign or otherwise, a jab at dark-skinned immigrants in a majority-White state so close to the election did not go unnoticed.

By early November, there were data available that showed that Trump was ahead in Pennsylvania and Michigan, two pivotal states in any presidential election due to their ability to tilt results one way or another. "Battleground" or "swing" states are so called because their voters are not committed to either the Democratic or the Republican Party. Therefore, depending on the election, they may "swing" in either direction, thus establishing a "battleground" for the parties. In addition to Pennsylvania, other swing states on the East Coast are New Hampshire, Virginia, North Carolina, and Florida; in the Midwest, Ohio, Minnesota, Michigan, and Iowa; Nevada and Colorado on the West complete the picture.

Another area of interest in presidential elections is that of the so-called "rustbelt states," which corresponds to the northeastern and Midwestern areas of heavy industry that had thrived at the turn of the nineteenth and twentieth centuries and had attracted millions to this country during the Great Immigration, but which have become economically depressed since the U.S. economy made the transition to postindustrialization, starting in the 1970s. The area includes upstate New York, Pennsylvania, Ohio, Michigan, Iowa, Illinois, and Wisconsin. Though some rustbelt states are also swing states, such as Pennsylvania, Ohio, and Wisconsin, others, such as Illinois, have traditionally voted for Democratic candidates. Although Hillary Clinton expected to win in North Carolina and Florida, based on the results of the 2012 election and the "analytics model" her campaign team had employed, she lost in both of them. In fact, Trump did better in most of the swing and the rustbelt states. Before midnight on election night, after early counts that had given Clinton an edge, Fox News declared Trump a winner in Wisconsin (Allen and Parnes 2017, 366; 375; 381).

THE ELECTORAL COLLEGE AND ELECTION RESULTS

Fewer than 60 percent of the voting population of Americans actually voted on November 8, 2016, which, though it seems to be a low turnout, is average for the United States and actually higher than the turnout four years before. Of all the votes cast, Donald Trump won 62,984,825 votes, as compared with Hillary Clinton, who received 65,853,516 votes. In other words, Clinton won 48.5 percent of the popular vote, which amounted to 2,864,974 more votes than Trump received (46.5 percent); the remaining 5 percent of votes went to "Other" or were blank (CNN 2016; Hubby April 20, 2018).

Had the election been conducted in another country, Hillary Clinton would have been declared the winner, albeit by a small margin. However, U.S. presidents are elected indirectly, in that voters cast ballots in the presidential primaries to determine the presidential nominee for their party to the Electoral College, which then decides who the winner is. In other words, although Clinton won the popular vote, she lost the election. Before 2016, that result had happened only three times (Fuentes-Rohwer and Charles 2001, 880): mostly recently, in 2000, when George W. Bush was declared president over Al Gore in a very contested election during which votes were recounted; in1888, when Benjamin Harrison won over Grover Cleveland, who was seeking a second term; and in 1876, when Congress and the Electoral College declared Rutherford Hayes the winner, even though he had fewer popular and Electoral College votes than opponent Samuel Tilden, they conceded disputed votes to Hayes, as a compromise for the federal government to end the Reconstruction, withdraw from the south, and leave the southern states free to enact laws that would disenfranchise Blacks (The Editors of Encyclopaedia Britannica October 31, 2019).

The Electoral College, this "lasting" and "unpopular institution" (Fuentes-Rohwer and Charles 2001), is as old as the U.S. Constitution. After much debate about how to choose the executive power, the constitutional convention settled on the plan to have electors in each state vote for two candidates: the candidate with the highest number of votes would be elected president; the second highest, vice-president; that is reflected in Article II, section I. The Electoral College was born out of "a compromise between the small and large states" (Fuentes-Rohwer and Charles 2001, 886). Part of the compromise was the decision to count one slave as three-fifths of a free man. Because the Constitution originally granted franchise solely to White propertied men, a state with a large slave population, such as Virginia, whose slave population was 60 percent of the total in 1787, and so many southern states would be automatically at a disadvantage in presidential elections (Roos July 10, 2020). According to Wills (2005), that deal had been a condition for southern states to recognize the U.S. Constitution and also guaranteed Thomas Jefferson's victory in the 1800 presidential election.

There are 538 electoral votes in total, which are distributed among the states "based on the number of representatives they have in the House plus their two senators" (Roos July 23, 2020). A minimum of 270 electoral votes are necessary to clinch the presidential election. Clinton gathered 232 votes against Trump's 306. Trump's win was secured by 7 of the 12 battleground states and in 5 of the rustbelt states (CNN 2016). As I show later, Trump owes his electoral success to the strength of the White vote, which toppled income and education, given that both the White working and middle classes favored him. Race even toppled gender, despite Trump's well-documented misogyny and the fact that his opponent was a woman. Indeed, although over 50 percent of women voters cast their ballot for Clinton, over 50 percent of White women voted for Trump (CNN 2016; Sims and Buncombe November 9, 2016). As Grenell (October 6, 2018) noted,

> In sum, the gender gap in politics is really a color line. That's because white women benefit from patriarchy by trading on their whiteness to monopolize resources for mutual gain. In return they're placed on a pedestal to be "cherished and revered," as Speaker Paul D. Ryan has said about women, but all the while denied basic rights.

CHARACTERISTICS OF TRUMP VOTERS

Donald Trump had a much wider appeal than among the expected White non-Hispanic working-class and Evangelical electorate; among the latter, 80 percent of them voted for him, the most since they voted for George W. Bush in 2004 (Bailey November 9, 2016). Overall, he garnered over half of voters who are male (52 percent), over 44 years of age (52 percent), and with less than a college education (67 percent), but he also did well among the college educated: while Clinton won 52 percent of their vote, Trump had a small advantage over her among college-educated Whites, at 49 percent versus 44 percent (CNN 2016; Tyson and Maniam November 9, 2016).

Among racial/ethnic minorities, the share of Trump supporters among both Asian Americans and Hispanic/Latino(a)s was 29 percent, very similar to their support for Mitt Romney, the Republican presidential candidate in 2012 (Sims and Buncombe November 9, 2016). It is safe to assume that the Latina population reacted against Trump's relentless attacks on immigration in general and Mexican immigration in particular, given the fact that Mexican Americans constitute the largest share of Hispanics/Latino(a)s in the United States. Still, support for Trump among Latinos was higher than expected by earlier predictions; while Clinton had been presumed to sweep the Latino vote, she ended up getting a lower share than Obama had four years earlier (Sonneland and Fleischner November 10, 2016).

Trump's draconian immigration policies also seem to have reinforced the American Jewish tradition of voting for Democratic candidates and led to their rejecting Trump: only 23 percent of the 3 percent who identified as Jewish voted for him (Newport August 27, 2019). Jewish voters made the connection between the threat of closed borders to certain groups and the plight of their ancestors who had been forbidden from entering the country during their flight from Nazism; they also saw similarities between White nationalism and anti-Semitism (Goldberg August 25, 2019). Less than a year later, when a White nationalist rally in Charlottesville, Virginia, left several injured and 1 dead, over 40 Jewish organizations and individuals organized as "Jews Stand Up to Hate," clamoring "Never again means never again!" (The Action Network).

When it comes to voting for the Democratic Party, African Americans make up the most loyal share of the electorate, and their voting behavior in 2016 was no different. Trump's openly racist rhetoric stood out after the first African American president's two tenures, which led them to overwhelmingly reject Trump, as only 8 percent of them veered toward him (Hubby April 20, 2018). African American voters also unique in that, unlike non-Hispanic Whites and Hispanics, fully four-fifths of the men favored Clinton, as did 93 percent of the women (Sims and Buncombe November 9, 2016). African

Americans remembered Trump's repeated attempts to undermine Obama's legitimate claim to the presidency with his promotion of "birtherism" and, then, during his own presidential campaign, stoking the fires of racial resentment. For them, "Make America Great Again" was code for "Make America White Again" (Abramowitz 2018, 123–124; Daniel and Kelekay 2017, 662).

Even though the largest proportion of votes Clinton received came from African Americans, they were lower than the proportion of votes they cast for Obama in 2008 and 2012. One of the reasons for the lower voter turnout among African Americans in 2016 is the series of impediments that have been put in place for some years. States have been passing laws, such as the requirement to present a government-issued identity card with a photograph in addition to one's voter registration card and the removal of posts where people could get identity cards, such as Department of Motor Vehicles centers, especially in areas heavily populated by African Americans. In addition, some states have closed poll places earlier, as it happened in the 2000 presidential election. The result is disenfranchisement, notwithstanding the Voting Rights Act of 1965. As legal scholar Carol Anderson (2018, 45) concludes,

> In the twenty-first century, the geography of voter suppression had clearly changed. It was no longer only a phenomenon of the Jim Crow South. Voter suppression had now gone nationwide as it became a Republican-fueled chimera that by 2017 had griped thirty-three states and cast a pall over more than half the American voting-age population.

Anderson argues that the larger the share of the non-White electorate, the more voter suppression manifests itself. She notes that the proportion of Blacks, Latino(a)s, and Asian Americans more than doubled in the 20 years between 1992 and 2012, from 13 percent to 28 percent. That, coupled with the tendency of non-Whites to vote for Democratic candidates, has led states dominated by Republican legislators to change laws so as to either discourage that population from voting or to actively prevent them from voting. As evidence, Anderson mentions the voting pattern of the 2000 presidential election among non-Whites, when all but 10 percent of African Americans, over 60 percent of Latinos, and over half of Asian Americans voted for Al Gore, the Democratic candidate. Since then, disenfranchisement has increased. For instance, data from the battleground state of Wisconsin showed that "8.4 percent of white voters who were surveyed said they were 'deterred' from voting in the 2016 election because of voter ID laws; that number more than tripled for African Americans (27.5 percent)" (Anderson, C. 2018, 70).

Smith and Hanley (2018) argue that the lower African American turnout in 2016 helped seal Hillary Clinton's defeat in the key states of Pennsylvania, Michigan, and Wisconsin, where Trump won "by less than one percentage point" (Allen and Parnes 2017, 387). Donald Trump's win "gave him 46 Electoral College votes and the election." Ultimately, Trump owes his victory to the strength of the White vote. In the next section, I discuss Trump's allure for those voters.

UNRAVELING THE WHITE VOTE: RACIAL RESENTMENT, REGION, AND AUTHORITARIANISM

Scholars have correlated Trump's presidential victory to sentiments that had been brewing in a portion of the White population as early as the 1970s. Although public opinion had favored the passing of civil rights legislation in the 1960s, including the Voting Rights Act in 1965 (Burstein 1979; Garrow 1978), southern states such as South Carolina, Mississippi, and Virginia contested the changes that would make racial inclusion more tenable (Anderson, C. 2018, 22–25); 10 years later, the argument that affirmative action policies amounted to "reverse discrimination" was popular enough to render the publication of a book devoted to it (Glazer 1975). In 1976, the overwhelming support southern Black voters gave to Democratic candidate Jimmy Carter assured his presidential win, but federal intervention was necessary to guarantee adherence to the Voting Rights Act of 1965 in a number of counties (Garrow 1978, xii–xiii). That was a sign that "racial resentment" was already growing (Abramowitz 2018). Ronald Reagan, Carter's successor, won over him aided by a thinly veiled attack on the welfare state. After Reagan's two successful tenures, he was followed by George Bush, his vice president, who also explored racial fears by exposing images of Willie Horton, an African American convicted of murder, who had committed rape while he was temporarily released from prison in Massachusetts. Bush emphasized the fact that his opponent, Michael Dukakis, was the governor of Massachusetts at the time; with the aid of television, newspaper, and magazine advertisements, he was able to convince a sizable portion of the electorate that Dukakis would be soft on crime if elected. By associating the face of a Black rapist to Dukakis, the Bush campaign successfully played on one of the most basic fears that Whites harbor of Blacks, that is, the stereotype of the beastly man who is out to harm White women's honor, which has led to countless lynchings since the late nineteenth century.

Abramowitz (2018, 129) defines "racial resentment" as the "subtle feelings of hostility toward African-Americans. It is different from old-fashioned racism, which involves beliefs about the white race's inherent superiority and right to dominance." He relies on the American National Election Survey (ANES), which operationalizes racial resentment as a scale that measures reactions to statements about how African Americans should mirror White ethnics and succeed based on their own merits, how slavery continues to affect African Americans' access to upward mobility, whether they have not gotten their fair share, and how African Americans fall behind Whites because they are less diligent. Examining longitudinal survey results from the early 1980s to the 2010s, Abramowitz notes that a high racial resentment level consistently went up from 42 percent in the Reagan-Bush years to 51 percent in the Obama years; among White Republicans, the figure reached a high of 64 percent in the Obama years, up from 44 percent in the Reagan-Bush years (129–130). In other words, racial resentment has been growing among White voters in general, but particularly among White Republicans.

Smith and Hanley (2018; 2020), who also analyzed the results of the 2016 presidential election, found that, even though the White working class had long been feeling left out (Rubin 1994), it would be too simplistic to think that it alone guaranteed Trump's victory. In fact, some of Trump's strongest supporters were solidly middle class, that is, those in the US$70,000 to US$120,000 annual income bracket. Moreover, they note that the White working class is far from an amorphous aggregate, since it behaves differently depending on the regions where it is located: less educated White voters from the northeast did not favor Trump over Clinton, whereas southern and Midwestern White voters clinched his victory, supporting him significantly more than they had Mitt Romney, the Republican candidate in the 2012 presidential election. Furthermore, the Midwest had both the largest percentage of White voters in the country and the largest percent of voters without college degrees, whereas the White population in the northeast was smaller and more educated. That led Smith and Hanley to suggest that a regional, more conservative culture affected people's voting behavior. In other words, they voted as Whites who resented the "undeserving," namely, Blacks, non-White immigrants, and Muslims; they engaged in the "anger games" (Smith and Hanley 2018) and were "Whiter than White" (2020), that is, they differentiated themselves from Whites who are located in other regions.

Smith and Hanley (2018, 196) suggested the inclusion of two statements in the ANES scale for the 2016 election, which together measure sympathy for a "domineering leader":

> "What our country really needs is a strong, determined leader who will crush evil and take us back to our true path"; and (2) "Our country will be great if we honor the ways of our forefathers, do what the authorities tell us to do, and get rid of the 'rotten apples' who are ruining everything." (Smith 2019, 202)

They also analyzed the responses to the question "Do you regard yourself as a strong supporter of the candidate you supported for President?," which allowed them to differentiate between "mild" and "strong" Trump supporters.

Statistical analysis revealed that the latter (about 75 percent of the total) were significantly more likely to agree with the aforementioned two statements from the domineering scale, tendencies which transcended education, age, and income. Smith and Hanley (2018) conclude that prejudice correlates with authoritarianism. Unlike the arguments about the "authoritarian personality" that Theodore Adorno popularized in the post–World War II period, Smith and Hanley suggest that "people with authoritarian tendencies follow domineering leaders less for the pleasure of submission than for the pleasure of forcing *moral outsiders* to submit" (196; emphasis in original). "Moral outsiders" are similar to the "line cutters" (Hochschild 2016), or the so-called "undeserving" people who have purportedly cut in line in front of "deserving" Americans. Given that most of those outsiders are racialized as non-White (e.g., Blacks, Mexicans, and Muslims), Smith and Hanley's analysis lends credence to my argument that White supremacy, as expressed by nativism, racism, and authoritarianism, helped to elect Donald Trump president. In their words, "Whether rich or poor, young or old, male or female, college or non-college educated, white voters supported Trump in 2016 when they shared his prejudices, and very seldom otherwise" (Smith and Hanley 2018, 197).

Before the night of November 8, 2016 was over, President Obama advised Hillary Clinton to concede victory to Donald Trump, but she decided to wait until morning. At 1:00 a.m., she received the official notice that she had lost in Pennsylvania; she maintained her stance nonetheless because she was waiting for the results from Michigan and Wisconsin and also because, according to Allen and Parnes (2017), she was in disbelief. Clinton finally conceded on the afternoon of November 9. During her speech, she asked her constituents to have an "open mind" toward Trump, mentioned the Constitution and the rule of law, and finished with a passage from the Bible: "'Let us not grow weary in doing good,' she said, paraphrasing Galatians 6:9, 'for in due season, we shall reap if we do not lose heart'" (Allen and Parnes 2017, 394).

THE INAUGURATION

Donald J. Trump was inaugurated as the 45th president of the United States in front of the Capitol Building, in Washington, DC, on January 20, 2017. Based on aerial photographs, analyses by experts, and the Washington Metropolitan Area Transit Authority, the crowd in attendance was estimated to be anywhere between 300,000 and 600,000, which would put it, at best, at about one-third of those who attended President Obama's 2009 inauguration (Ford January 21, 2017; Frostenson January 24, 2017). However, true to his penchant for hyperbole, President Trump believed the words of his press secretary, Sean Spicer, who claimed that "this was the largest audience to ever witness an inauguration, period, both in person and around the globe" (Robertson and Farley January 24, 2017). When reports contradicted that conclusion, Kellyanne Conway, Trump's campaign comanager and now White House counselor, offered that Spicer had relied on "alternative facts"; in turn, Trump charged that the media were trying to undermine his appeal (History.com January 4, 2018; Robertson and Farley January 24, 2017).

Surrounded by all of his children in addition to his wife, Trump was sworn in with his hand on his own Bible and the one that Abraham Lincoln had used in his own ceremony. Former presidents Barack Obama, George W. Bush, Bill Clinton, and Jimmy Carter were present. The man who had emphasized his status as a Washington "outsider," who never held political or military posts, and who by then was 70 years old, added another "first" to that list: "the oldest man to assume the presidency" (History.com January 4, 2018).

While Hillary Clinton had extolled the public to give President Trump a chance, Kellyanne Conway had declared on the morning of the inauguration that his speech would reveal "a man of action, a man of resolve in what we know to be a divided country" (Time January 20, 2017). Echoing his campaign slogan, President Trump started his speech by calling out "the citizens of America" to be "joined in a national effort to rebuild our country and restore its promise for all of our people." He thanked the former president and First Lady for having been "magnificent" in "their gracious aid throughout this transition." In fact, Barack and Michelle Obama's poise and courtesy toward the new First Lady Melanie Trump was noticed by those who watched the ceremony live and was a topic of discussion in the news media.

Trump then alluded to his persona as a political outsider and assumed a populist tone when he promised to return the country to its people and out of the hands of greedy and uncaring traditional politicians:

> Today's ceremony, however, has very special meaning because today, we are not merely transferring power from one administration to another or from one party to another, but we are transferring power from Washington, D.C. and giving it back to you, the people.
> (APPLAUSE)
> For too long, a small group in our nation's capital has reaped the rewards of government while the people have borne the cost. Washington flourished, but the people did not share in its wealth. Politicians prospered, but the jobs left and the factories closed. The establishment protected itself, but not the citizens of our country. Their victories have not been your victories. Their triumphs have not been your triumphs. And while they celebrated in our nation's capital, there was little to celebrate for struggling families all across our land.
> (APPLAUSE)

That all changes starting right here and right now because this moment is your moment, it belongs to you.

(APPLAUSE)

TRUMP: It belongs to everyone gathered here today and everyone watching all across America. This is your day. This is your celebration. And this, the United States of America, is your country.

(APPLAUSE)

What truly matters is not which party controls our government, but whether our government is controlled by the people.

(APPLAUSE)

January 20th, 2017 will be remembered as the day the people became the rulers of this nation again.

(APPLAUSE)

The forgotten men and women of our country will be forgotten no longer.

(APPLAUSE)

Everyone is listening to you now. You came by the tens of millions to become part of a historic movement, the likes of which the world has never seen before. (*Time* January 20, 2017)

Trump continued with his exaltation of "the people" by promising to put an end to job loss, embattled families, and neighborhoods ravaged by crime. There was also an allusion to his nativist campaign promise to build a wall to prevent the entry of Mexicans when he uttered that he would defend the U.S. borders and put its workers first. He was explicit about the Muslim threat, another one of his oft-repeated campaign concerns, when he vowed to "unite the civilized world against the radical Islamic terrorism, which we will eradicate completely from the face of the Earth."

Despite Trump's record of racial divisiveness, he brought back, toward the end of his 16-minute speech, the populist theme under the guise of patriotism that transcends race and class:

It's time to remember that old wisdom our soldiers will never forget, that whether we are black or brown or white, we all bleed the same red blood of patriots. We all enjoy the same glorious freedoms and we all salute the same great American flag.

He ended his speech by calling upon the whole country to unite and "make America great again" (*Time* Staff January 20, 2017). In sum, as I mentioned before, Trump appealed to the downtrodden who was implicitly or explicitly White. His inaugural speech conjured up a Jacksonian type of nativism that had been present throughout his campaign. In fact, his speech was believed to have been fashioned after Andrew Jackson's own inaugural speech in 1829 (History.com January 4, 2018).

Breitbart.com, the site once edited by Trump's campaign comanager Steve Bannon, published an almost minute-by-minute report of the day's events, from the arrival of the crowd early in the morning to the last of the three inaugural balls that the president, the First Lady, vice president Mike Pence and his wife attended, complete with pictures republished from Twitter accounts of Trump supporters. A photograph showed two smiling men arriving at the swearing-in site; one of them, clad in a MAGA baseball hat, carried a sign that read, "I VOTED FOR TRUMP! I SWEAR NO RUSSIAN TOLD ME TO."

In the morning, the president, the vice president, and their wives attended a "private family service" at St. John's Church presided over by Dr. Robert Jeffress, who preached on "When God Chooses a Leader." From there, Donald and Melania Trump proceeded to the White House, where they were met by the outgoing First Couple. Mrs. Trump, clad in powder blue, brought a Tiffany gift box for Mrs. Obama. The two kissed on the cheek; the two men shook hands and kissed each other's wives. Much was made of Obama's chivalry, who offered a hand to Mrs. Trump, whose husband had left her behind in the drizzly stairway.

The festivities were accompanied by protests. According to pictures on Breitbart.com, there were signs that read "Feminists against Fascism" and "Don't Normalize Trump," in addition to street disturbances the site attributed to "anarchists" and "Black Bloc protesters." On the other hand, there were plenty of Trump sympathizers in the crowd, such as a White man who held a poster with a drawing of a cat's face in blue, stars for eyes and mouth, and the saying, "Day #1 of Making America #1. Now Grab Your Pussy And Go Home." Identified as "John from Maryland," he claimed he was there "protesting the protesters." Unsurprisingly, security was tight, so the lines to get to Capitol Hill were long, which generated many complaints. The police maintained their presence amid the "anarchists" who broke windows on Starbucks' and McDonald's and parked limousines.

For what would have been her victory speech two months earlier, Hillary Clinton had wanted to wear white in homage to suffragettes (Allen and Parnes 2017). She did it for her opponent's inauguration, and so did his two daughters, although it is not clear whether they had done so with the same intention. On the other hand, Kellyanne Conway made the news with a red-white-and-blue outfit called "Trump Revolutionary Wear," which she attributed to the Gucci fashion house. On social media, however, her outfit was mocked as resembling the Nutcracker, Molly the American Girl Doll, and Paddington Bear (Real January 20, 2017).

Vice President Mike Pence was sworn in by Justice Clarence Thomas. Right after noon, President Trump was sworn in by Justice John G. Roberts Jr. Some shouted, "Not my president!" As it is customary, religious figures took part in the swearing-in ceremony. Among the six who were present in Trump's inauguration, one was a Latino Evangelical pastor and the other was a rabbi. The Reverend Samuel Rodriguez, who heads the National Hispanic Christian Leadership Conference and whose congregation is located in California, was quoted as being "the first Latino Evangelical to participate" in a presidential inauguration. Rabbi Marvin Hier, also from California, claimed he was "the first rabbi, since 1985, to take part in an inauguration," which was an honor for him (Gayle January 19, 2017).

The presence of the two clergy members at once catered to two constituencies that had favored Trump and nodded to another. Though neither the pastor nor the rabbi declared themselves Trump supporters, they brought attention to Evangelicals, who constituted an important category for Trump's victory. By inviting a Latino Evangelical, the Trump camp might be attempting to take away the accusation of White supremacy leveled at him and some of his vitriol against Mexican (i.e., Latina) immigration. In turn, having a rabbi officiate again favored Evangelicals, who, as I showed in the previous chapter and will show again in the next one, have a fondness for Judaism and Israel because they believe Jesus's second coming will take place there.

After the inauguration luncheon, the parade that would take the First Family to the White House began. Later in the afternoon, General James Mattis was confirmed as secretary of defense and General John Kelly, as secretary of homeland security.

Early in the evening, President Trump signed his first executive order, the curtail of Obama's Affordable Care Act (known as Obamacare), thus fulfilling a campaign promise. Specifically, Trump's order halted the parts of the act that added financial burdens to organizations, states, and individuals. In a clear effort to dismantle measures from the Obama administrations, Trump suspended the decrease of mortgage rates, a policy that would have made it easier for more Americans to become homeowners (Chamberlain January 20, 2017). Evidently, such measures ran counter to Trump's populist promise to return the government to "the people" and put people first. Another attention-grabbing act on Trump's first day as president was the removal of the pages dedicated to climate change and LGBTQIA+ civil rights from the White House's website (Silverstein January 24, 2017).

At the end of the Armed Services, the third and last inaugural ball, President Trump spoke remotely to the troops in Afghanistan. The First Lady complemented, "Thank you for your service. I'm honored to be your first lady. We will fight. We will win. We will make America great again" (CNN January 20, 2020).

President Trump's cabinet was composed of 15 members; all were confirmed by the Senate with varying degrees of ease. The aforementioned General John Kelly, secretary of homeland security, mentioned in his hearing that he disagreed with President Trump about registering Muslims. General James Mattis, secretary of defense, disagreed with Trump about the U.S. relations with Russia and Iran. Thomas Shannon was recommended by Condoleezza Rice, secretary of state in President George W. Bush's tenure, to fill that position; he did so for less than a month, and was replaced by Rex Tillerson, who left himself in March 2018. Jeff Sessions was attorney general. During Sessions's confirmation hearing, Representative John Lewis (1940–2020) identified "racial undertones" in his speech. Steven Mnuchin was appointed secretary of the treasury. Ryan Zinke was appointed secretary of the interior; unlike Trump, he believes that climate change is real. The secretary of agriculture was Sonny Purdue; Wilbur Ross was secretary of commerce.

The only Latino cabinet member was R. Alexander Acosta. The former dean of Florida International University College of Law, Acosta replaced Andrew Puzder, whose nomination was marred by allegations that he had hired an undocumented immigrant to work as his housekeeper. Although he claimed he was ignorant of her status, fired her upon learning about it, and "fully paid back taxes to the IRS and the state of California and submitted all required paperwork" (Merica February 7, 2017), he ended up withdrawing from the process.

For the Office of Health and Human Service, Trump appointed orthopedic surgeon Tom Price, who sided with his criticism of the Affordable Care Act. Trump selected Ben Carson, the neurosurgeon who had competed with him for the Republican Party nomination in the 2016 presidential elections, to be secretary of housing and urban development. Carson was the only African American in Trump's cabinet and had no experience with housing, but Trump said of him, "Ben Carson has a brilliant mind and is passionate about strengthening communities and families within those communities." Carson was described as "one of Trump's most loyal supporters" (Biography.com Editors June 23, 2020), and agreed with him about nullifying the Affordable Care Act well before he crossed paths with Trump. For instance, in 2013, Carson characterized Obama's health policy thus,

> Obamacare is really I think the worst thing that has happened in this nation since slavery. And it is in a way, it is slavery in a way, because it is making all of us subservient to the government, and it was never about health care. It was about control. (in Strauss March 17, 2017)

To equate a policy that extends health benefits to more Americans (including African Americans) with the worst that has happened in the nearly 150 years since the Emancipation is shocking enough, even more when we consider that the author of that phrase is an African American man who was 14 years old when voting rights were finally granted to all.

Perhaps equally controversial was the selection of Betsy DeVos to head the Department of Education. Former chairperson of the Republican Party in Michigan, DeVos is famous for her lack of support of public education, what with her defense of "school choice," school vouchers, and charter schools and for being against a common-core curriculum. She reacted to her nomination by tweeting, "I am honored to work with the president-elect on his vision to make American education great again. The status quo in ed is not acceptable" (in Zernicke November 23, 2016). The Senate confirmed DeVos with the smallest margin of 51 to 50. Early on in her tenure, she hailed Historically Black Colleges and Universities (HBCUs), the institutions of higher learning that Negroes founded starting in the nineteenth century because Jim Crow laws forbade them from attending schools with Whites, as "real pioneers when it comes to school choice," when it was exactly their lack of choices that led to their creating schools of their own:

> They started from the fact that there were too many students in America who did not have equal access to education. They saw that the system wasn't work-ing, that there was an absence of opportunity, so they took it upon themselves to provide the solution. HBCUs are real pioneers when it comes to school choice. They are living proof that when more options are provided to students, they are afforded greater access and greater quality. Their success has shown that more options help students flourish. (in Strauss March 7, 2017)

Two weeks before DeVos's statement, the Twitter account of the Department of Education had already shown unfamiliarity with the history of African Americans when it spelled the name of W. E. B. Du Bois as "DeBois" (Strauss March 7, 2017). In addition to having been the first Negro to receive a doctoral degree in sociology from Harvard University, in 1895, DuBois went on to cofound the National Association for the Advancement of Colored People (NAACP) and pioneer the study of U.S. race relations. He was also famous for his debate with Booker T. Washington, who defended vocational education for Negroes, whereas Du Bois was a staunch defender of higher education for them. Despite his many accomplishments, legal segregation restricted his options, so that the only teaching appointment DuBois secured was at Atlanta University, in Georgia, an HBCU founded in 1865. The lack of national visibility afforded to an HBCU has prevented the recognition of DuBois's role as the pioneer U.S. sociologist whose Atlanta School of Sociology precedes the Chicago School of Sociology and whose book *The Philadelphia Negro* (1899) located the causes of Negroes' lower socioeco-nomic status in "racism" rather than in "racial inferiority" (Morris 2015).

Less controversial was the appointment of Elaine Chao for secretary of transportation, the same position she had held in George W. Bush's presidency. Rick Perry, a former governor of Texas, headed Energy. Finally, David Shulkin was selected to be secretary of veteran affairs; he was the only candidate unanimously confirmed (*New York Times* May 11, 2017).

Another seven cabinet-level officials were confirmed by the Senate: Robert Lighthizer as U.S. Trade Representative; Dan Coats as director of national intelligence; Nikki Haley as ambassador to the United Nations; Mick Mulvaney as director of the office of management and budget, whose main assignment was to cut governmental spending, including the Affordable Care Act; Mike Pompeo as director of the Central Intelligence Agency; Scott Pruitt as administrator of the environmental protection agency, someone at once with ties to the coal industry and a believer in climate change; and Linda McMahon, the former CEO of the World Wrestling Entertainment, as Administrator of the Small Business Administration (*New York Times* May 11, 2017).

President Trump appointed 10 additional positions to his government. For White House chief of staff, he selected Reince Priebus, former chair of the Republican National Committee, who was expected to aid him on policy making. Trump rewarded the comanagers of his campaign with key positions: he named Stephen Bannon chief strategist, with the expectation that he would collaborate with Priebus "as equal partners"; Kellyanne Conway became the president's Counselor. Donald F. McGahan II was White House Counsel, an "adviser on legal matters." Peter Navarro, a professor of economics, was Director of Trade and Industrial Policy. Michael Flynn was National Security Adviser; he resigned after one month once his connection to the Russian ambassador was discovered. Thomas Bossert, who had been a "top national security aide" in President George W. Bush, was appointed as Homeland Security Adviser, a position with the same status as the National Security Adviser. Sean Spicer was Press Secretary and Special Assistant to the President. In addition, Trump had two appointments closer to home: his daughter Ivanka as his Adviser, and Jared Kushner, her husband, as his Senior Adviser. Both positions were unpaid.

Finally, President Trump created one more position. Before inauguration, the announcement came that Omarosa Manigault had landed the job of "assistant to the president and director of communications for the Office of Public Liaison" (Puente January 4, 2017). As we recall from chapter 3 of this book, Omarosa is a former cast member of *The Apprentice* who went on to work as senior adviser to Trump's presidential campaign; specifically, her role was to encourage Blacks to vote for Trump. Subsequently, she was part of his transition team. When Trump won the election, she said, "Every critic, every detractor will have to bow down to President Trump." However, by the end of Trump's first year as president, Omarosa was gone, fired by General John Kelly. Because she refused to leave, she was dragged out of the White House.

She retaliated by writing a tell-all book, *Unhinged: An Insider's Account of the Trump White House* (2018), which was summarized as "attacks on the physical and mental health of the president" and prompted charges by Trump that she was a liar (Griffin August 15, 2018). However, hers was but one of the many unflattering books ousted members of Trump's network wrote about him, including one by his personal lawyer, Michael Cohen, who ended up serving time in prison, and another by his niece Mary L. Trump (Cohen 2020, Trump, Mary 2020).

AGAINST MISOGYNY: THE WOMEN'S MARCH

In the previous chapter, I related how Donald Trump's presidential campaign had suffered a potential blow when the *Access Hollywood* tape leaked that registered Trump's voice bragging about the freedom his notoriety gave him to "grab [women] by the pussy." I also mentioned that the incident ended up having little effect on his campaign. Nevertheless, there were enough women who were outraged by it and wanted to display their outrage in a national platform.

Proof of the power of the internet to mobilize large numbers of people today, a movement against Donald Trump's victory was born on November 9, 2016, when Teresa Shook, an Indiana native and retired lawyer who resided in Hawaii, posted on Facebook an event page calling for women to march on Washington, DC; soon, a number of similar pages sprang up and thousands of women were adhering to them. Mari Lynn Bland, called "Bob Bland," a New Yorker described as a "left-of-center millionaire" and "fashion designer" (Influence Watch.org), organized the several pages into the Women's March movement. Bland recruited Tamika Mallory, an African American activist and former executive director of the National Action Network, headed by Al Sharpton, Carmen Perez, a Mexican-American criminal reform activist and founder of Justice League NYC, and Linda Sarsour, a Palestinian-American who is the former executive director of the Arab-American Association of New York, to cochair the march; Teresa Shook did not organize the march, but was scheduled as one of the speakers. They selected January 21, 2017 for the event, the day after Trump's inauguration (Influence Watch.org).

Attendance of the march surpassed all expectations, in that half a million people descended upon the country's capital. Additionally, there were simultaneous demonstrations all over the country and the world, totaling over four million in the United States and 300,000 in "more than 30 foreign countries, ranging from Antarctica to Zimbabwe" (History January 5, 2018). On the West Coast, Los Angeles drew the largest contingent at 750,000. On the

East Coast, New York had 400,000 marchers. And in the Midwest, Chicago counted 150,000 present.

A notable characteristic of the demonstrations was the head gear that many of the women wore: a pink knitted hat with small pointy ears resembling a cat's. The hats were called "pussyhats," a word play alluding to a common term for "cat" and the infamous expression Trump had uttered on the *Access Hollywood* tape. The hat was the idea of Krista Suh and Jayna Zweiman, two friends from Los Angeles who enjoy knitting and combating gender inequality. According to Zweiman, "It's reappropriating the word 'pussy' in a positive way. It's a pussyhat -- one word. This is a project about women supporting women." The Pussyhat Project was born when they approached their knitting teacher, Kat Coyle, who also owns The Little Knittery. Coyle recalls, "I designed a hat that was simple enough that beginners could make it, or modify it, and make it their own. We put together the website, and then I got on Instagram, let my knitting community know, and it just took off from there" (Hamasaki January 20, 2017). Knitters from across the world donated over 60,000 hats, accompanied by messages to the ultimate wearer about women's rights; #PussyhatProject flooded social media with images of volunteers displaying their work before mailing them to The Little Knittery. Some women wore the hats on inauguration day.

The Women's March is considered "the largest single-day protest in U.S. history" (History January 5, 2018). Speeches emphasized not only gender inequality and the threat to women's rights that were expected from the Trump administration, but also "criminal justice, defense of the environment and the rights of immigrants, Muslims, gay and transgender people and the disabled (History January 5, 2018). The organizers had hoped that the march would catapult higher political engagement and become a yearly event. While the march took place again in the following years, a clash ensued between Teresa Shook and the leaders of the march when they refused to disassociate themselves from Nation of Islam's head Louis Farrakhan. Shook claimed they "allow[ed] anti-Semitism, anti-LGBTQIA+ sentiment and hateful racist rhetoric to become part of the platform by refusing to separate themselves from groups that espouse these racist, hateful beliefs" (Influence Watch). On January 18, the march took place under new leadership, with a focus on "climate, reproductive justice and immigrants' rights" (Sarmiento January 17, 2020).

The hundreds of thousands of women who expressed their discontent over Donald Trump's election on marches starting in 2017 were not alone. Every display of blatant sexism, nativism, or racism from the part of the president was met with social dissent. For instance, after only one week in office, Trump "signed an executive order that prohibited citizens from seven Muslim-majority countries from entering the United States for 90 days, suspended the entry of all refugees for at least 120 days, and barred Syrian refugees indefinitely" (Cheng December 6, 2017). Actually, that was a modification of his presidential campaign; in December 2015, he had clamored for a ban on the entry of the entire Muslim population (Berenson December 7, 2015). Trump's executive order found resistance both from the public and from the courts. Throughout the nation, people flocked to airports, where they chanted "Let them in!," while federal judges disqualified Trump's order that had been challenged by the American Civil Liberties Union (ACLU) (Cheng December 6, 2017). Trump issued another executive order aimed at banning Muslims two months later, which was also challenged in the courts. Trump signed yet another order, in September 2017, banning the entry of citizens of Iran, Syria, Libya, Yemen, Chad, and Somalia. This time, the Supreme Court upheld the ban.

In addition to his attempts at excluding Muslims, Trump showed his sympathy for White supremacists during a deadly confrontation in Charlottesville, VA in August 2017. White nationalists carrying tiki torches and chanting "Jews will not replace us" and "White lives matter" marched through the University of Virginia campus, where they were met by counterdemonstrators who chanted "No Nazis! No KKK! No fascist USA!." In addition to the face-to-face altercations, which lasted for days, violence escalated when James Alex Fields, a White man, plowed his car on the crowd, injuring many and killing Heather Heyer, a White woman who was protesting against White nationalism. While vice-president Pence condemned the attack and Terry McAuliffe, the governor of Virginia, declared that White nationalists, "Let's be honest, they need to leave America, because they are not Americans," President Trump argued that there were good people on both sides of the confrontation, that the rally organizers had permits unlike the counterdemonstrators, and that the rally was in protest against the removal of statues of Confederate figures. By equating White supremacists with those who confronted them, Trump favored the actions of the former, even if he later admitted the clashes had been "terrible" (Yan, Sayers, and Almasy August 14, 2017).

Trump would make racist remarks concerning foreign countries in January of the following year, when he referred to African countries, El Salvador, and Haiti as "shithole countries" whose citizens should be prevented from migrating to the United States, as opposed to Norwegians. On his Tweeter account, Trump denied he had uttered those words after the United Nations, politicians from several African nations, and even members of the Republican Party condemned them as racist (Yan, Sayers, and Almasy August 14, 2017).

To sum up, Trump's election and governing style clearly placed him on the far right, anchored by a disregard for diplomacy, a disdain for minority racial/ethnic groups, and an emphasis on nativism. As the following two chapters show, those characteristics made him an inspiration and a role model for Jair Bolsonaro, who was elected president of Brazil two years after Trump's victory.

Chapter 5

"Make Brazil Great Again"
Jair Bolsonaro's Presidential Campaign

*Still regarded by some as a joke, as it happened to Donald Trump in
the United States in 2016, the candidacy of Bolsonaro must be taken
seriously.*—Saint-Clair 2018, 13

Published before Jair Bolsonaro's election as the 38th president of Brazil in
October 2018, journalist Clóvis Saint-Clair's words proved to be prophetic.
In this chapter, I examine Bolsonaro's life from soldier to exonerated captain
to politician prior to his presidential candidacy as well as his presidential
campaign.

BEFORE THE "MYTH": BOLSONARO'S
INSERTION INTO POLITICS

Jair Bolsonaro presents himself first and foremost as a military man. Indeed,
the man from Glicério, a small town in the countryside of the state of São
Paulo, where he was born in 1955, had frequented the School for Army
Cadets as an adolescent and, later, trained as a skydiver. Compared with
Donald Trump, Bolsonaro had much humbler beginnings, as he was the son
of a lay dentist who descended from Italian immigrants and a homemaker;
he started to work as a preteenager in order to help out his family, both as a
field hand and as a fisherman (Saint-Clair 2018, chapter 2). Even before he
joined the army, young Bolsonaro had already displayed a fondness for the
military dictatorship, the political regime that ruled Brazil with an iron fist
from 1964 to 1985: he "loathed João Goulart, the president ousted by the
dictatorship, and saw the military who confronted Lamarca [an army captain

who had famously joined the anti-dictatorship forces] as heroes" (Saint-Clair 2018, 17).

As a cadet in the town of Resende, located in the state of Rio de Janeiro, between 1974 and 1977, Bolsonaro was not a stellar student, with grades at first fluctuating between 51/100 in Portuguese and 78/100 in drawing. He tended to do better in mathematics courses, such as statistics, but he excelled in sports, so much so that his superiors nicknamed him *Cavalão*, or "big horse" (Saint-Clair 2018, 24). He graduated in 19th place out of 68 graduates in artillery (Sassine November 19, 2018).

Upon graduation, Bolsonaro was transferred to a barracks in the city of Rio de Janeiro, which would eventually serve as the headquarters of his political career. Between 1979 and 1981, he was based in Nioaque, in the state of Mato Grosso do Sul, in the Brazilian hinterland. Back to Rio de Janeiro in 1982, he finally excelled in the School of Physical Education, as a diver and skydiver (Saint-Clair 2018, chapter 3).

Despite his taste for military life, which is based on a strict hierarchy, Bolsonaro established a reputation as one who confronted his commanders even as a student. There are several accounts of his having defied those in command, to the point of being imprisoned in 1986 for having criticized the alleged low salaries of military personnel (Saint-Clair 2018, chapter 3) as well as having engaged in gold mining in the early 1980s; for his superiors, that was demonstration of "an excessive ambition to succeed financially and economically." According to a report by *Folha de São Paulo*, Colonel Carlos Alfredo Pellegrino, Bolsonaro's immediate commander, also noted that Bolsonaro's intention to be a leader repeatedly failed due to "the aggressive way he treated his comrades as well as his lack of logic, rationality, and equilibrium in the presentation of his arguments" (Valente May 16, 2017). In 1986, he was accused of insubordination for revealing military goings-on to newspapers. Although found not guilty, Captain Bolsonaro left the army as a persona non grata. Rather than being subjected to a new military trial in 1988, he began his political career by campaigning for a seat as a councilman for the city of Rio de Janeiro (Saint-Clair 2018, chapter 6).

Like Donald Trump's, Jair Bolsonaro's candidacy was also seen as "unconventional." However, if something is unconventional about Bolsonaro's trajectory, it ought to be the ease with which he has changed allegiances: Between 1988 and 2018, he was affiliated with no fewer than nine political parties (Saint-Clair 2018, 63). Bolsonaro's first party was the Christian Democratic Party (*Partido Democrata Cristão* [PDC]). Founded in 1945, it was banned 20 years later by the Second Institutional Act (*Ato Institucional 2* [AI 2]), which Marshal Castelo Branco signed one year after the coup that had established a military dictatorship in Brazil. AI 2 restricted political parties to only two: National Renewing Alliance (*Aliança Renovadora Nacional—Arena*), the party of the military dictatorship, and Brazilian Democratic Movement (*Movimento Democrático Brasileiro*). In addition, AI 2 subordinated the legislative to the executive power (Historiaresumos.com) and eliminated direct presidential elections, in response to the 1965 elections of over half (6 out of 11) of gubernatorial candidates who opposed the military regime, including the winners in the states of Minas Gerais and Guanabara, where Rio de Janeiro, the former capital of the country, was located (Memorial da Democracia 2015–2017).[1] In 1985, after the end of the dictatorship, multi-partisanship was reestablished, which led to reemergence of the PDC. The new Democratic Christian Party had a middle of the road platform, "situated between liberalism and Marxism, and preaching the 'establishment of a new social order without the destruction of liberty.'" In sum, the party was about "'Respect of the dignity of the human person,' 'private property,' and the 'Evangelical message,' besides 'peace and love among men, regardless of racial differences'" (FGV CPDOC). We will see that, during Bolsonaro's presidential campaign, the themes of private property and the dignity of the human person appear as the defense of *cidadãos de bem*, that is, well-heeled citizens, whom he would claim were losing ground to allegedly morally loose people. We will also see that the Evangelical vote, like in Trump's campaign, was fundamental for Bolsonaro's presidential election.

According to Saint-Clair (2018, chapter 9), Bolsonaro launched his candidacy to councilman in 1988 with the goal of eventually becoming a congressman by counting on the military vote. With a small number of votes, he was elected to councilman only because his party as a whole got more than 140,000 votes.[2] The year 1988 remains an emblematic election year because that was when *Macaco Tião*, a chimpanzee at Rio's zoo, garnered 300,000 votes, enough to finish in fourth place for the mayoral election (Saint-Clair 2018, chapter 7).

In 1990, the army once again accused Bolsonaro of insubordination, having also curbed his access to the barracks in order to campaign as a politician (Saint-Clair 2018, 49). It was then that the high echelon of the army saw him as a *bunda-suja*, literally a "dirty butt," or someone who failed to be promoted to higher ranks. As a result, "That group never supported his plans to get to Planalto Palace nor does it approve of his attempt to personify the savior of the country" (50).

Bolsonaro's first tenure as a councilman was characterized by an extreme absenteeism, although he attended an event for human rights and against violence and often wrote to newspapers against the Workers' Party (*Partido dos Trabalhadores* [PT]) (Saint-Clair 2018, 53–54; 57). According to Saint-Clair (2018, chapter 9), Bolsonaro aimed at becoming a congressman as soon as he was elected councilman, by counting on the military and firefighters' vote in order to spend less money on his campaign. Indeed, as early as 1989, that is, one year after having been elected councilman, Bolsonaro was elected congressman, thus forfeiting the remaining three years of his tenure. From the start, he advocated the use of violence to combat violence and longed for a return to the military dictatorship regime.

One example of his predilection for violence was his reaction to the Carandiru Massacre, which took place in the city of São Paulo in October 1992, when 111 prisoners were murdered by the Military Policy after a prison mutiny.[3] According to Saint-Clair (2018, 70), Bolsonaro said then, "Too few died. The Military Police should have killed a thousand!" He also consistently voted for the death penalty and for sterilization as a form of birth control in order to prevent future crime. That makes him a proponent of eugenics, which had been so popular in the United States, and in Brazil too, at the turn of the nineteenth to the twentieth centuries.

As for Bolsonaro's longing for the military dictatorship, as early as 1993, he defended the closing of Congress due to the "lack of preparation of the parliamentarians" and the institution of an exception regime, that is, one that suspends civil rights, by claiming, "There are too many laws that get in the way. In an exception regime, a ruler, who doesn't need to be from the military, grabs a pen and crosses out the disturbing law" (Saint-Clair 2018, 70). The tone of his declarations attracted the attention of *The New York Times*, which published on July 25 of the same year "Conversations/Jair Bolsonaro: A Soldier Turned Politician Wants to Give Brazil back to Army Rule" (in Saint-Clair 2018, 71). Another example of Bolsonaro's predilection for dictatorships was his praise, in a 1998 magazine interview, of other totalitarian South American regimes: of General Augusto Pinochet's government in Chile (1973–1981) Bolsonaro once wished that more than the 3,000 persons should have been killed during his tenure; of Alberto Fujimori's having closed the Peruvian Congress through military intervention while president in 1992, Bolsonaro called him a "model" (De Ferrari November 5, 2019; Sousa 2019, 79). He also advocated the assassination of President Fernando Henrique Cardoso (1995–2002) more than once as punishment for his "corruption." Meanwhile, Bolsonaro continued to generate the wrath of the high military echelon against him. For instance, in a 1998 interview, General Ernesto Geisel, the penultimate president of the military regime in Brazil (1974–1979), referred to Bolsonaro as "a bad military man": "Currently, who are the military in Congress? Let us not count Bolsonaro because Bolsonaro is a completely abnormal case, including being a bad military man" (Nossa Política December 29, 2017).

In 1993, PDC merged with the Social Democratic Party (*Partido Democrático Social*), which became the Progressive Reformer Party (*Partido Progressista Reformador—PPR*). Bolsonaro remained a member of PPR until 1995, when that party merged with the Progressive Party (*Partido*

Progressista [PP]) and became the Brazilian Progressive Party (*Partido Progressista Brasileiro* [PPB]). From there he moved on to the Brazilian Labor Party (*Partido Trabalhista Brasileiro* [PTB]) in 2003, where he remained for two years before leaving for the Liberal Front Party (*Partido da Frente Liberal—PFL*) and the PP, the former PPB, in 2005. Bolsonaro remained there until 2016, when he joined the Christian Social Party (*Partido Social Cristão* [PSC]) for a little over one year. Though brief, that tenure was significant in that it marked his association with Evangelicals, which would prove crucial for his presidential election two years later (Saint-Clair 2018, 61); it was also when he declared his pre-candidacy to the 2018 presidential election (*Extra* March 2, 2016). However, in mid-2017, Bolsonaro left for the National Ecological Party (*Partido Ecológico Nacional—PEN*), which, at his request, changed its name to Patriot (*Patriota*). Finally, in March of 2018, he became a member of the Liberal Social Party (*Partido Social Liberal—PSL*), the party from which he ran as a presidential candidate in 2018 (Saint-Clair 2018, 63). Inaugurated in an Evangelical-like ceremony, he was then called "Myth!" by those in attendance (Saint-Clair 2018, 66).

What explains so many political departures and affiliations in such a relatively short time? According to Saint-Clair (2018), Bolsonaro shopped for the party with the most money and the most coalitions, which could also offer political positions for his adult sons, namely, Flávio, a state deputy from Rio de Janeiro; Carlos, a councilman from the city of Rio de Janeiro; and Eduardo, a congressman from São Paulo. The members of Patriot, in particular, felt betrayed given Bolsonaro's promise to be its presidential candidate; his promise was captured on video on November 23, 2017, when he declared to the president of the party,

> Final decision. A word is much worthier than a piece of paper. Everything is ready for our membership in March of next year, and together we will go toward a project for a different Brazil. When we do that, a marriage, everyone loses some so that as a whole we will win. (Saint-Clair 2018, 64)

The president of Patriot, Adilson Barroso de Oliveira, declared that Bolsonaro and his team had ultimately requested control of 23 out of the 26 Brazilian states, an ambition which annoyed longer-term members of the party, in addition to vying for the presidential candidacy (Saint-Clair 2018, 65).

Another reason for Bolsonaro's unprecedented party migrations may have been his desire to be elected president of the House of Representatives. In 2005, 2011, and 2017, he tried, never to be elected. Altogether, he was elected to the House seven times (*Gazeta do Povo* October 28, 2018), but his tenure was deemed inexpressive in that, in 27 years, only 2 out of his 171 bills were approved: the elimination of taxation over computer products and the use of the so-called "cancer pill," a synthetic medication (*Rede Brasil Atual* May 6, 2018). Among his failed bills were those of a misogynist nature, such as the nullification of the 2013 law that grants medical treatment to victims of sexual abuse, including rape, in public hospitals; according to him and his Evangelical colleagues, the law makes it easier for abortion to become legal in Brazil (Megale October 12, 2018). He also introduced bills of a homophobic nature, which would "eliminate the use of a social name for transvestites and transsexuals in police reports and also in educational institutions" (*Rede Brasil Atual* May 6, 2018). For Antonio Augusto Queiroz, the director of documentation of the Interunion Department of Parliamentary Advisory (*Departamento Intersindical de Assessoria Parlamentar—Diap*),

> having only two approved bills is extremely negative. As inexpressive a member of parliamentary may be, he manages to convince his peers to turn his bills into laws. In 26 years [*sic*], to approve only two inexpressive bills is too little. He has total interest in safety, and he is totally inefficient about it, unable to approve anything.

As a congressman, then, Bolsonaro was regarded as part of the *baixo clero*, or "low clergy," which Oyama (2020, 8) defined as "the periphery of Congress, formed by representatives of dwarfish parties, without influence or relevant projects under their belt and dismissed by the parliamentary leaderships, who only remember them when they need a quorum in an election." Moreover, journalists who work in Brasília included Bolsonaro in what they called the "folkloric quota of Congress—parliamentarians who often call attention by histrionics, verbal explosions at the plenary, and by the troubles they get into" (Oyama 2020, 9). Thus, the presidential candidate who would run based on the promise to save the country not only had a dismal record as a legislator, but was also seen by some as unstable. Evidently, that did not hinder his ability to convince a significant portion of the electorate that he was indeed the best person to become the 38th president of Brazil.

In order to understand how and why an obscure politician came to be seen as the only solution to the country's problems despite his lack of an agenda, it is necessary to go back to the early 2010s and examine the state of unrest that befell Brazil.

SEEDS OF DISCONTENT: URBAN UNREST AND A TURN TO THE FAR RIGHT

On March 14, 2009, President Luiz Inácio Lula da Silva visited the White House. President Barack Obama opened his remarks to the press thus,

The President and I just had a wonderful meeting. I have been a great admirer of Brazil and a great admirer of the progressive, forward-looking leadership that President Lula has shown throughout Latin America and throughout the world. We have a very strong friendship between the two countries, but we can always make it stronger in areas like energy and biofuels, in the interest in increasing the standards of living in impoverished countries throughout Latin America, expanding trade relationships—you know, the President and I had a wonderful meeting of the minds. And I'm grateful that he took the time to visit with us. We intend to have a host of meetings at a ministerial level in the coming days and weeks, both in preparation for the G20, to coordinate our activities to strengthen global economic growth; also in anticipation of the Summit of the Americas that will be taking place in April, so that we can have a proactive strategy that uses the strength of the U.S.-Brazilian relationship to strengthen ties throughout the hemisphere. So I'm very grateful to him for taking the time to visit, and I'm looking forward to reciprocating in a visit to Brazil sometime soon. (The White House March 14, 2009)

The two presidents met once again at the G20 Summit, the meeting of the 20 wealthiest nations in the world, in London, England, on April 2, 2009. On that occasion, Obama said, "That's my man right there. I love this guy. He's the most popular politician on earth" (YouTube April 3, 2009). True to his word, Obama would reciprocate Lula's visit two years later, when he, First Lady Michelle R. Obama, and their two daughters landed in Brazil. On March 19, he met with then President Dilma Rousseff, Lula's successor (Calmes and Barrionuevo March 19, 2011).

The international prestige that Brazil was enjoying then was notorious. For instance, the cover of *The Economist* from November 12, 2009 had been a picture of the statue of Christ the Redeemer, one of Rio de Janeiro's post-cards, shooting upright from Mount Corcovado, as if it were a spaceship, on which the following headline was printed: "Brazil Takes off." The article lauded Brazil's booming economy, its successful handling of a world recession, its many mineral riches, and the prediction that Brazil would "become the world's fifth-largest economy, overcoming Britain and France" by 2014. The deep socioeconomic inequality for which Brazil is famous decreased between 2003 and 2014, when nearly 30 million people experienced upward mobility from poverty and the income of the general population went up over 4 percent (World Bank October 14, 2019). However, despite so much optimism, as of 2017 Brazil was the eighth economy in the world, right behind Britain and France (*The Economist* 2017).

By 2013, there were signs that Brazil was weathering economic stagnation and political unrest. As I noted elsewhere (Penha-Lopes 2017, 145–146), protest against the increase in the prices of bus fares—an increase of

R$0.20—led to demonstrations throughout the country starting on June 6. Teixeira (2018) has linked those demonstrations to global unrest manifested two years earlier in movements such as the Arab spring, "Occupy Wall Street," in New York City, and in manifestations in Europe and Africa as well as to initiatives to take over public space such as squares and parks in major urban centers in Brazil. All of them, he argues, were "struggles for the radicalization of democracy," that is, a rejection of party politics. What came to be known as the "June journeys" (*jornadas de junho*) garnered more and more demonstrators, often called to action via social media.

By January 2014, the protest had become violent, with police intervention and the destruction of property such as the facades of banks and stores. It had also turned against the federal government, especially against the costs of hosting the Soccer (Football) World Cup in midyear, given the precariousness of public services in health and education. From the "Twenty Cents Is Too Much!" chant was added "There Will Be No Cup!" (Penha-Lopes 2017, 146). President Rousseff responded by scheduling an emergency cabinet meeting while overseas at the World Economic Forum in Davos, Switzerland (Previdelli January 27, 2014). In early June, she declared that demonstrations are a sign of democracy (Terra.com.br June 4, 2014). Finally, on June 21, Rousseff went on national television to address the protests. She reiterated that they were pertinent in a democratic country, something that had taken so long for Brazil to become. She stated that "the voice of the streets must be heard and respected," but she also pointed out that the violence perpetrated by a minority must be stopped. Addressing the concerns about the lack of public services, she announced a plan for urban transportation, the application to education of "100 percent" of the gains from oil, and the hiring of medical doctors from overseas to attend to the lack of health care in the country. She favored the demonstrations against corruption, but she also asked that the population receive the teams of the countries that would take part in the Cup with "respect, tenderness, and joy" (*Veja* June 21, 2014).

By then, Rousseff's popularity had gone down from 79 percent in March 2013 to 31 percent in June 2014. Still, she was ahead in the voting preferences for the presidential elections in October of that year: 39 percent, as compared with 21 percent for Aécio Neves, a senator from the southeastern state of Minas Gerais, affiliated with PSDB (*Partido da Social Democracia Brasileira*, Brazilian Social Democarcy Party) and 10 percent for Eduardo Campos, former governor of Pernambuco, from the Brazilian Socialist Party (*Partido Socialista Brasileiro—PSB*) (*O Dia* June 19, 2014). Both Neves and Campos came from political families; Neves was the grandson of Tancredo Neves (1910–1985), the first president elected through direct ballot after the end of the military dictatorship, who died of diverticulitis before he had a chance to be sworn into office. In turn, Campos (1965–2014) was the son of

Ana Arraes, a former congresswoman, and grandson of Miguel Arraes, former congressman and former governor of Pernambuco. On August 13, 2014, three days after turning 49 years old and two months before the presidential elections, Campos died in a plane crash over the city of São Paulo; his death was seen as "a blow to Brazil's politically disenchanted youth" (Fusion August 14, 2014). Marina Silva, his running mate, proved incapable of garnering electoral support vis-à-vis Rousseff and Neves. A major polarization among the electorate ensued. Aécio Neves was dubbed "Aécio Never" by the pro-Rousseff camp; Rousseff's opponents vehemently demonstrated against her government in what came to be known as *panelaços*, that is, demonstrations characterized by the beating of pots and pans by a populace wearing yellow jerseys of the Brazilian national soccer team (Penha-Lopes 2017, 146). On social media and in person, pro-Aécio and pro-Dilma sympathizers fought with each other to the point where even close relatives cut ties with each other.

In October 2014, Rousseff was reelected by a very tight margin: 51.64 percent of the valid ballots; Neves garnered 48.536 percent of the votes overall (Pereira October 26, 2014). In an obvious show of polarization, Rousseff won 70 percent of the votes cast in the northeast, whereas Neves won in the southeast, south, and center-west, although Rousseff won in Neves's home state of Minas Gerais (Vi o Mundo October 24, 2014). Overseas, Neves won in Miami, Florida; in France; and in England as well as overwhelmingly in Israel and Tokyo; Rousseff won in Palestine and Cuba (Redação RBA October 27, 2014).

Soon after the election, anti-Rousseff forces started to organize themselves. *Panelaços* continued throughout Brazil. For instance, on November 15, 2014, the 125th anniversary of the proclamation of the Republic, over 2,000 persons occupied Praça da Sé (See Square), a main square in downtown São Paulo, and Paulista Avenue, in order to protest against Rousseff's victory and PT's maintenance in power. Visibly pro-PT persons were verbally and physically attacked, and told to "go back to Cuba." The crowd shouted "Out with Dilma" and "Out with PT." The polarization that had been established during the presidential campaign was maintained with reciprocal name calling (Neves November 15, 2014). Rousseff reorganized her cabinet, ousting ministers, such as Antônio Palloci, who were investigated over claims of corruption. Moreover, she focused on investing on education, public health, urban housing, and the family allowance program as well as on economic growth (*Gazeta do Povo* October 26, 2014). However, in the first year of her second tenure, Rousseff struggled against falling approval rates; on December 2015, she had a 70 percent rejection rate (Matoso December 15, 2015). The spectrum of corruption charges loomed over her, to the point where Marina Silva, Eduardo Campos's running mate, who had finished in third place, claimed Rousseff's victory was an example of "electoral fraud":

What won the election were the structures, the marketeers, the money misappropriated from Petrobras and from the pension funds. I hope that, with the *Lava Jato* operation [Operation Car Wash], all that is being investigated leads to the cooling of electoral corruption. (Campos November 27, 2017)

In an earlier work (Penha-Lopes 2017, 146), I argued that "part of the resentment of those against the Rousseff government was the proliferation of social welfare programs such as aid to lower income families with children ('*Bolsa Família*'), which opponents claim did little beyond inflate the number of PT voters." In other words, the focus on corruption and its association with PT masked the conviction that the social programs that had sprung in the years that party was in power benefited the undeserving. After all, the Lula-Rousseff tenures were the first in Brazilian history to promote a comprehensive set of policies geared toward decreasing social and racial inequality in Brazil, such as ProUni, the scholarship program for enrollment in private universities; Pronatec, the scholarship program for enrollment in technical schools; Fies, low-interest student loans for higher education; and Science without Borders, scholarships for study abroad, all of which would be dismantled after Rousseff's impeachment. Undoubtedly, the most radical of the policies during the Lula-Rousseff tenures were the implementation of university quotas, which, for the first time, opened up real opportunities of higher education for scores of students of African and indigenous descent and the poor. The approval in 2012 by the Senate of the university quotas bill over a decade after it had been presented in Congress, followed by the signing of it as a federal law, was met with the continuing resistance from Brazilians who, despite reliable evidence of tremendous racial disparities in life chances, insist that Brazil is not a racist country.

IMPEACHMENT

The two years that preceded the 2018 presidential elections in Brazil were witnesses to dramatic events that left deep marks in the political scenario of the country. That was when Dilma Rousseff was impeached during her second tenure as president of Brazil under corruption charges. Rousseff was the former president of Petrobras, the federal oil company. Since 2014, a number of Petrobras officials had been arrested under *Operação Lava Jato* (Operation Car Wash), which concerned suspicions of money laundering. The head of the investigation, Sergio Moro, a judge from the city of Curitiba, in the southern state of Paraná, was labeled a "hero" by scores of Brazilians, especially by those who opposed PT, Dilma Rousseff's party. On the streets, a mostly White middle-class populace again dressed in the official yellow jerseys of the Brazilian soccer team marched against corruption and "communism."

On September 1, 2015, Janaina Paschoal, a law professor from São Paulo; former minister of justice Miguel Reale Júnior; and Hélio Bicudo, a founder of PT who had left the party, filed a formal request for the impeachment of President Rousseff in the House of Representatives (Migalhas September 1, 2015). On April 4 of the following year, the trio of accusers took part in an event at the University of São Paulo's Law School during which Paschoal gave an impassioned speech that led to her being compared, on social media, to the possessed character in *The Exorcist* (Sanches April 6, 2016). On that occasion, Paschoal equated the PT government to a government of "snakes": Janaina said that

"the snakes that are in power are taking advantage in order to perpetuate themselves." According to her, "they get stronger out of our fear, out of the excessive ambition." She also affirmed we are at a moment of reflection. "More than stopping to reflect on the impeachment, for which we have plenty of reasons, do we want to serve a snake?"

Paschoal then infused her speech with religious tones by invoking God:

We are not going to lower our heads. Since I was little, my father has told me, "Janaina, God doesn't give wings to snakes." And I say, Father, sometimes, the snake grows wings, but God sends a legion to finish with the snake.

Paschoal ended her speech with a call against PT and against jararacas, a type of venomous snake from Brazil (Aguiar April 4, 2016). Some, such as University of São Paulo philosopher Vladimir Saflate (April 8, 2016), criticized Paschoal's speech as a dangerous mix of Evangelical discourse with fascism that compares opponents to vicious animals, and philosopher Marcia Tiburi (in Scirea April 15, 2016) interpreted Paschoal's "histrionism" as a fascist manifestation of hatred rather than of insanity. Others, such as Hélio Bicudo, insisted that her speech "was a civic exaltation. She has an explosive temperament, but she is lucid and doesn't miss the boat" (in Sanches April 8, 2016).

On May 12, 2016, the House of Representatives recommended impeachment based on "crime of responsibility due to the so-called 'fiscal pedaling' and the publication of decrees without the authorization of Congress" (Dw .com August 31, 2016). For 12 hours, a procession of 43 congresspersons manifested their allegiance to that recommendation with increasingly long and unusual justifications, voting for impeachment in the name of their grandchildren, and invoking God's will. Those who voted against impeachment, such as Vanessa Grazziotin, from the Communist Party of Brazil (*Partido Comunista do Brasil—PcdoB*) regarded it a "coup" (Cipriani August 31, 2016).

One of the vociferous votes came from congressman Jair Bolsonaro. In his speech, the retired army captain uttered, "In memory of Colonel Carlos Alberto Brilhante Ustra, Dilma Rousseff's terror, for Caxias' army, for the armed forces, for Brazil above everything and for God above us all, I vote yes" (Barba and Wentzel 2016). It turns out that Colonel Ustra (1932–2015) was not only Rousseff's torturer when she was part of the resistance against the military dictatorship; he is also "the first military to be recognized by Brazilian justice as a torturer" (Barba and Wentzel 2016). Records estimate that he was responsible for the torture of 500 persons between 1970 and 1974; about 50 of those perished. Before Ustra, Luís Alves de Lima e Silva (1803–1880), called "The Pacifier" and "The Iron Duke," had a decorated military career which included his leadership of the Brazilian army during the Paraguay War (1864–1870). For his service, he was given a nobility title, Duke of Caxias (*Duque de Caxias*); Vila do Porto da Estrela, where he was born, was renamed Duque de Caxias, in his honor. In 1962, he was named patron of the Brazilian army (Ministério da Defesa). In a few words, then, Bolsonaro praised the army and made an apology to the military dictatorship that the Brazilian Bar Association (*Ordem dos Advogados do Brasil— OAB*) labeled "terrifying"; the OAB also called for the suspension of Bolsonaro's tenure (Barba and Wentzel 2016).

Unlike other countries that had survived military dictatorships, such as Chile and Argentina, Brazil has never made it a crime to praise those regimes. Therefore, it is no wonder that Bolsonaro the congressman was never suspended. Instead, on August 31, 2016, the Senate voted for President Rousseff to be impeached by 61 to 20 votes, even though no evidence of corruption ever surfaced against her (Garcia et al. 2016). The fact that an investigation concluded in June 2016 had cleared Rousseff of any crime of responsibility lends credence to Rousseff's claim, echoed by many, that her impeachment had been a coup d'état (Simões July 6, 2016). Internationally, the impeachment was classified as "a tragedy and a scandal" (*The Guardian* April 18, 2016).

On the eve of that decision, Janaina Paschoal gave a speech during which she cried when she apologized to Rousseff, but asserted that the president would one day realize that the impeachment was beneficial even to her grandchildren (YouTube August 30, 2016). Ironically, many of Rousseff's accusers, including Eduardo Cunha, the president of Congress at that time, ended up having their mandates revoked due to corruption charges. On March 30, 2017, Cunha was convicted of corruption and money laundering, as a result of the *Lava Jato* investigations (Garcia, Janaina, and Lopes March 30, 2017).

On July 22, 2018, Bolsonaro announced he was running for president, under the claim that his "mission" was "to rescue Brazil." The audience at the headquarters of the Liberal Social Party in Rio de Janeiro greeted him with shouts of "Myth!" (Solé 2018). According to Saint-Clair (2018), the image of Bolsonaro as a "myth" was forged during his various campaigns against the Workers' Party and his defense of salary raises for military personnel in the 1990s, in such a rude way as to justify his nickname of *Cavalão* (i.e., "big horse").

BOLSONARO'S PRESIDENTIAL CAMPAIGN

The "Prosperity Way": The Economy, Education, and Public Safety

Bolsonaro started his campaign for president on March 1, 2016, when he joined the Social Christian Party (*Partido Socialista Cristão* [PSC]). The president of the party, Pastor Everaldo, announced Bolsonaro's pre-candidacy as "the mission of representing the Social Christian Party in the 2018 elections." According to Datafolha Institute, if the elections had been held then, Bolsonaro would secure about 5 percent of votes, behind Senator Aécio Neves, who had lost to Dilma Rousseff in the presidential elections two years earlier, Geraldo Alckmin, and José Serra—all from PSDB—Marina Silva, from Rede, and, most important, Lula, the former president from PT (*Extra* March 1, 2016). Moura and Corbellini (2018, 90–91), who analyzed longitudinal Datafolha data on "intention of spontaneous votes" through October 2018, observed that the intention to vote for Bolsonaro grew from 3 percent in July 2016 all the way to 31 percent on October 4, 2018; only once (between November 2017 and January 2018) did that percentage go down, and only 1 percentage point. With the exception of June 2018, Lula was winning until late August 2018, even though he had been arrested on April 7, 2018 on corruption charges linked to the Operation Car Washtion. Fernando Haddad, the PT candidate who replaced Lula, never got close to Bolsonaro: on October 9, 2018, 4 percent of those polled intended to vote for him, compared with 9 percent for Lula and 20 percent for Bolsonaro. By October 4, Haddad's portion had grown to 17 percent; Lula still had 1 percent of intended votes, but Bolsonaro had 31 percent. Undecided votes went down from a high of 64 percent in July 2016 to a low of 22 percent on October 3 to 4, 2018; the proportion of null and blank votes also decreased. That led them to conclude that Bolsonaro's success in October 2018 was the outcome of long-term conditions rather than a complete surprise; including in those conditions is the polarization between *"Lulismo"* (i.e., an intense predilection for former president Lula) and the "*Lava Jato*" party (i.e., the anti-corruption dimension). Moura and Corbellini (2018, 50–51) also note that PT and PSDB were the two parties that defined the presidential elections from 1994 to 2014; in that sense, then, Bolsonaro's candidacy, ascendancy, and eventual victory reflected a crisis in both parties, not just PT.

As noted earlier, Bolsonaro ended up leaving PSC and Patriota before joining PSL and clinching his candidacy in 2018. He named his platform "The Prosperity Way," a way that would be "decent, different from all that has thrown us in an ethical, moral, and fiscal crisis; a government without *quid pro quo*, without spurious agreements; a government formed by persons who are committed to Brazil and to Brazilians" (Pleno.news October 8, 2018). The platform claimed PT had left Brazil in an economic deficit that could only be eliminated by a "democratic liberal" economic plan with less state control; it also planned to lower the number of ministries in order to tend to the "legitimate interests of the Nation," thus eradicating corruption. Those promises confirmed his alignment with the claims that "Communism" was a threat spearheaded by PT and symbolized by its red flag, an idea that had gained momentum during the campaign for Rousseff's impeachment.

The chant "Our flag will never be red!" had been heard in demonstrations as early as August 2015, when a group gathered near Pedro Ernesto Palace, the headquarters of the City Town Hall, located at Cinelândia, a large square in downtown Rio de Janeiro, and burned a red flag (YouTube August 15, 2015). Another episode worth mentioning happened the following year, in Brasília, on November 17. During a visit to the National Congress, a woman interpreted the juxtaposed flags of Brazil and Japan, on permanent display ever since the 100th anniversary of Japanese immigration to Brazil in 2008, as proof that the Brazilian flag had already become "a symbol of communism." The video that depicted her warning to "unwary" Brazilians is quite popular on YouTube (YouTube November 17, 2016). In late 2019, director Pablo López Guelli premiered *Our Flag Will Never Be Red* (*Nossa Bandeira Jamais Será Vermelha*), his documentary about the role of the mass media in distorting the goals of the 2013 demonstrations up until Bolsonaro's campaign in 2018, at the Rio Festival 2019 (Festival do Rio 2019). Critics and scholars such as Noam Chomsky and Jessé Souza as well as journalist Glenn Greenwald took part in a debate then (Mathias December 13, 2019).

Deep aversion to the color red also led to physical attacks against passersby wearing red clothing. For example, during the highly contested 2014 presidential dispute, between Dilma Rousseff and Aécio Neves, Enio Barroso Filho, a wheelchair-bound man, was accosted in São Paulo on October 14 by a group of men who recognized him as a pro-PT blogger and got out of their car after they taunted him to remove his red shirt and he refused. According to Barroso, the men proceeded to shake his wheelchair so he would fall out, and called him a "shitty *petralha*" (*petralha de merda*).[4] Before that, on October 5, a pro-Rousseff voter was insulted when, wearing all red attire, she went to cast her vote (Guimarães October 17, 2014). Rousseff was reelected, but ostensibly PT supporters would continue to be victims of verbal and physical aggression beyond the next presidential election, in 2018, as PT-opponents adopted the Brazilian Soccer Team yellow jersey as an "anticommunism" symbol.

Besides the economy, Bolsonaro's campaign targeted education and public safety. For Bolsonaro, it was necessary to rid Brazilian education of the influence of Paulo Freire's ideas. Paulo Freire (1921–1997) had been a Brazilian historian and philosopher of education who developed the "pedagogy of the oppressed," a critical system in which learning is dialogical and engaged with one's cultural and economic circumstances. His work was considered subversive by the military regime, which led to his imprisonment in 1964 and exile from 1964 to 1979 (goodreads.com; Freire Institute 2020). Freire is internationally known as an authority in innovative pedagogy. Like the military in power during the dictatorship, Bolsonaro equates Freire's body of work with communism. In fact, in August of 2018, he vowed to "go in with 'a flame-thrower in the Ministry of Education and Culture in order to kick Paulo Freire out of there'" (*Veja* January 2, 2019:47). His plan was to create a "school without parties," that is, an educational system free of the influence of leftist ideas, from grade school to the university level.

It is worth mentioning that Bolsonaro has been consistently against university expansion and university quotas. About the former, that was a widespread policy during the PT years in government. During President Lula's two tenures, the number of university students grew from nearly 4 million to close to 6 million. Most of them went to private universities, made affordable by scholarships and low-interest student loans (Cieglinski December 24, 2010). Dilma Rousseff adopted the slogan "Brazil: Educating Country" and created Science without Borders, a study-abroad program financed by the federal government to support scientific and technological development (www.cienciasemfronteira.gov.br). After Rousseff's impeachment, Michel Temer, her former vice president who turned against her and assumed the presidency of the country, sought to discontinue those programs. In other words, though Bolsonaro is suspicious of higher education, a disregard for it did not start in his campaign.

About university quotas, Bolsonaro said on *Programa do Ratinho*, a television variety show broadcast on the SBT channel, in March, 2014 that he was "totally against them. What do Blacks have below me?" Asked about how slavery had kept Brazilian Blacks behind, Bolsonaro replied,

> Ask any member of my family whether they want to go back to Italy. Ask any
> Black whether he wants to go back to Angola. All of us are much better off here

than in our countries of origin! We have to start from the principle that we are all equal before the law. (Pedroso March 7, 2014)

Bolsonaro has since manifested himself against other types of university quotas (i.e., for the physically disabled, public school students, and indigenous students) as well as against quotas in civil service. Before that, in 2009, his son Flávio, a state representative from Rio de Janeiro, had already questioned the constitutionality of quotas (Junqueira 2009); two years later, he admitted that the country had a "historical debt to certain segments of the population . . . the poorest ones," but any measure should be temporary; those who benefit from it "should not keep sucking on the teats of the state forever" (Bolsonaro, Flávio October 21, 2011).[5]

Critics of this approach interpret it as "anti-intellectualism," that is, an association of thinking with snobbery, elitism, and the left. According to Alonso (2019), the main articulator of Bolsonaro's campaign was Olavo de Carvalho. Born in the state of São Paulo in 1947, Carvalho has resided in the state of Virginia, in the United States, since 2005. According to a biographical site, he is mostly self-taught, never having finished his undergraduate education in philosophy. A member of the Brazilian Communist Party during his youth, he went on to denounce that doctrine. Before joining Bolsonaro's campaign, Carvalho worked as an astrologer and a journalist for a number of Brazilian newspapers and news magazines. He is also described as "a lover of hunting and a compulsive smoker" (Biografiaresumida.com.br). Another biographer (Frazão 2019) indicates that

> one of Olavo de Carvalho's main ideas is that the conscience of the individual must be preserved from the collectivism represented by the state, the institutions, and the means of communication, or by any opinion group. He is avowedly a conservative thinker who combats the tyranny of dictatorships and of communism.

Presented as a "philosopher" by Record, the publisher of his book, Carvalho is for Alonso "less of a thinker and more of a public figure who repeats everything that has already been said. Proof that he is not an intellectual are his videos, the main means of propagation of his ideas." Among his nearly two dozen books, Carvalho is the author of *O Mínimo que Você Precisa Saber para Não Ser um Idiota* (The least you need to know in order not to be an idiot, 2013), a 616-page collection of 193 essays Carvalho published between 1997 and 2013 about national and international current affairs. The book has been a success: 300,000 copies were sold in 2013 and 100,000, in 2017 (Alonso 2019). Carvalho would go on to indicate six members of Bolsonaro's cabinet once elected, including the first minister of education, Ricardo Vélez

Rodriguez, whom Carvalho described as "the most knowledgeable person of Brazilian political-social thought in the world," and Carlos Nadalim, indicated to the secretariat of literacy, whom Carvalho touted as "having made more for Brazilian education 'than all the other enlightened of the ministry of education'" due to his development of a distance learning methodology.

As for public safety, it is indeed a concern in Brazil. According to the World Health Organization, Brazil has the 9th highest homicide in the world, with over 30 cases per 100,000 inhabitants (Chade 2017). In addition, a report by Amnesty International pointed out that most of the deaths were caused by firearms (Amnesty International May 4, 2017). Citing 2018 data from the Institute of Applied Economic Research (*Instituto de Pesquisa Econômica Aplicada—Ipea*) and the Brazilian Forum of Public Safety (*Fórum Brasileiro de Segurança Pública—FBSP*), Schwarcz (2019, 152) compares the daily number of casualties in Brazil to "the crash of a filled-to-capacity Boeing 737–800." Most of them die from gunshot wounds.

Violence in Brazil is widespread and not a new phenomenon. Between 1980 and 2003, homicide rates went from 40 percent to over 70 percent of the deaths (Schwarcz 2019, 154). That led to the implementation of a gun control law in 2003, the Statute of Disarmament, which restricts gun ownership by only allowing it

> in cases of confirmed need, which will still have a predetermined duration. Yet, the license may be revoked at any moment, especially if the bearer is caught drunk or under the influence of drugs or medication that may alter one's intellectual or motor skills. (Schwarcz 2019, 154)

The law has been contested ever since and is often ignored, under the justification that the civilian population must arm itself against the heavily armed criminals.

While homicide rates had decreased in 2004, they started to go up again after 2012 (*Veja* January 2, 2019, 46), which correlates with the increase in gun sales despite the statute (Schwarcz 2019, 155). According to Carvalho (2019), cofounder of the Igarapé Institute, which monitors violence reduction in Brazil, Latin America is the only region in the world where violence is increasing; Brazil alone accounts for 14 percent of homicide in the world.

Violence in Brazil interacts closely with race. As of 2015, most of the victims of homicides in Brazil were young Black men. Moreover, a significant number of them happened by the hands of the police. For example, in the two largest Brazilians cities, São Paulo and Rio de Janeiro, homicides by the police amounted to 25 percent and 20 percent, respectively (Amnesty International May 4, 2017). Those numbers were expected to increase and indeed they did: data from the Brazilian Forum of Public Safety show that "of the 6,357 victims of police violence [in 2019], 99% were men." Close to 80 percent of them were Black or Brown. Moreover, "23.5% were between 15 and 19 years of age; 31.2% were between 20 and 24; and 19.1% were 25 to 29 years old" (Dias and Adorno October 18, 2020).

Violence in Brazil also interacts closely with class. The reason for such a large number has to do with the concentration of the Black and Brown populations in favelas (i.e., low-income, often hillside, urban communities), and also the growth of the number of drug dealers and the *milícia* (i.e., paramilitary groups formed by former and active military and civil police officers) who make those communities home. When the police venture into those areas, it is not uncommon for them to be received by bullets or to start shooting themselves; the victims are often law-abiding residents, most of whom are not White. Often, neither are the police officers, be they civil or military. As a matter of fact, the military police corps has been a career path for non-White Brazilians for a long time. French (2013) notes that "in São Paulo, the military police force has been largely nonwhite since the 1860s. Rather than engage immigrants, the state first hired free men of color, and after 1888, the police became a category to be filled by ex-slaves."

By 2018, public safety had become the priority issue for voters. Preoccupation with widespread violence was a major reason for the growth of Bolsonaro's popularity among voters, over and above the other candidates' platforms, be they managerial expertise, such as Gerald Alckmin, or the promise of job creation, such as Henrique Meirelles. For Moura and Corbellini (2019), the fact that Bolsonaro lacked a clear plan to foment public safety was less important than his willingness to face criminal violence with equal force, characterized by his hand gesture simulating a gun. Interestingly enough, although he declared he would govern "without *quid pro quo*," he approached violence as an eye for an eye. As a middle-class voter from Brasília responded to a poll, "Whoever really wants safety and doesn't want the police to impose themselves doesn't want any change, only sameness" (Moura and Corbellini 2019, 77).

Brazilians personalize violence. Class inequality and racist stereotypes interact to make Blacks and the poor the poster children of violence and the main threat to public safety. Amanda Pimentel, a researcher at the Brazilian Forum for Public Safety, concluded, "When we try to think of violent deaths, especially those by the police, they happen both because we live in a country with a slavery past and because race affects those violent events" (in Dias and Adorno October 18, 2020). I agree with Pimentel. Rather than a mere coincidence, such occurrences denote the continuing significance of Brazil's slavery past. The last country to abolish slavery in the Americas, in 1888, Brazil at once denies the existence of racism, by claiming to be a racial democracy, and stigmatizes Afro-Brazilians, especially those with darker skin, as remnants of a past that the country would like to erase. Moreover, a not-so-distant dictatorial past may lend credence to the proposal to allow the population to defend itself. Therefore, a candidate who promises to grant that to the people can garner appeal. As a member of Congress, Bolsonaro had been part of the pro-gun block (*bancada da bala*, in Portuguese) (Kadanus October 4, 2018). Due to his pronouncements for almost three decades, he was already known as one who believed human rights should not be extended to criminals even before he launched his presidential campaign. For instance, he had declared, in 2015, that "'violence is to be combated with violence and not with human rights banners' such as the ones defended by Amnesty International, which he considered to be formed by 'scoundrels' and 'idiots'" (Sousa, Judite 2019, 79). As a presidential candidate, he promoted a change in the gun control law that would make it easier for civilians to carry firearms in order to defend themselves; in fact, he vowed to defend the right of "everyone to have a firearm at home" if elected (Gunkel 2017). Moreover, he continued to express that, because not all lives are worth the same, police killings are justified. For example, in an interview for *Mariana Godoy Entrevista*, on Rede! TV channel, on October 27, 2017, Bolsonaro was asked how he would combat crime while respecting human rights. He replied, "Nowadays, the human rights policy focuses on the defense of thugs, not well-heeled citizens. That is what the people say! I'm not the one saying that." Asked whether he believed a police officer must shoot first and negotiate later, he brought up U.S. laws as his model for police procedure, that is, the right to shoot to kill:

Look, I copy the American legislation a lot. What the police officer must have— not only the civil, but the military police too—is the exclusion of liability. In an operation, if there is a reaction, he has the right to shoot. And if he kills with two, three, or 20 shots, he presents himself, but there is no punishment. As long as we don't give him that carte blanche, for him to shoot to kill, to kill someone who is firing at him or at someone in society, we won't be able to reduce violence in Brazil. . . . The thug is better armed than the police officer! (Rede TV! October 27, 2017)

What Bolsonaro failed to explain was how sophisticated armament such as rifles and hand guns produced overseas get to the hands of Brazilian criminals.

On the same television program, Bolsonaro promised to have leaner laws so that farmers can defend themselves against land invasions by indigenous persons armed with rifles who, he claimed, are controlled by the Landless Movement (*Movimento dos Sem-terra—MST*). He even affirmed that, in hinterland states such as Pará and Mato Grosso do Sul, MST members murder indigenous persons in order to blame the farmers. For him, farmers must bear arms in order to protect their land, for "private property is sacred!"

Videos and photographs of his gesturing as if he had a gun in each hand and even teaching a little girl how to imitate him became popular. Opposing presidential candidate Ciro Gomes, of the Working Democratic Party (*Partido Democrático Trabalhista* [PDT]), condemned that as typical of a "fascist" (*247* May 21, 2018). Close to the presidential elections, Fernando Haddad, the PT candidate, equated Bolsonaro to "violence, . . . bullet, . . . disrespect. He is the representation of all that is worst in terms of violence in this country" (Roxo October 12, 2018). Haddad also recalled that Bolsonaro had said that he would be a member of the Nazi army had he lived in the 1930s.

A HOMOPHOBIC STANCE

Another way Bolsonaro attacked Brazilian education during his campaign was to claim it promoted a gay lifestyle. Especially through social media, Bolsonaro's camp was successful in convincing plenty of voters that Fernando Haddad, the PT candidate, had created and adopted a "gay kit" to combat homophobia and turn school children into homosexuals during his tenure as mayor of the city of São Paulo. A video in non-Standard Portuguese containing a bottle with a nipple shaped like a penis and a scrotum spread over social media, urging people to vote for Bolsonaro in order to combat Haddad's invention:

> Your 5- to 6-year-old son in daycare will drink out of a bottle with this. To combat homophobia. You've got to vote for Bolsonaro, man. Bolsonaro, so as to make our son man and woman [*sic*]. PT and Haddad, Lula, Dilma, they only want this for our children. This is part of the gay kit, Haddad's invention, you see?" (Redação Pragmatismo October 5, 2018)

In fact, however, the Ministry of Education had elaborated pamphlets as part of a program to expose school children to diversity, including sexual diversity, but they never got to be distributed due to pressure from conservative sectors (Bellloni 2017). Even though the Electoral Supreme Court ruled the video "manifestly untrue and outrageous" and banned it from exposure in September 2018, it was viewed "4.9 million times and shared 96 thousand times" by the following month (Redação Pragmatismo October 5, 2018). Spread so many times over WhatsApp and other digital means, the "gay kit" came to symbolize to conservative voters (especially Evangelical voters) an affront to the family of the *cidadão de bem*, which was being dismantled by *gayzism* and "immorality." To opponents of Bolsonaro, it was yet another example of the "misinformation" and a "hate discourse" that characterized his campaign (Wyllys and Solis December 12, 2019).[6]

Actually, Bolsonaro had alleged the existence of a gay conspiracy years earlier, while still a member of Congress. In June 2011, in his interview in *Playboy* magazine, Bolsonaro justified his combat of homosexuality as a crusade against the Human Rights and the Education commissions. According to him, "a group of homosexuals" had rejoiced at a meeting the previous November over the issuing of "material with films, posters, and books to be distributed in primary schools," which amounted to 190,000 in the entire country. Bolsonaro alleged that the material was pornographic and was aimed at corrupting minors (in Saint-Clair 2018, 89–90).

Bolsonaro's personal aversion to LGBTQ persons is notorious. Amid a number of examples, that aversion was famously etched in his 2011 *Playboy* magazine interview. He claimed government—"the Ministry of Education, the Secretary of Human Rights, and the Ministry of Health"—gave "superpowers" to "homosexuals" with "proposals to benefit them" and that the Supreme Court ruling that legalized gay unions was "a joke" (in Saint-Clair 2018, 91). He justified his position by adding that the presence of gays in a neighborhood was detrimental to property values (terra.com.br June 8, 2011):

That is a personal question of mine. For example, I live in a condominium. All of a sudden, a homosexual couple moves next to me. That will devalue my house! . . . Yes, it will. If they walk hand in hand, kiss each other, it will lower my property value because, if someone would like to buy my house who is adopting a child, they will see that and run away. Nobody says that because they're afraid of being labeled homophobic, but it's a reality. I'm not obligated to like anybody. I have to respect them, but liking them no, I don't. It so devalues [property] that bill no. 122 reads that, if you don't sell or rent a house to a homosexual, you may get one to three years in prison. If it didn't devalue it, that wouldn't be there. (in Saint-Clair 2018, 91)

Running against current views, in another passage Bolsonaro speculated that being gay is mostly the result of a promiscuous environment, such as drug use, where "anything goes" (in Saint-Clair 2018, 91); he also insisted he did not discriminate against gay employees, presumably as long as they behaved according to what he considered proper. In 2014, however, Bolsonaro stated that being gay is the result of a "lack of spanking," that he would be incapable of loving a gay son, and would rather see him dead (YouTube.com March 6, 2014). In other words, he advocated conservative childrearing methods to guarantee heterosexuality, clearly a homophobic stance. Given that an important part of his platform was the protection of the right to private property, Bolsonaro's conflation of a defense of property values and "proper" childrearing methods as well as a repudiation of drug use as justification for anti-gay attitudes and behavior framed homophobia as a defense of capitalism.

MISOGYNY

As I have mentioned, two other similarities between Trump and Bolsonaro are their views on women and racial/ethnic minorities. Regarding women, although I have found no record of accusations of physical sexual abuse against Bolsonaro, his contempt for women was apparent well before he launched his candidacy for president. In 2003, congressman Bolsonaro had called Maria do Rosário Nunes, a PT congresswoman from the state of Rio Grande do Sul, a "tramp" ("*Vagabunda!*") and told her he would not rape her because she "didn't deserve it" for being so "ugly"; in 2014, he repeated the same insults (*O Globo* December 9, 2018). Then, on June 13 of 2019, he apologized to her via Twitter, claiming that it was all the result of a heated "ideological sparring between two parliamentarians," during which, he claimed, she had called him a "rapist." The apology was the result of a federal judicial order which also intimated him to pay R$10,000 fine to cover "moral damage" (*danos morais*). Here is an excerpt of his apology:

> I take up the opportunity to manifest my integral and unrestricted respect for women. I recall that, when the facts at hand first happened, I had just defended in the Chamber of Members a more severe penalty for rapists and crimes against sexual dignity . . . always a constant struggle in my years in parliament. Anyone can verify that; all they need to do is look back at the bill I presented in 2013, which proposed chemical castration to rapists, precisely as a measure for the protection of women, so as to avoid recidivism.
>
> On the day of my inauguration as President, a woman was the protagonist, since the First Lady gave a speech even before the President, with the naturalness with which we deal with those issues in our lives. In the first months of my tenure, I reinforced the Maria da Penha Law, allowing the adoption of protective measures for women and their dependents. . . .
>
> Therefore, I reiterate that the Brazilian women are a priority in my govern, something that has been and will continue to be demonstrated with concrete actions.
>
> Thus, I reinforce my respect to all women.
>
> Thank you very much and a big hug! (in Oliveira, June 14, 2019)

Maria do Rosário called the judicial decision a victory over *machismo* and vowed to donate the money to organizations that protect women from violence. Seven organizations, from the states of Rio Grande do Sul, Rio Grande do Norte, São Paulo, Rio de Janeiro, Maranhão, and Brasília received R$2,873.43 each (Revista Forum.com November 19, 2019). She declared at a ceremony that day: "Even when men rise up in a *machista* way with hatred and devaluation, when they try to despise us, know that we are women who will never lower our heads." However, Maria do Rosário also objected to Bolsonaro's letter because, she argued, it contained "untrue information," such as claiming he had reacted to her first having called him a rapist (Oliveira 2019). She requested that he write a new apology, but a judge denied that.

It is clear that Bolsonaro turned a judicial reprimand into an opportunity to present a more agreeable position as a defender of women's rights, and for that he omitted other incidents of misogyny, such as his controversial speech at Hebraica Club in Rio de Janeiro in April of 2017, during his presidential campaign, when he said he "had five children. It was four men. Then, the last time, I got weak and a woman was born" (Gunkel 2017). Later, he and his third wife, Michelle, claimed he was joking.

Bolsonaro is also against equal pay. During his 28-year tenure as a congressman, he declared on a television program that he "would not hire a woman with the same salary as a man because she gets pregnant" (Catraca Livre October 31, 2018). As a congressman he was part of group that proposed a bill to nullify the 2013 law that grants medical treatment to victims of sexual abuse, including rape, in public hospitals. According to Bolsonaro and his Evangelical colleagues, the law makes it easier for abortion to become legal in Brazil (Megale October 12, 2018).

After Bolsonaro's election, his wife came to his defense, insisting he was not misogynist. However, she clearly showed ignorance of the meaning of the term by affirming he could not be a misogynist because he was married to her, the daughter of a man from the Brazilian northeast (*Catraca Livre* October 31, 2018), thus clearly showing ignorance about the meaning of the term. Comprised of seven states, covering an area of 1,558,196 km² (601,622.839 square miles), the northeast is the poorest region in Brazil; northeasterners face constant regional, social, racial, and economic discrimination in the southeast and the south, the wealthiest regions, where they are called a number of pejorative terms that attempt to erase the rich cultural variation that characterizes the area. Regardless of the First Lady's vouching for her husband's lack of prejudice against northeasterners, once elected, Bolsonaro would clearly display it. During an official meeting, Bolsonaro was distinctly heard telling Onyx Lorenzoni, his Presidential Chief of Staff, "Among the governors from Paraíba, the one from Maranhão is the worst. We don't have to have anything to do with that guy" (*Extra* July 31, 2019, 3). Bolsonaro was referring to Flávio Dino, a member of the Communist Party of Brazil (PcdoB). "Paraíba" is the name of a northeastern state located between Rio

Grande do Norte and Pernambuco. It is also the pejorative name inhabitants from the southeastern state of Rio de Janeiro apply generically to all
northeasterners. Therefore, when Bolsonaro referred to the entire region as
if it were only one state, he was being ostensibly prejudiced against all its
inhabitants.

RACISM

Just as he claims to be for women's rights, Bolsonaro claims he is not a racist,
offering as evidence the time when he saved a Black comrade's life during an
army exercise (Saint-Clair 2018, 25). However, Bolsonaro has used openly
racist language and referred to Black Brazilians as if they were still enslaved.
There is also plenty of video and audio evidence of prejudiced statements
on racial/ethnic minorities by Bolsonaro. For instance, on March 28, 2011,
Bolsonaro was interviewed on "The People Want to Know" (*O Povo Quer
Saber*), a segment on *CQC*, a program on the Band TV channel. One of the
questions came from Preta Gil, a singer who is a daughter of Gilberto Gil,
a famous singer/composer who is Black and was the Minister of Culture in
President Lula's first tenure. She asked Bolsonaro what he would do if one
of his sons fell in love with a Black woman. He replied that would never
happen because he had raised his sons well, not in a "promiscuous" environment (YouTube March 29, 2011). Yet his followers insisted that the video,
shown on a television program, had been edited and, thus, was "fake news."
Preta Gil vowed to sue Bolsonaro for defamation. However, on May 25,
2015, the Brazilian Supreme Court dismissed the case for lack of evidence,
alleging that the television program had supplied an edited copy of the segment, for interpreting "promiscuity" as a term with sexual rather than racial
connotations, and for Bolsonaro's privilege as a legislator, which granted him
"immunity" in his pronouncements (Ramalho May 27, 2015).

During his infamous Hebraica speech, Bolsonaro referred to descendants
of enslaved Brazilians who live in *quilombos* as if they were cattle, a discourse reminiscent of the 1824 Constitution. Bolsonaro claimed that they
were lazy, useless, and too fat: "I went to a *quilombola* [*sic*][7] in Eldorado
Paulista. Look, the lightest Afro-descendant there weighed 7 arrobas.[8] They
don't do anything. I don't think he's good even for procreation anymore" (in
Arcanjo and Tavares January 26, 2020). In addition, Bolsonaro complained
that "More than 1 billion reais [are] spent on them per year" (Tavares May
3, 2018). Finally, Bolsonaro declared that "the minorities must bow to the
majority" and that "not a centimeter" of *quilombola* or indigenous land
would be left if he were elected. It is worth recalling here that the Brazilian
Constitution of 1988 covers the protection both of *quilombos* and of

indigenous land. Nevertheless, land dispute and murders are commonplace in such areas, pointing to a disregard for the law which comes from the belief that Afro-descendants and the indigenous population are worth less than other Brazilians.

There are over 10 *quilombos* in Eldorado Paulista, in the state of São Paulo. They rely on bananas and other crops as their main economic means. According to residents of a number of them, Bolsonaro never visited them; in turn, Bolsonaro's press office never released information about his itinerary. Therefore, residents displayed disgust at Bolsonaro's attitude and his presidential candidacy (Tavares May 3, 2018). Bolsonaro's pronouncement led to a charge of moral damage against him. A judge from Rio de Janeiro ruled that he must pay R$50,000 in compensation for his offense "to *quilombola* communities and to the general Black population" (Affonso and Macedo October 3, 2017). However, in September of 2018, Bolsonaro's conviction was nullified, on the grounds of "parliamentary immunity" (Último Segundo June 7, 2019).

After the negative repercussions of his speech at Hebraica Club, Bolsonaro recruited the presence of Hélio Lopes, a dark-skinned candidate to congress from the National Working Party (PTB) known as "Hélio Negão," to deny that he was a racist.[9] By late August 2018, Hélio Negão, a military man himself, had adopted Bolsonaro's last name, claimed to be his "brother," and often positioned himself behind Bolsonaro in public appearances (Iraheta August 26, 2018). He also switched to PSL, Bolsonaro's party at the time, and ran successfully in the October 2018 elections. On a video that he himself posted, Hélio Negão states, "Let's end this class division: Black against White, rich against poor, homo against hetero. We are one Brazil only" (Iraheta August 26, 2018). Since Bolsonaro's 2018 victory, Hélio Negão has accompanied him even on international trips. For instance, in October 2019, when planning an official visit to China, Bolsonaro joked, "Is there a problem? All you have to do is this [pulling his eyelids to the sides] and no one will find you in a crowd" (Arcanjo and Tavares January 26, 2020). Pulling one's eyes to signify a person of Asian descent is a well-known stereotype; making a joke out of that stereotype by using a dark-skinned Black man compounds that offense.

Another group Bolsonaro targeted during his speech at Hebraica were Japanese Brazilians. Bolsonaro rhetorically asked the crowd whether anyone had ever seen "any Japanese" begging; he himself responded that the Japanese are a race with a strong sense of shame. As I showed in chapter 1, the myth of the model minority is a stereotype that plagues Asian Americans. According to Brazilian historian Rogério Dezem, Bolsonaro grew up in a region in the countryside of São Paulo with a large concentration of Japanese Brazilians; Bolsonaro's view "represents an idea shared by a large part of the Brazilian population" (Arcanjo and Tavares January 26, 2020).

If Bolsonaro appeared to be praising Japanese Brazilians then, he would be unequivocally negative toward them when he called Thais Oyama, a Brazilian journalist of Japanese descent, "that Japanese." In 2020, Oyama published *Tormenta: O Governo Bolsonaro: Crises, Intrigas e Segredos* (Torment: The Bolsonaro Government: Crises, Intrigues, and Secrets), about Bolsonaro's first year as president of Brazil. Dissatisfied with her account, Bolsonaro reacted thus, "That's that Japanese's book, whom I don't know what she does in Brazil, who now does it against the government. . . . There in Japan, she would starve out of journalism, writing books" (Arcanjo and Tavares January 26, 2020). Brazil has the largest population of Japanese descent outside of Japan; Oyama was born and raised in the state of São Paulo. By referring to her as "that Japanese," Bolsonaro attempts to annul her Brazilian identity and citizenship, which reinforces the idea that, for him, racial and ethnic minorities can be excluded from the nation. As I showed in chapter 2, that type of discourse runs counter to the inclusionary ideas specified in the 1988 Constitution; it does, however, reflect an age-old longing for the country to have a majority-White population.

THE EVANGELICAL CONNECTION

Like Donald Trump, Jair Bolsonaro has a strong connection to Evangelicals, though neither was brought up in that faith. Unlike Trump, however, Bolsonaro has converted to it. Bolsonaro seems to have approached Evangelicals via his third wife, Michelle de Paula Firmo Reinaldo. They met in 2007, when he was a member of the Progressista Party and she was the party's secretary. Accounts claim they started dating and, in the same year, he transferred her to his office in order to work for him. Soon after, they got married, after having signed a pre-nuptial agreement. Six years later, "she convinced her husband . . . to have an Evangelical wedding ceremony" (Saint-Clair 2018, 163). Michelle Bolsonaro was a member of the Assembly of God Victory in Christ Church, headed by Pastor Silas Malafaia, who officiated the wedding. During the ceremony, Malafaia emphasized, "Family is a man, a woman, and their offspring. . . . Man is only complete with a woman and a woman is only complete with a man. . . . Nothing more and nothing less" (164).

There is a clear connection between Bolsonaro's discourse about education, homosexuality, women, and minorities and his appeal to Evangelicals. According to Alonso (2019), Bolsonaro's campaign appealed to a "moralization of customs," that is, a rejection of the "ideology of gender," of feminism, and of "abortionists and gayzists," all of which it saw as the products of years of a leftist government. For instance, against the prominence of so-called "feminazi bitches" (i.e., feminists), the Evangelical discourse proposes the "princess" and the "queen of the home" (*rainha do lar*). For years, Evangelical politicians have promoted the "gay cure," that is, a bill, approved in the state of São Paulo, that overrules the decision of the Federal Council of Psychology to refrain from engaging in projects that see homosexuality as a disease that needs to be treated. The bill was proposed by João Campos, of PSDB, and embraced by Evangelicals, some of whose churches have long claimed the power to restore wellness by turning gays into straight persons (explica.tumbler.com). Pastor Marco Feliciano, a congressman from PSC who headed the Chamber of Human and Minorities Rights, was one of the supporters of that idea. Feliciano was the same parliamentary who had claimed, years earlier, that Africa had been "cursed by God" (YouTube May 29, 2016). He also claimed, as a "prophet" and a "parliamentarian," that the Devil had infiltrated government and that "AIDS is a gay disease" (Rubens Júnior Oficial March 11, 2013).

Moura and Corbellini (2019), who published the first book to come out about Bolsonaro's presidential election, point to the strength of Evangelical voters: they constitute about a third of the Brazilian electorate and are sexually and politically conservative. For Evangelicals, Brazil had become "too liberal" and immoral, promoting an ideology of gender. As a presidential candidate, Bolsonaro capitalized on that discourse. His motto was "Brazil above all and God above everything." Once elected, he would fill his cabinet with Evangelicals, such as Pastor Damaris Alves, whom he named minister of Women, Families, and Human Rights. She had worked in Congress for 20 years, as a judicial aid. Openly anti-feminist, Alves became infamous for her many bombastic declarations, such as "girls should wear pink and boys should wear blue." She also warned parents about the danger Brazil presented for raising daughters given the level of violence against women in the country: "If I had to give a piece of advice for who is a father of girls, a mother of girls, get out of Brazil. You are in the worst country in South America to raise girls" (in Otta February 15, 2019).

JEWS AND ISRAEL

Both Donald Trump and Jair Bolsonaro have professed a love for Israel; both have visited the country officially and promised to transfer their embassies from Tel Aviv to Jerusalem. That appeals to Evangelicals and to a number of American and Brazilian Jews, but the Evangelical fondness for Israel is not because it is a Jewish country, but because they believe it is the place of the Second Coming, according to which everyone has to convert to Christianity or go to hell.

In both countries the Jewish community is divided. As I discussed in chapter 3, in the United States, many Jews object to Trump's far right associations, which are too close to Nazism. In Brazil, after Bolsonaro's speech at Hebraica Club in 2017, the fission between Jews on the left and the right widened; protest against Bolsonaro's presence at the club would give birth to *Judeus pela Democracia* (Jews for Democracy) the following year (Instituto Brasil-Israel February 13, 2020). Quite active on social media, the group aims at denouncing anti-Semitism, especially in Brazil, keeping the memory of the Nazi Holocaust alive, and positioning itself against any kind of prejudice and discrimination not only against Jews, but also against the other racial/ethnic minorities, women, and the LGBTQ+ population. Its motto is, "Jews for the defense of the democratic rule of law; in the struggle against fascism, racism, *machismo*, and LGBTphobia!" (Facebook February 7, 2020). In fact, according to Maria Fiszon, a member, *Judeus pela Democracia* arose out of the self-titled movement "#NotHim" (*#elenão*), which, on social media and on the streets, repudiated Bolsonaro's misogynistic, homophobic, and racist pronouncements and campaigned against his election. The movement garnered support from ordinary persons and celebrities alike, including Madonna. As of 2020, the group, based in Rio de Janeiro, had 140 active members and 8 million followers on Facebook (Ohana January 27, 2020); on February 7, 2020, the group announced there that it had started a Twitter account.

One major point of contention for the group is Bolsonaro's insistence that Nazism was a leftist movement if only because its full name was "National Socialism." When he went to the Holocaust Museum in Jerusalem, during an official visit to Israel in April 2019, Bolsonaro affirmed that he was sure that Nazism was the party of the German left. Even though the museum explains the roots of Nazism in a brochure, Bolsonaro held on to his error (Catraca Livre April 2, 2019). It is worth mentioning that, about one month before the presidential elections, the German embassy in Brazil had released a video explaining the Nazi reality (Queiroga September 17, 2018); evidently, like a number of right-wing Brazilians, Bolsonaro ignored that information.

Furthermore, Brazilian Jews have objected to Bolsonaro's display of Israel's flag in his public appearances. The association of Jewish symbols with the far right eliminates the diversity of attitudes in Israel, which, compared with other countries, is quite open about abortion and the LGBTQ community, as noted Michel Schlesinger, rabbi of the São Paulo Israelite Congregation (*Congregação Israelita Paulista*) (Venceslau and Galhardo August 25, 2019). Likewise, Fiszon (in Ohana January 27, 2020) adds that Bolsonaro's fondness for Israel is more personal toward Benjamin Netanyahu, its right-wing prime-minister, than toward the country itself:

> He has a great closeness with the current government of Israel, of [Benjamin] Netanyahu. It does not mean, for example, that would be maintained should there be a change in government. It is very similar to what happens in the United States. He [Bolsonaro] has a closeness with President [Donald] Trump.

If Trump is not reelected this year, will this closeness be maintained? His closeness is of a personalist character.

Visiting Israel and getting to know the country, Lula did that too. That doesn't demonstrate a closeness. Bolsonaro situates himself very close to Israel from a Christian idealization. It is a much bigger relationship with the Evangelical electorate, which also has this closeness with Israel, than in fact with the country that exists there. Tel Aviv has one of the largest LGBT parades in the world; it's gigantic. Homoaffective unions have been recognized for a long time [since 1993]. Abortion is legal in Israel. So, what Israel is this that Bolsonaro is close to, but that it is a much different state that he defends here. That closeness is more complex than a friendship with Israel.

"A STABBED POLITICIAN IS EITHER KILLED OR ELECTED"

As of 2019, there were 35 political parties in Brazil (Lenzi n.d.); that number is expected to increase, for, in that same year, 76 more applied for registration (Humberto November 25, 2019). The existence of so much political divergence that would necessitate so many different parties is questionable. In fact, there are those who attribute the applications to get-rich-quick schemes, because, according to Brazilian electoral law, all parties are eligible to receive campaign funds (Sanches August 7, 2018).

Evidently, the large number of parties creates problems during electoral campaigns when it comes to televised debates. For instance, in 1989, out of 34 political parties, 22 had presidential candidates. The difficulties in allotting time to all of them led the Brazilian Association of Radio and Television Corporations (*Associação Brasileira das Empresas de Rádio e Televisão—ABERT*) to solicit the right to broadcast debates "even without the presence of all candidates" (Muller n.d.). In 1997, a new law required the presence of all candidates whose party had congressional representation, which could still yield a cumbersome number. After many attempts at reaching an equitable arrangement, the Electoral Reform of 2009 allowed for the broadcast corporations to invite candidates for debates as long as "the rules could be approved by two-thirds of the suitable candidates, defined by the Supreme Electoral Court . . . as those who, (a) are affiliated to a political party with representation in the House of Representatives and (b) who have requested registration of their candidacy" (Muller n.d.). Moreover, a 2014 modification, which prohibited businesses from making financial contributions to televised campaigns, together with the issue about congressional representation, also led to a shortening of television time.

PSL, Bolsonaro's party, did not meet the criterion of representation. However, in the Brazilian coalition system, Bolsonaro would qualify if PSL joined forces with another party, thus raising its congressional quorum to two more representatives. He could also participate in debates if television channels invited him (Tiagoleite and Vogel March 21, 2018). As of August 2018, among the 13 presidential candidates, Geraldo Alckmin of PSDB had the longest slot, at 5:32 minutes, whereas Ciro Gomes of PDT and Avante had 38 seconds; Jair Bolsonaro had only 8 seconds (Equipe HuffPost July 20, 2018). Yet, outspoken as he was, Bolsonaro avoided taking part in debates with the other several presidential candidates. Instead, he had a marked presence on social media, not only personally, via his Twitter account, but also through his sons' accounts as well as on messages shared profusely on the WhatsApp platform. For that reason as well as the shortened airtime, Moura and Corbellini (2018, 95) regarded Bolsonaro's absence from television immaterial for his campaign and detrimental for the other candidates.

Then, on September 6, 2018, an event would grant Bolsonaro a lot more airtime than the mere eight seconds of televised debate to which he was entitled ever could. During a campaign stop in Juiz de Fora, in the state of Minas Gerais, Bolsonaro was stabbed when he was being carried on the shoulders of a crowd. Police officers promptly arrested the perpetrator of the attack, Adélio Bispo de Oliveira, who, according to newspaper reports, was about to be lynched. Oliveira was identified as a 40-year-old man from Minas Gerais who had been a PT supporter and was once affiliated with the Socialism and Liberty Party (*Partido Socialismo e Liberdade—PSOL*).[10] Given Oliveira's claim that his act had been at once "ordered by God" and due to "personal reasons" (Iraheta September 6, 2018), it is no wonder that the Public Ministry argued he was only partially guilty by reason of insanity (*Gazeta do Povo* April 10, 2019). In June 2019, Oliveira "was recognized as the author of the crime, but he could not be legally responsible due to a mental illness, 'persistent delirious syndrome.'" In March 2020, it was announced that his transference to a "more adequate" prison facility was approved where he could be properly treated (Romanews March 2, 2020).

Stabbed in the abdomen, Bolsonaro reportedly hemorrhaged and had surgery to repair damage to his intestine. He was in intensive care for 10 days and remained in the hospital for another two weeks (Sousa 2018, 75–76). From then on, Bolsonaro claimed that his doctors forbade him from participating in television debates, which would justify his missing the last televised debate before the presidential elections, on TV Globo (Favaro October 10, 2018; RTP October 5, 2018). However, his interview was aired at the same time of the debate on TV Record, a station owned by Edir Macedo, head of the Universal Church of the Kingdom of God (*Igreja Universal do Reino de Deus*), the largest Evangelical congregation in Brazil. His two eldest sons,

Flávio and Eduardo, to whom he refers as "01" and "02," coordinated it online (Sousa 2018, 80).

Citing a Brazilian journalist who wrote that "a stabbed politician either dies or is elected," Sousa (2018, 77) seems to agree that the attempt at Bolsonaro's life helped him win the election by propelling him into the spotlight. On the other hand, Moura and Corbellini (2018, 95; 57) give less weight to the attack, arguing instead that Bolsonaro's victory was already determined by then, given the steady upward trend in his favor and "the structural marks that were already given for that election," including the Operation Car Wash, accusations of corruption against PT, and the electorate's lack of faith in PSDB and other traditional politicians.

NOTES

1. With the inauguration of Brasília as the capital of Brazil in 1960, the state of Guanabara was created. Composed solely of the city of Rio de Janeiro, Guanabara was a city-state. In 1975, after the construction of the Rio-Niterói Bridge, Guanabara became extinct by its fusion with the state of Rio de Janeiro, resulting in the state of Rio de Janeiro, the capital of which is the city of Rio de Janeiro.

2. According to the official site of the federal government (Brazil.gov.br), "Brazil uses two different system—majority and proportional—to define the winners of the election depending on the office being elected. All Executive positions (the president, governors and mayors) and Senate races are decided according to the majority system, in which the candidate with the most votes wins. The remaining votes, i.e. those for the Chamber of Deputies and municipal and state legislatures, are decided according to the proportional system. . . . In the proportional system (in a quick summary) the overall votes are distributed proportionately among the competing political parties."

3. The feature film *Carandiru* (2003), by Héctor Babenco, is an acclaimed fictionalized account of the massacre based on the book *Estação Carandiru*, by Dr. Dráuzio Varella, the medical doctor who pioneered the treatment of inmates infected with HIV/Aids who for years worked at Carandiru Prison.

4. *Petralha* is a pejorative term for one who votes for PT.

5. For a comprehensive analysis of the controversy over the Brazilian quotas policies and the results of their implementation, see Penha-Lopes (2017).

6. Jean Wyllys, an openly gay congressman who clashed with Bolsonaro over Rousseff's impeachment and later left Brazil over repeated death threats, reflected, "Without the gay kit, Bolsonaro would not have gone beyond the mediocre congressman he had always been and I would not be in exile" (Columbia University Seminar on Brazil, December 12, 2019).

7. *Quilombo(s)* is the name of the settlement(s); the term *quilombola(s)* refers to the inhabitants of *quilombos*. Therefore, Bolsonaro confused the two terms.

8. *Arroba* is a measure to weigh cattle. One *arroba* weighs 15 kg. In pounds, 7 *arrobas* equal 231 pounds.

9. *Negão* is a corruption of the augmentative of the word *negro*. It may be both a term of endearment or a very insulting pejorative term to designate dark-skinned Black Brazilian men.

10. PSOL was founded in 2005 by PT dissidents who disagreed with the party's political leaning once it assumed the presidency of the country in 2003. The pivotal event occurred when Heloísa Helena, a senator from the northeastern state of Alagoas, and Babá, Luciana Genro, and João Fontes, three congresspersons, were expelled from PT for having voted against the pension reform it had promoted "because they saw it as stripping civil servants of their rights." They went on to form PSOL in 2004, with Heloísa Helena as its president. Two years later, she would run for president of Brazil against Lula (Silva, Débora November 7, 2015).

Chapter 6

"Brazil above All and God above Everything"

Jair Bolsonaro's Presidential Victory

PRESIDENTIAL ELECTIONS, BRAZILIAN STYLE

If the importance of delegates in U.S. presidential elections is difficult for Brazilians to grasp, having to cast a ballot twice in Brazilian presidential elections confuse Americans. In Brazil, presidential elections run for two rounds, unless a candidate achieves over 50 percent of valid votes in the first round. This chapter discusses the 2018 presidential election in Brazil, which took place over two rounds, on October 7 and 14, when Jair Bolsonaro sealed his victory.

The designation of two rounds was stipulated in the 1988 Constitution, according to which "the president elect shall be the candidate who, registered by a political party, garners the absolute majority of the votes, not computing the blank and null votes" (in UOL September 9, 2018). Fernando Henrique Cardoso (1995–2002), founder of PSDB, is the only candidate ever elected in the first round: in 1994, he won 54.3 percent of the valid votes (Ebiography.c om); in 1998, 53 percent. In both cases, his closest opponent was Luiz Inácio Lula da Silva, who would succeed him for eight years (2003–2010).

THE FINAL STRETCH

In the few weeks between his stabbing on September 6 and the first round of elections on October 7, Bolsonaro convalesced first in the hospital and then at home. From then on, in the words of Judite Sousa (2019), a Portuguese journalist who went to Rio de Janeiro in order to cover the Brazilian presidential elections of 2018, Bolsonaro's campaign took an unexpected and unprecedented turn in that it was "frozen," or, according to political science professors Sousa interviewed, "in automatic pilot." By that she meant that Bolsonaro stopped making in-person appearances and giving interviews altogether; although she and other journalists set up a daily vigil in front of Bolsonaro's home at a gated community in Barra da Tijuca, a neighborhood in the West Zone of Rio de Janeiro, she notes that he never once went outside to meet with any of them. For all intents and purposes, Bolsonaro had become "invisible" (Sousa, Judite 2019, 99), purportedly to avoid taking part in televised debates, which would unmask his lack of a plan, despite his insistence on bringing change to the country.

However, Bolsonaro remained quite visible on television, due to the constant updates on his medical condition. Moreover, Bolsonaro ended up benefiting the most from "The Brazil that I Want" (*O Brasil que Eu Quero*), a series of vignettes put forth by voters and broadcast by TV Globo in which they described what they were looking for in a candidate. According to Moura and Corbellini (2018, 115), the two most common wishes that emerged were "the end of corruption and the combat of violence." As I showed in the previous chapter, those were the themes that characterized Bolsonaro's campaign, even if he did not have a concrete course of action to execute them.

More than the traditional television medium, the tipping point for the 2018 presidential election were the social media, that is, all means of communication available through the internet and disseminated through smartphones, such as WhatsApp, Facebook (both of whom are owned by Mark Zuckerberg), and Twitter. The effect of social media was so powerful that Moura and Corbellini (2018, 109–133) refer to it as "the WhatsApp election," though they clarify that platform is but one element in a conglomeration of technology, calculated direction of information, and the presence of a frustrated electorate. In sum, Bolsonaro's "victory was not exclusively a 'WhatsApp product,' but the result of a new juncture, both political and technological, in which this great transformation in the platforms of communication was one of the central elements" (Moura and Corbellini 2018, 120).

Unlike TV ads, social media information is constant; moreover, its dissemination is interactive (Messenberg 2017). Thus, the technology of social media allows for the easy propagation of that information (Wyllys 2019). Between August 16 and October 28, 2018, Bolsonaro's Facebook fans grew from nearly 5.5 million to over 8 million (in Moura and Corbellini 2018, 117). Thus, when Carlos Bolsonaro, who is credited as the manager of his father's internet campaign, went online to ask for prayers for him after the stabbing (1News Brasil September 6, 2018), he was able at once to reach not only Bolsonaro's strong Evangelical base, but also part of the electorate who agreed with his view that violence is to be combated with violence and was frustrated over traditional politics and the possibility of the election of a *Partido dos Trabalhadores* (PT) candidate.

Carlos Bolsonaro was but one social media manager in Bolsonaro's well-articulated campaign. Several sources (e.g., Alonso 2019; Fellet December 15, 2016; Messenberg 2017; Moura and Corbellini 2018) recognize the importance of Olavo de Carvalho's internet presence, what with his half a million followers as of 2016 (Fellet December 15, 2016)—including 6,000 YouTube subscribers—and his close to 2,200 Facebook posts in 2015 alone, which were significant for the mobilization of participants in right-wing street demonstrations in that year (Messenberg 2017). In fact, when interviewed about the demonstrations in 2016, Carvalho identified himself as the "midwife" of the so-called new Brazilian right (Fellet December 15, 2016).

Another major influencer in Bolsonaro's internet campaign was Steve Bannon, exponent of the online presence of the Far Right and a crucial figure in Donald Trump's campaign, as we have seen. Although Bannon claimed not to be associated with Bolsonaro's camp, a fact that Bolsonaro himself confirmed, Eduardo Bolsonaro affirmed that "the two had met and that Bannon was an 'enthusiast' of his father's candidacy and they would 'unite forces against cultural Marxism'" (*The Guardian* October 12, 2018). On a campaign video for Fernando Haddad from a few days before the second round, the narrator named Bannon as someone who was "side by side" with Bolsonaro and who had a reputation for undermining democratic governments the world over by spreading "fake news" (YouTube October 16, 2018). Louault (2019) also recognizes Bannon as the founder of "The Movement," an initiative he started in 2017 in order to gather together the radical right from European countries. One of the goals of that initiative, according to Louault, is "to redefine the notion of truth," which he recognizes as having played a role in Bolsonaro's campaign. Solis (2019) suggests that Bannon was behind the role of fake news in defining the 2018 presidential election.

Evidently, the significance of social media for political campaigns over traditional means of communication is their capacity to disseminate news as fast as it happens, be it factual or not. The more contemporary people communicate via social media, the more they come to rely on them for any kind of information; the more that information is spread, the more it is believed to be "real." In fact, the producers of news need not even be human at all; after the elections, WhatsApp deactivated 400,000 accounts whose "owners" were robots (Solis 2019). Increasingly, it is becoming more difficult to differentiate between what is "real" and what is "made up," evidenced by the coining of the paradoxical term "virtual reality." "Fake news," then, can mean both made-up information and any information that runs counter to one's way of thinking, that is, a type of "post-truth."

An example of the power of fake news would be the postmortem treatment of Marielle Franco's image. Marielle Franco (1979–2018) was a councilwoman from Rio de Janeiro who was elected in 2017 under the slogan

"Woman, Black, and from the *favela*." Having been born and raised in the Maré Favela, in Rio's North Zone, Franco focused on denouncing police brutality and discrimination against Afro-Brazilians, women, and LGBTQIA+ persons during her brief tenure. On March 14, 2018, she and her driver were shot to death after her participation in an event organized by Afro-Brazilian women in downtown Rio. An outcry reverberated first in the city, then in the whole country, and, eventually, throughout the Americas and Europe. A year later, after the arrests of Ronnie Lessa and Élcio Queiroz, both former military police officers, a year later, the call "Who murdered Marielle?" was replaced by "Who ordered Marielle's murder?" As of this writing (2021), the question remains unanswered.

According to Wyllys (2019), hours after Franco's assassination, the creation and dissemination of fake news about her ensued. A photograph of her sitting on the lap of Marcinho VP, a well-known drug dealer, was spread to lend credence to the lie that Franco, a lesbian woman, was his lover and had had a child by him. In addition, Marília Castro Neves, a judge from Rio de Janeiro, claimed the Franco had been in cahoots with *Comando Vermelho*, a criminal faction that controls Maré, while Alberto Fraga, a congressman from the Democráticos Party and an ally of Jair Bolsonaro, called her a "marijuana user." Wyllys argues that the goal of those actions was "to drain the sympathy that people felt when they learned of Marielle's brutal murder." Solis (2019) adds that the physical elimination of Marielle was followed by an attempt to eliminate her image with the goal of preventing the rise of Afro-descendants, women, LGBTQIA+ people, and the poor. Especially in a country with a relatively recent authoritarian past, we can conclude that fake news may facilitate the reinstallation and legitimation of a dictatorship in that it creates the illusion that the production and the consumption of ideas are egalitarian, since all one needs to participate in their making is internet access.

Bolsonaro's robust internet presence was countered by #EleNão ("not him" in Portuguese), a social media movement that sprang from the Facebook group entitled *Mulheres Unidas Contra Bolsonaro* (United Women Against Bolsonaro). The group was created in September 2018 by Ludmilla Teixeira, an advertising agent, and Rosa Lima, a businesswoman, whose goal was to congregate women, regardless of political affiliation, who opposed Bolsonaro's candidacy based on his misogynistic, racist, and homophobic pronouncements. Two weeks after its formation, the group counted over one million members, which reflected women's dislike of Bolsonaro: research by Datafolha released on September 10 revealed that 49 percent of women voters rejected him. In fact, Jairo Nicolau, a political scientist, declared that the gender gap among voters regarding Bolsonaro was the largest at least since the 2010 elections (Seta September 12, 2018). By the end of September, Mulheres Unidas had nearly four million Facebook members. Discussions centered around the agreement that "[Bolsonaro] represents everything that is backward in the fight for women's rights; he directly attacks maternity leave, [and] the wage difference between men and women," as Teixeira stated (Seta September 12, 2018). Hence, not him.

#EleNão was the call on street demonstrations that took place on September 29, 2018 in 114 Brazilian and international cities. In Rio de Janeiro, it garnered about 25,000 demonstrators, and São Paulo, the largest city in Latin America, 100,000 people were estimated to have shown up. Demonstrations also took place in Europe (in Lisbon, Paris, and London) and in the United States (in New York City). According to historian Céli Regina Jardim Pinto, "#EleNão . . . was the biggest demonstration by women in the history of the country," focusing not only on women's rights, but also on the fight against fascism and the threat of the return to a dictatorship. By then, gender polarization over Bolsonaro was even stronger: 52 percent of women, but only 37 percent of men, were against him. #EleNão differs from other social media phenomena such as #MeToo in that it spilled over to the streets (Rossi, Carneiro, and Gragnani September 30, 2018). Eventually, #EleNão, to which was added #EleNunca ("Never him"), attracted 40 Brazilian celebrities, mostly singers and actresses, but also a famous right-wing journalist, Rachel Sheherazade, who thus justified her stance: "I am a woman. I raise two children by myself. I was raised by my mother and my grandmother. No. We are not criminals. We are HEROINES! #elenao" (Warken September 18, 2018). Furthermore, the movement was embraced by a number of international figures, such as actors Stephen Fry, who had interviewed Bolsonaro in 2013 for a documentary on homophobia, and Ellen Page,[1] who had done the same three years later (iG São Paulo September 27, 2018); even Madonna joined in.

The fact that the Mulheres Unidas group only allowed women leads to the conclusion that gender was its most important characteristic. However, there seems to be also an intersection of gender with race. Brum (September 24, 2018), a journalist, noted that "it is no wonder that the creator of the . . . page is Black," given that Black Brazilian women have the lowest income, but are also among the ones who have benefited from university quotas policies and changes in labor law concerning domestic workers. On the other hand, Souza (2019, 255) argues that most of the #EleNão demonstrators were "women from the more critical and engaged middle class." Thus, even though working-class women had been against Bolsonaro's candidacy, they were turned off to the movement by manipulated images that ran counter to their ethos. According to Souza, the Far Right was able to create images that mixed scenes from the demonstration with those that would be highly offensive to poorer and religiously conservative women, "such as transvestites breaking saints, shirtless women, etc." He concludes that the fake news created a moral divide between women that proved effective in Bolsonaro's election.

In fact, a countermovement of women who supported Bolsonoro, self-entitled #EleSim (yes, him), ensued, garnering women who were antiabortion and those against the supposed "immorality" in society that threatened children's upbringing (Alonso 2019).

ELECTION RESULTS

Bolsonaro won both rounds of the presidential election, on October 7 and 28, 2018. In the first round, he obtained 46.3 percent of the valid votes, ahead of Fernando Haddad (29.28 percent) and Ciro Gomes (12.47 percent). Bolsonaro won in 17 of the Brazilian states, covering all of the south, southeast (the wealthiest regions of the country), center-west, and all but one northern state; he also won in Brasília, the capital of the country. Haddad won in all but one northeastern state (the poorest region of the country), plus one northern state. Gomes, who descends from a prominent political family from Ceará and is himself a former mayor of Fortaleza, the capital of Ceará, and former governor of that state, won the majority of the votes there (Rossi October 8, 2018). The White nationalist tone that had characterized Bolsonaro's campaign was reflected in the attacks some voters from his party perpetrated on social media against northeasterners, by calling them "stupid," "alienated," and deserving of the difficult conditions they face due to the semiarid climate of the region, which the Bolsonaro sympathizers claimed were evidence of God's wrath (in *O Povo Online* October 8, 2018). It bears repeating that the northeast is the Brazilian region with the largest contingent of people of African descent. Therefore, when Bolsonaro voters, who were mostly White, attacked northeasterners, they were also attacking Afro-Brazilians. Evidently, the fact that racial discrimination is a crime in Brazil did not deter them.

The promotion of violence during Jair Bolsonaro's campaign materialized into physical attacks against those who were perceived to be Fernando Haddad's supporters. Such was the case of Anielle Franco, sister of assassinated councilwoman Marielle Franco, who reported being accosted by men in Bolsonaro shirts who called her "loose" (*piranha*), "feminist," and "shitty leftist" (*esquerda de merda*). The day after the #EleNão demonstrations, Maria Tuca Santiago, who had helped organize them, was allegedly robbed and beaten by a group of Bolsonaro supporters who proceeded to attack her on social media as well. In addition, there were reports that "130 journalists were attacked or threatened on social media during the electoral press coverage" (Redação RBA October 8, 2018).

The most violent occurrence was the murder of 63-year-old Romualdo Rosário da Costa, in Salvador, capital of the state of Bahia and the city with the largest percentage of Afro-Brazilians in the country. Costa, known as

Moa do Katendê, was a capoeira master, the martial arts created by enslaved Africans in Brazil. In the morning after the votes were cast, Costa was sitting at a bar when in went 36-year-old Paulo Sérgio Ferreira de Santana, praising Bolsonaro. The fact that Costa defended PT, pointing out the gains Brazilian Blacks had achieved during the PT years, was enough for Santana to stab Costa 12 times in the back (Redação RBA October 8, 2018). Santana was arrested soon after, as the police were able to follow the blood stains from the bar to his house. In Brazil's racial schema, Costa, a dark-skinned man who heavily identified with Afro-Brazilian culture, was clearly Black. His murderer, a lighter-skinned man with a shaved head and a curly-to-coarse goatee, might call himself *pardo* (Brown) or even *moreno* (brunette). During an interview after his arrest, Santana denied that the motives for the crime were political. Instead, he claimed that he stabbed Costa after he repeatedly called him a *"viadinho negro"* (i.e., a Black little faggot) and the two had physically fought (in Salles October 11, 2018). Two days before Santana's arrest, Bolsonaro replied to a reporter that he had been a victim of a stabbing, and that he was sorry for the murder, but he had no control over his sympathizers' actions. He asked that "people stop practicing that" (*Veja* October 10, 2018).

After the first round, two moves occurred: the losing candidates realigned themselves around Bolsonaro and Haddad and the two remaining opponents sought to conquer a chunk of the blank and null votes, which amounted to nearly 9 percent of the total (Mori October 16, 2018).

Right after the results were revealed, on October 7, none of the losing candidates endorsed either Bolsonaro or Haddad, although Ciro Gomes, who ended up in third place, vowed never to vote for the winner of the first round (Melo October 7, 2018). However, three days later, Gomes's party, PDT, announced its endorsement of Haddad. PSOL, *Partido Socialista Brasileiro*, and *Partido Comunista do Brasil*, all left-wing parties, also declared their support for Haddad, whereas *Partido Trabalhista Brasileiro* went for Bolsonaro (Alagoas 24 Horas October 10, 2018). Geraldo Alckmin, who obtained less than 5 percent of the votes, declared that his party would be neutral in the second round, leaving its members free to support either candidate. João Amoêdo, who ended up in fifth place, had run as a candidate from New (Novo). The party "declared neutrality, but said it was against PT" (Bertoni October 11, 2018). In such an unusually polarized election, it would be fair to assume that being against one of the candidates almost automatically meant support for the opposing candidate.

As for the blank and null votes, the burden to grasp them was with Haddad. That was because, according to social scientists, "those votes help whoever is ahead in the dispute—because they are not computed among the valid votes, they facilitate the leader's conquering the majority in the polls" (Mori October 18, 2018). In particular, a reversal was observed in between the two rounds, in that the percentage of those who said they would not vote for Bolsonaro decreased. The unusual characteristics of the 2018 election, that is, the relevance of social media over television for the presidential race and the voters' strong rejection of both final candidates made experts uncertain about the impact of blank and null votes.

To complicate matters, there was also the issue of abstention. In Brazil, voting is a duty as well as a right. An irregular voting registration (*título de eleitor*) may lead to a number of serious restrictions, such as the prohibition to acquire real estate, get an identification card and a passport, and apply for a civil service job. In turn, failure to vote is also problematic, in that it may lead to the cancellation of a voting registration if it happens in three elections in a row. Those who cannot vote must justify it up until two months after the election either in person or online; a plausible justification is being away from one's voting area on Election Day (TRE-RJ). Upon justification, one must pay a fine of R$3.51, which amounted to a little over US$1.00 in 2018. At such low financial cost, we can imagine how disgruntled Brazilians might have opted to stay home when they rejected both candidates so vehemently.

Bolsonaro's share of the electorate in the second round grew to 55.13 percent, or nearly 58 million votes, against 44.8 percent of votes for Fernando Haddad. Bolsonaro took 15 states and Brasília, whereas Haddad maintained his influence in the northeast (Rossi October 8, 2018; Máximo October 28, 2018; Poder360 October 28, 2018). For the purposes of this analysis, it is worth noting that, unlike previous elections, the 2018 results showed a clear racial and class divide: out of all 5,500 Brazilian municipalities, Bolsonaro won by a large margin in the 10 wealthiest cities, whereas Haddad prevailed in the 10 poorest cities, as defined by wages and literacy rates. Furthermore, Bolsonaro was victorious in overwhelmingly White municipalities, mostly located in the south of Brazil, where there is a concentration of descendants of German immigrants. Haddad "obtained minimal results in those cities, but won in all municipalities where Whites represented less than 20 percent of the population" (Llaneras October 30, 2018). Given such results, we can conclude that Bolsonaro's campaign discourse was quite effective after all.

Internationally, probably as a result of the ongoing emigration of Brazilians in this century, voting was significant for the final results. In South America, Bolsonaro won in Montevideo, Uruguay. In Europe, Bolsonaro won in Lisbon, Portugal; Madrid, Spain; Rome, Italy; Geneva and Zurich, Switzerland; Frankfurt and Munich, Germany; London, England; and Istanbul, Turkey. In Asia, Bolsonaro won in Tokyo, Japan. His most impressive win was in the United States, where the majority of the expatriate Brazilians who are eligible to vote reside. He won in New York, with 76.39 percent of the votes, and in Washington, DC, with over 69 percent of the votes; Miami, Florida, proved to be Bolsonaro's strongest ground, where he garnered over 90 percent of the votes. Haddad won only in Paris, France; Berlin, Hamburg, and Cologne, in Germany (Fernandes October 28, 2018; *Gazeta do Povo* October 7, 2018; *Veja* October 28, 2018).

Bolsonaro's election was accompanied by the election of 52 state and federal congresspersons from his party, including Janaina Paschoal, the lawyer who had submitted the request for President Dilma Rousseff's impeachment. With two million votes—the most by any congressperson—she was elected to the São Paulo chamber with the largest number of votes ever recorded in Brazil (Pessoa and Saldaña October 7, 2018); Eduardo Bolsonaro was her equivalent in the elections for federal congressperson, with over 1.8 million votes. Wilson Witzel was elected governor of the state of Rio de Janeiro with over three million votes, soaring from obscurity after endorsing Jair Bolsonaro's presidential campaign (Solano 2019, 10–11). After the 2018 elections, the right was firmly ensconced in Brazilian politics.

CHARACTERISTICS OF BOLSONARO VOTERS

While Bolsonaro's victory may give the impression that most Brazilians turned out for him, another reading of the election results questions that conclusion. Nearly 61 percent of eligible Brazilian voters did not vote, voted blank, or nullified their vote; those who nullified their votes, about 7 percent, made up "the highest level of spoiled votes since 1989" (Junge 2019, 3). Only 29 percent of the electorate actually voted for Bolsonaro (Junge and Mitchell 2019). Moreover, "PT lost about 7 million votes in relation to the dispute of the last presidential second round, in 2014" (Máximo October 28, 2018); in other words, the bulk of the electorate chose neither candidate (Sousa, Judite 2019, 86). Together, those facts lend credence to Moura and Corbellini's (2018) conclusion that Bolsonaro's victory had more to do with the public's desire to break with the traditional political system than with an affinity for Bolsonaro, a disenchantment that had been brewing since 2003, that is, since PT first came to power on an anti-corruption platform, but ended up operating on the basis of corruption. Bolsonaro's campaign emphasis on "changing all of it" without any clear plan appealed to a large enough part of the electorate who no longer believed in the traditional campaign performances of career politicians such as Geraldo Alckmin and Ciro Gomes. In sum, Bolsonaro's election was "disruptive."

Still, Bolsonaro voters were far from homogeneous. Several researchers (e.g. Alonso 2019; Junge and Mitchell 2019; Koister and Eiró 2019; Solano 2019) have noted the socioeconomic and even political variation among those who helped to elect the new president of Brazil. Alonso (2019) notes that 57 percent of men, 50 percent of those who earn more than three times the monthly minimum wage,[2] 45 percent of Whites, and 36 percent of Evangelicals approved of Bolsonaro; together, they constitute about 12 percent of Brazilians aged 16 years and over. She calls them "Bolsonarists from the heart" who form a "moral community." They are, according to her, the so-called *cidadãos de bem*, that is, well-heeled citizens, whose ethos is based on binary distinctions that had characterized Bolsonaro's campaign. Among the voters, Alonso further identified the following categories: participants in social liberal movements; professionals; industrial, agricultural, and financial elites; Pentecostals; the military; and the police. What united them was a way of thinking based on a series of simplistic oppositions which she calls "binarisms," namely, a "belligerent nationalism," a "hierarchical moralism," and an "anti-elitism."

A belligerent nationalism opposes "nationalists" to "communists," under the idea that "communism" is a global phenomenon that must be combated. It also emphasizes the nation as a whole over and above any social inequalities, as illustrated by the slogan "Brazil Above All;" whoever is against that is politically corrupt and must be stopped. I should mention the similarities between that way of thinking and the official governmental propaganda during the military dictatorship (1964–1985). In particular, President Emílio Garrastazu Médici's tenure, which came to be known as the "lead years" (1969–1974) due to its extremely oppressive measures against "subversives," promoted the slogan "Brazil: Love it or Leave it," meaning that those against the regime should voluntarily emigrate or risk being arrested, tortured, or murdered.

A conflation of mores, the role of the state, and the economy characterizes "hierarchical moralism." Corruption is immoral and must be eradicated by a new economic program that decreases the role of the state. In other words, the investment in social programs during the Lula-Dilma years, which Bolsonarists call "governmental leftism" (*esquerdismo governamental*), must be replaced by a neoliberal state that emphasizes individual initiative and corporate investment. The goal, according to Alonso, is the "moralization of customs" that includes an attack on the "ideology of gender" that champions feminism, the fight for abortion laws, and gay rights. Feminists were labeled "feminazi bitches" (*cadelas feminazis*) and contrasted with stay-at-home women (*rainhas do lar*). Williams, a British journalist, traces the term "feminazi" to Rush Limbaugh, tright-wing radio personality who coined it in the 1990s

to describe, in his improbable phrasing, "a feminist to whom the most important thing in life is ensuring that as many abortions as possible occur." More broadly, the word was meant to indicate women who shut down their opponents with authoritarian orthodoxies, against which ramparts an ordinary interlocutor had no hope. And, more recently, this is how it has surfaced, a word around which people—Men's Rights Activists (or MRAs)—can mobilise when they feel that a feminist has gone too far. (Williams September 15, 2015)

The fact that Bolsonarists use a foreign term to describe in a pejorative way Brazilian women who fight for their rights implies the conclusion that they truly believe they are combating global enemies of a Communist stance; after all, as I have mentioned, Bolsonaro has insisted that the German Nazi regime was left-wing. Yet, the reliance on the translation of a foreign term is paradoxical, given their claim to strong nationalism. Their action thus betrays their own global connections with the Far Right.

Finally, anti-elitism refers to the emphasis on seeing Bolsonaro as an ordinary man, as "a Brazilian like any other" (Alonso 2019). For instance, when Bolsonaro justified his lack of an economic plan by claiming to be ignorant about economics and vowing to leave the planning to Paulo Guedes, the man who would occupy that post were he to be elected, he came out as honest rather than incompetent.

In her research on Bolsonaro's voters, Gallego (2019) found that what unites them is the sense that *cidadãos de bem* constitute the Brazilian people and that the state had abandoned them in favor of the *bandidos*, that is, criminals. Therefore, for them, the state is the "enemy" of the Brazilian people. In general, her respondents were in favor of civil rights for LGBTQIA+, but they should keep their marriages and families in private rather than flaunt them in public. Evangelicals, who constitute about a third of the voters (Moura and Corbellini 2018, 80), identified with Bolsonaro's campaign both for his moral stance and for the resentment they felt toward the left, which they believe disrespects them and find them less intelligent. Moreover, many of Gallego's interviewees had voted for PT in previous elections, attracted by Lula's charisma and promise to govern without corruption; by 2018, they had become disenchanted with that promise. Regarding class distinctions on Bolsonaro's promise to fight violence with violence, Gallego found that lower-class voters were more at ease with changes in the gun ownership law because they felt they were vulnerable to the power of criminals, who often lived in their communities and were heavily armed. Finally, Gallego concluded that a deciding point was the White heterosexual men's feeling of being unprotected for "not being women, Black, or homosexual." Evidently, Bolsonaro's campaign promise that "the minorities must bow to the majority" resonated with those who fit in the majority, but felt excluded by all the public policies that the federal government had given priority for over 10 years, seeking to decrease social inequality in Brazil.

Lest we think only White, well-to-do Brazilians thought that way, data show that some of those whose income was low enough for them to qualify for aid to families (*Bolsa Família*) and also those who had experienced upward mobility during the PT years, whom Junge and Mitchell (2019) call "the new middle class," expressed similar attitudes.[3] In their ethnographic research on Bolsonaro voters from the northeast, Koister and Eiró (2019) found that, while religiosity was a major factor for those who listened to their Evangelical pastors, an overall feeling of "disenchantment" over traditional politics, especially with the corruption charges against PT, was also significant. Some felt that "the PT only benefited gays, lesbians, and lazy people," whereas others saw *Bolsa Família* as a synonym of *Bolsa Preguiça* (literally, a fund for laziness), that is, a pronatalist policy that led people to apply the funds toward the purchase of appliances. On the other hand, Bolsonaro appeared to some of them as the one capable of combating violence, a provider of law and order, which they saw as the purview of the state.

Similarly, Junge and Mitchell (2019), who did both ethnographic and large-scale research in the northeast (Recife, in the state of Pernambuco), the southeast (Rio de Janeiro and São Paulo), and the south (Porto Alegre, in the state of Rio Grande do Sul), sought to understand why persons who had emerged from poverty and were now fragile due to the economic recession had adopted a conservative ethos. Though most of those "previously ascendant Brazilians" agreed that their life chances had improved under the PT regime, they voted for Bolsonaro nonetheless. Like the other researchers I discussed earlier, Junge and Mitchell (2019) also find among their informants a sense that Brazil was lacking in morality of late. In the Recife part of their research, Junge (2019, 8–9) noted a discourse that longed for a time when Brazil was less corrupt and more rigorous, the result of the application of "binary logics" that pitted politicians (corrupt) against the military (rigorous) and parents against their young, both of which firmly planted on a view of masculinity that felt threatened by the expansion of LGBTQIA+ rights. We see here the classification of Bolsonaro as a military man over and above his long-term political career, which elevated him in their eyes to a moral stance, while also dismissing the social transformations brought forth by the PT years which allowed for economically depressed families to ascend.

Recurrent in the analyses of Bolsonaro's victory are both a lack of interest in the presidential election (evidenced by the large absenteeism) and a reaction to the expansion of rights to minority groups writ large. The concession of rights to minority groups is often interpreted as antimeritocratic, and the most contested such program in Brazil has been affirmative action in the form of social policies aimed at decreasing racial and social inequality. Unlike in the United States, affirmative action in Brazil has mostly taken the form of a university quotas program. First demanded by Afro-Brazilians as reparation for the centuries of slavery and the lack of insertion programs for former slaves and their descendants once slavery was abolished in 1888, university quotas were first implemented in Rio de Janeiro in 2003 for Afro-descendants and the poor and were signed into federal law in 2012 by President Rousseff. Since then, they have expanded to include "the physically disabled . . . and, in the case of Rio de Janeiro, even the children of police officers killed in the line of duty" (Penha-Lopes 2017, 143). However, they continue to be seen as antimeritocratic and unnecessary purportedly because Brazil is not a racist country; rather, quotas policies are thought to incite the emergence of racial hatred. Therefore, implicit in the reaction against the years when PT was in the federal government is also a critique of affirmative action programs that have allowed for the largest number of Afro-Brazilians to graduate from college and for low-income students to enroll in public universities. It is also a reaction to the expansion of rights that have seen more women enter the professional labor market, allowed same-sex couples to marry and adopt children, allowed for transgendered persons to change their names legally, and allowed for the previously poor to ascend enough to acquire middle-class consumer habits, such as owning cars and traveling by airplane. All of those changes took place in the Lula-Dilma tenures. As I have mentioned, the social media played a crucial role in forging an articulation of several fears (Moura and Corbellini 2018, 82), namely, a purported lack of morality, an imagined threat of communism, and corruption, and also a release of racial prejudice that has been ever-present in Brazil, which Bolsonaro was able to capture to his advantage (Silva and Larkins 2019).

A lack of interest in the election and the impetus to break from traditional politics that characterized the Bolsonaro victory in 2018 was not exclusive to Brazil. It had also occurred in the United States in 2016, when the presidential elections were marked by a very low voter turnout. As we have seen, many Bernie Sanders's sympathizers, especially the young, chose either to stay home or to vote for Donald Trump rather than vote for Hillary Clinton. Although Sanders has had a longer career as a senator than Clinton did, he was able to portray an image of freshness and vigor, highlighted by the "Feel the Bern" slogan, that Clinton never did. In the end, Trump, who had never held a political post, managed to capitalize on being "different" from traditional politicians, much as Bolsonaro also did two years later in Brazil. Despite having lost the popular vote to Clinton, Trump won the Electoral College. The results of both elections surprised most political pundits and social scientists. However, Moura and Corbellini (2018, 143–144; 82) suggest that, while professional observers interpreted both Trump's and Bolsonaro's discourses as so divisive as not to be taken seriously, the electorate in both countries focused on their essence rather than on their incendiary phrases. For instance, Trump's promise of a tough stance on immigration, not his verbal attacks on Mexicans and Muslims, was what stuck in U.S. electors' minds. In turn, Bolsonaro's promise to address public safety, not his slogan that "a good criminal is a dead criminal," was what allowed voters to turn a blind eye to his aggressiveness and prejudice, even though that was so glaring that it led David Duke, the avowed White supremacist, to praise Bolsonaro for his "totally European" ancestry and his defense of "heteronormality" (Senra October 16, 2018). Moreover, the verbal spontaneity that both candidates displayed gave credence to their presentation as different from traditional politicians such as Clinton in the United States and Alckmin in Brazil.

THE INAUGURATION

On October 28, 2018 Bolsonaro was elected president of Brazil. The next day, Trump tweeted that he had called Bolsonaro to congratulate him; he added that he expected to "work closely" with him:

> Had a very good conversation with the newly elected President of Brazil, Jair Bolsonaro, who won his race by a substantial margin. We agreed that Brazil and the United States will work closely together on Trade, Military and everything else! Excellent call, wished him congrats! (President Donald J. Trump, on Tweeter, October 29, 2018)

Steve Bannon, the articulator of Trump's presidential campaign who had since parted ways with him, declared that he expected Bolsonaro to practice "enlightened capitalism" in a populist government, which he saw as a global trend (*Exame* October 29, 2018).

On January 1, 2019, Jair Bolsonaro was inaugurated as the 38th president of the Federative Republic of Brazil. I was in Rio de Janeiro then and watched the ceremony on television.

Following protocol, the caravan of the president traversed from the Granja do Torto, one of the official presidential homes, on to the Cathedral of Brasília, through the Esplanade, and up to the National Congress. Sitting on the convertible presidential Rolls Royce with Bolsonaro were the First Lady, Michelle Bolsonaro, and his son Carlos. Eduardo Bolsonaro later justified his brother's presence thus, "He is the family's pit bull." At one point, Bolsonaro lifted a boy from the crowd and had him ride with them. The president's car was followed by that of the vice president, General Hamilton Mourão, and his wife, Paula. They were covered by "the largest security scheme ever put together in Brasília," including sharp shooters (*O Globo* January 2, 2019). In the trajectory, in military style, Bolsonaro saluted even the officiating priest. He also made a hand gesture imitating a gun, which had become emblematic of his campaign, but also made a gesture of a heart to the crowd, which counted about 115,000 people.

In the National Congress, where he had acted for nearly 30 years, Bolsonaro was sworn in as president. In his speech, he started by "thank[ing] God for being alive." He proffered his defense of democracy and his compromise with combating corruption, discrimination, and the "ideology of gender." In a populist fashion, he asked those present for their support in "uniting the people" and respecting "our Judeo-Christian tradition." He also brought up the target of his campaign, the *cidadão de bem*, "who deserves to avail himself of the means to defend himself, respecting the 2005 referendum, when he opted in the ballot boxes, for the right to self-defense." President Bolsonaro followed that with the plea that the National Congress "judicially support police officers to do their job. They deserve to be respected, and they should be." He closed his speech by invoking God again:

> With God's blessing, the support of my family, and the strength of the Brazilian people, I will work tirelessly for Brazil to meet its destiny and become the great nation that we all want. Thank you very much to all of you. Brazil above everything, God above all. (*O Globo* January 2, 2019, 10)

From there, the president and his entourage moved on to the Three Powers Square to meet Michel Temer, the president in exercise after Dilma Rousseff's impeachment, and the former First Lady, Marcela Temer, in order to receive the presidential sash. Many of those present screamed, "Myth!" and "The captain is back!"

When they got off the car, Bolsonaro at first ignored his wife, who remained in the back, just like Donald Trump had treated his wife Melania two years earlier. However, unlike Mrs. Trump, Mrs. Bolsonaro had a central role in the inauguration in that she gave a speech before the president gave his own; that was the first time that ever happened in a presidential inauguration in Brazil. Mrs. Bolsonaro, who works with the deaf, delivered her speech both orally and in Brazilian Sign Language (*Linguagem Brasileira de Sinais—Libras*); at some point, she kissed her "beloved spouse, our president." Below are some of the highlights of her speech:

> It is a great satisfaction and privilege to be able to contribute and work with the entire Brazilian society. The voice of the ballot box was clear in the sense that the Brazilian citizen wants safety, peace, and prosperity, in a country where all are respected.
>
> I thank the Brazilian people for the prayers, which gave us so much courage to forge ahead. . . . We are all on the same side. Together we will reach a Brazil with education and freedom for all. (*O Globo* January 2, 2019, p. 8)

The First Lady spoke under strong applause. By having his wife be the first speaker of the ceremony, Bolsonaro seemed to aim at dispelling his misogynistic and anti-feminist image.

Afterward, it was time for the national anthem. Most guests had their cell phones pointed at the stage, and many applauded at the end, which, in Brazil, is a sign of disrespect.

The president spoke next. His new speech echoed his first, in that he promised to "lift our homeland," freeing it forever from the "oppression of corruption"; he also promised to rule without party favoritism. He added, "I place myself before the entire nation, today, as the day when the people started to be free from socialism, from the inversion of values, of state gigantism, and the politically correct." To emphasize his combat of socialism and communism, and his allegiance to religious voters, Bolsonaro uttered,

> This is our flag, which will never be red. It will only be red if our blood will be necessary to keep it green and yellow. . . . I ask the good Lord to give us wisdom to lead the nation. May God bless this great nation. Brazil above everything, God above all.

Michelle Bolsonaro did not applaud her husband's speech.

General Hamilton Mourão, the vice president, spoke next. For some reason, he spoke in a very loud voice, almost in screams, promising to "maintain, defend, and comply with the Constitution." The former president of the Senate, Elcidio Nogueira, made a number of grammatical errors during his very long speech.

The only former presidents who attended Bolsonaro's inauguration were José Sarney and Fernando Collor de Mello (1990–1992), who sat together. The former is touted as the Brazilian politician with the longest career—59 years—and also the first president after the end of the dictatorship; Sarney was vice president to democratically elected Tancredo Neves (1910–1985), who died before he was sworn in. Sarney was succeeded by Collor, who is infamous for having been impeached. Both have had careers as senators after their presidencies. Also absent were the governors-elect from nine northeastern states, all of whom scheduled their swearing-in ceremonies for the same time of the presidential inauguration.

As for foreign dignitaries, 10 attended the ceremonies. Brazil uninvited the president of Nicaragua to the inauguration with the claim that it would not endorse a government that oppresses its people; it did not invite the Venezuelan president either. On the one hand, Evo Morales, president of Bolivia, and Tabaré Vázquez, president of Uruguay, both of whom are leftist, were present. On the other hand, so were right-wing statesmen, such as Benjamin Netanyahu, prime minister of Israel; Viktor Orbán, prime minister of Hungary; and Sebastián Piñera, president of Chile. Mike Pompeo, the U.S. secretary of state, represented President Trump. However, Trump was present in a large green-and-yellow banner that two Bolsonaro sympathizers took to the inauguration: the banner read, "President Bolsonaro 17. Vice General Mourão"; the number 17 is the number of Partido Social Liberal, Bolsonaro's party at the time. On one side of the banner, there was a picture of Bolsonaro; on the other, a picture of Donald Trump (Diário do Centro do Mundo, January 1, 2019). That was not the first time some Brazilians gave the impression they wanted Trump to run their country, however. During the demonstrations against PT and President Rousseff in 2016, some displayed banners pleading for President Trump to take over Brazil.

In what would be recurrent in Bolsonaro's government, much like in Trump's, there were accounts of hostile behavior toward journalists, both Brazilians and the foreign press, who were there to cover the event. The French and Chinese presses left the inauguration for having been treated "like garbage." The journalists alleged that they were left without water and prohibited from going to the bathroom without permission. Brazilian journalists corroborated those allegations (*Brasil 247* January 1, 2019).

As part of the official ceremony, Bolsonaro posed with 21 of the 22 ministers who composed his government; seven of them were military officers. Among them were some who had been very close to Bolsonaro during his presidential campaign, such as Paulo Guedes (Economy), Onyx Lorenzoni (presidential Chief of Staff), Gustavo Bebbiano (general secretariat of the Republic), and Damaris Alves, the Evangelical pastor (Woman, Family, and Human Rights). In fact, Bolsonaro appointed ministers with ties to his main areas of support: in addition to Paulo Guedes, Ernesto Araújo, who was appointed to the Office of Foreign Affairs, and Ricardo Vélez Rodríguez, minister of Education, had been recommended by Olavo de Carvalho; Araújo was approved by Eduardo Bolsonaro as well. The "ruralist" sector, which lobbied for landowners, was represented by Teresa Cristina in Agriculture and Ricardo Salles as minister of the Environment. From the military branch, General Fernando Azevedo e Silva was appointed to Defense, General Augusto Heleno to Institutional Security, Tarcísio Gomes de Freitas to Infrastructure, and Carlos Alberto Santos Cruz to Government Secretariat (Fellet January 10, 2019); the latter replaced Bebbiano when Bolsonaro ousted him after less than two months in office (Terra.com.br January 29, 2020).[4] Despite its significant support, the Evangelical branch had only Damaris Alves as its representative. Sérgio Moro, the federal judge who had presided over the *Lava Jato* corruption inquiry and who had insisted he had no political aspirations, was the first to be sworn in. Despite Bolsonaro's vow to combat corruption, two of the ministers he appointed—Onyx Lorenzoni and Luiz Henrique Mandetta, minister of Health—had been involved in shady operations: the former had confessed "to having received slush funds for electoral campaigns," whereas the latter, at inauguration time, was "investigated by the Federal Prosecution Office for having supposedly benefited two firms in a public contract of R$9.9 million when he was health secretary of Campo Grande" (*O Globo* January 2, 2019, 15).[5] In all, Bolsonaro's cabinet stood out in that it contained only two women (Tereza Cristina, agriculture, in addition to Alves); according to Brazilian racial classification, all were White (*Extra* January 2, 2019, 8).

Donald Trump was quick to congratulate Jair Bolsonaro after his presidential inauguration on January 1, 2019. Later, on January 19, while addressing the convention of the American Farm Bureau Federation in New Orleans, Trump stated, "They say he's the Donald Trump of South America. Do you believe that? And he's happy with that. If he wasn't, I wouldn't like the country so much. But I like him" (Gearan March 19, 2019). Bolsonaro liked Trump too; he would choose the United States as the destination of his first official visit two months later.

President Bolsonaro would become even more internationally visible when *Time* magazine listed him as one of "the 100 most influential people" in the world in its April–May 2019 issue. Editor-at-large Ian Bremmer characterized him as "a complex character," acknowledging him both as "Brazil's best chance in a generation to enact economic reforms that can tame rising debt" and as "a poster boy for toxic masculinity, an ultraconservative homophobe intent on waging a culture war and perhaps reversing Brazil's progress on tackling climate change" (Bremmer 2019, 92). However, just like Trump, Bolsonaro met with plenty of resistance. Even though that would make it difficult for him to fulfill his campaign promises, his Far Right stance was unabated.

NOTES

1. In 2020, Ellen Page came out as a transgender man and changed his name to Elliot Page.

2. In 2018, the federal minimum wage was R$954.00 per month, which corresponded to US$300.00 (ADVFN 2018; G1 January 4, 2018).

3. Junge (2019, 1) defines the new Brazilian middle class as "the estimated thirty-five million people who rose above the poverty line during fourteen years of rule by the left-leaning Workers' Party, but whose prospects have since become precarious."

4. Other ministers would have the same fate. Ricardo Vélez was replaced by Abraham Weintraub, also an *Olavista*. Santos Cruz was exonerated after attrition with the *Olavista* branch of government.

5. Campo Grande is the capital of the state of Mato Grosso do Sul, a state in the center-west region.

Conclusion

Mr. Bolsonaro Goes to Washington

On March 17 to 20, 2019, President Bolsonaro made his first state visit to Washington, DC, where he met President Trump. Trump acknowledged how much of a role model he had been when he stated that Bolsonaro "has done a very outstanding job, ran one of the incredible campaigns; somebody said it a little bit reminds people of our campaign, which I'm honored by" (Gearan March 19, 2019).

Not since 1962 had a Brazilian president chosen the United States as his or her first destination. At the time, João (Jango) Goulart (1962–1964) is said to have gone north to request financial help from the U.S. government. Although President John F. Kennedy even went to the airport to receive Jango, he offered him not enough funds and soon plotted to oust Jango, who, from Kennedy's standpoint, was openly leftist and could turn Brazil into a "new Cuba" (Uchoa March 27, 2014). Classified documents attest that the Central Intelligence Agency was behind the 1964 coup d'état that instituted a military dictatorship in Brazil for 21 years and also trained the military and the police on torture techniques. On Twitter, Bolsonaro wrote, "For the first time in a very long time, a Brazilian president who is not anti-American arrives in Washington. It is the beginning of a partnership for freedom and prosperity, as Brazilians have always wished" (Shalders March 19, 2019).

Besides the opportunity for Trump and Bolsonaro to express their mutual admiration, the visit aimed at securing a commercial and political alliance between the two countries. For example, Bolsonaro announced the end of visa requirements for U.S. Japanese, Canadian, and Australian nationals, as a way of increasing tourism revenues to the country (*G1* March 19, 2019). As is well-known, diplomatic relations usually operate under the principle of quid pro quo, or reciprocity. However, Bolsonaro's gesture was not reciprocated; the United States is notorious for imposing restrictions on issuing visas to

Brazilians. Bolsonaro justified his decision by stating that, unlike Brazilians who go to the United States in search of jobs, Americans are unlikely to go to Brazil for that. He added that someone had to extend his hand first, and that person was him. That decision did not sit well with some Brazilian senators, such as Randolfe Rodrigues, from the northern state of Amapá, who asserted, "It seems to me that Australia, Canada, and Japan only got in to justify the subservience of the Brazilian government, of the president of the republic, not to the North American government, but, in particular, to Mr. Donald Trump" (*G1* March 19, 2019). Bolsonaro's decision was upheld.

On the commercial front, the two presidents considered China's increasing influence over Latin America, which is a disadvantage for the United States. Politically, the two presidents discussed Venezuela, as both were against Nicolás Maduro's socialist government; instead, both favored opposition leader Juan Guaidó as the country's legitimate president and were enamored of the idea of military intervention in the country. Finally, Bolsonaro agreed to cede the space base in Alcântara, in the northeastern state of Maranhão, for the United States to use (*NPR* March 17, 2019; Gearan March 19, 2019).

The following month, it was vice president Hamilton Mourão's turn to visit the United States. On April 8, he met with Vice President Mike Pence, and then went to the Woodrow Wilson International Center for Scholars, in Washington, DC, the next day. Mourão praised the Brazil Institute, housed at the Center, for being "the only think tank in D.C. exclusively dedicated to Brazil" and for its "role in advancing understanding about the agenda of reforms presented by our administration, and how that agenda will enable our country to reap more benefits from closer cooperation with the United States and other strategic partners" (Wilson Center April 9, 2020). He also defended neoliberalism, criticized Venezuela as "an emblematic example of the destruction that the so-called socialists can do," and emphasized the need for Brazil to rid itself of the "corruption" and "incompetence" left behind by the previous governments "that believed that the state should do everything." In a passage that sounded very much like the slogan "Make Brazil Great Again," Mourão named Bolsonaro's election as the result of "a vigorous movement to rescue our country, our pride, our values" and proceeded to list the measures the new government had already taken, such as eliminating thousands of appointments and shortening the number of cabinet members. He praised Paulo Guedes, the minister of the economy, and Sérgio Moro, the minister of justice, for having already taken the country to a new direction by tackling the stagnant economy and public safety. Mourão ended his speech by drawing similarities between Brazil and the United States, such as their affinity for "the same democratic principles and values." Both in the beginning and in the end of his speech, Mourão said he was confident Bolsonaro would fulfill his commitment to securing "greater freedom to the Brazilian people."

During the question-and-answer period, anthropologist Benjamin Junge asked the vice president how he would "address the concerns of LGBT Brazilians," given the rise in attacks against them and the death threats against Jean Wyllys, the congressman who left the country in order to protect himself from those threats. Mourão's response ran counter to Bolsonaro's campaign and presidential pronouncements, thus making himself sound insincere:

> Thank you for your question. Well, President Bolsonaro firmly and truly believes that he was elected for everybody who is in Brazil. So, there is no problem, there is no case about minorities, our government has no policy to—okay, we are going to persecute minorities? That is not the way we behave. Everybody who is Brazilian must be able to stay in Brazil, like I said, free from fear. And, in the specific case of Mr. Wyllys, I particularly think that he should have stayed in Brazil and believed in our law and our police, so that we could protect him. That is the task of the state.

The protection of individuals "is the task of the state," but that is often lacking, especially when it comes to the LGBTQIA+ population. Between 2008 and 2019, Brazil ranked number one in the murders of transgender persons, according to the National Association of Transvestites and Transexuals (*Association Nacional de Travestis e Transexuais—Antra*). In 2018, there were 14 murders; in the following year, the number of murders grew to 21. Almost 60 percent of the victims were young, between 15 and 45 years old; over four-fifths were Black and Brown, and close to 98 percent were trans women, which shows the intersection of racism and transphobia. Antra considers the murders a manifestation of the "ideology of gender" propagated by the "conservative sectors of the State" (Putti January 29, 2020).

Six months into his tenure, President Bolsonaro nominated his son Eduardo Bolsonaro, a congressman, to the post of ambassador in Washington, DC, who also presides over the Committee of Foreign Affairs in the House of Representatives, had visited the United States with his father in March. Reporters claim that Trump was so taken by Eduardo Bolsonaro that he invited him to join the private meeting between the two presidents, an honor denied to Ernesto Araújo, Brazil's minister of foreign affairs. President Bolsonaro argued that his son would be perfect for the position because he had lived in the United States, where he had "fried hamburgers," because he spoke English, and because he was friends with Trump's sons. The announcement was met with controversy and charges of nepotism. Although the nomination does not constitute nepotism according to the Brazilian Constitution, it does go against the principles of "legality, impersonality, morality, publicity, and efficiency." Lawyers, professors, and a minister of the Brazilian Supreme Court considered the nomination inadequate not the least of which because of the diplomatic importance of the United States for Brazil (Marchao July 11, 2019). In the end, nothing came of it.

Fascination with Trump was in full force again on August 7 of the same year, when vice president Mourão gave a speech in Santa Cruz do Sul, in the state of Rio Grande do Sul. At some point, he compared Donald Trump to the German prime minister Angela Merkel. The month before, she had been shown shaking during some public appearances. Pointing to a picture of a meeting of world leaders, Mourão said, "It's the picture of the most developed [countries]. *Our president*, Donald Trump, staring at Merkel. I think that is why Merkel started to have tremors from time to time" (Mendes 2019, 11; emphasis mine). It is at least curious that a president who was elected on the banner of extreme nationalism would so blatantly yield to a foreign power, but that became commonplace. In rallies and other public appearances, President Bolsonaro is often surrounded by U.S. and Israeli flags besides the Brazilian flag. On July 4, 2020, Independence Day in the United States, after he had lunch at the U.S. embassy in Brasília, he congratulated "[his] friend," President Trump, for his "gorgeous and courageous speech" ("*belíssimo e corajoso discurso*") about the date, called him "a great statesman," and prayed that "the legacy and the values of the founders of this great nation remain solid and may never be erased by radicals" (*Brasil 247* July 4, 2020).

TURNOVER IN THE TRUMP AND BOLSONARO GOVERNMENTS

Besides Bolsonaro's avowed admiration for Donald Trump, he seems to emulate him in the high turnover of members of their governments. According to a report by the Brookings Institution, as of November 9, 2020, President Trump's "A Team" (i.e., the executive office, excluding cabinet secretaries) had suffered a turnover rate of 91 percent, the highest among all of his predecessors since Ronald Reagan. Sixteen "resigned under pressure" (13 in the first year of Trump's presidency alone), such as National Security Adviser Michael Flynn, who was later convicted for having lied to the Federal Bureau of Investigation (FBI) about Russian collusion during the 2016 election; Deputy Chief of Staff Katie Walsh; Press Secretary Sean Spicer; and Chief of Staff Reince Priebus, to name a few. The report labeled 23 positions "serial turnovers" because they were occupied by at least three different officers, such as senior director of intelligence, and by as many as six officers, such as deputy national security adviser and communications director (Tenpas November 2020).

Trump's penchant for hyperbole has led him to praise appointees to the highest only to lower them to the ground when they disagree with him. Examples abound, but two are particularly worth bringing up for the pivotal roles they played in Trump's administration and their subsequent fall from grace: Attorney General Jeff Sessions and Chief Strategist Steve Bannon. A former Alabama senator and attorney general, Sessions was "one of the first major politicians to back Trump's campaign." However, Trump ousted him after he refused to testify about the Russian interference in the election and proceeded to call him "a total joke," "mentally retarded," "a dumb southerner," and "Mr. Magoo" (Raymond and Stieb February 13, 2020). Steve Bannon, whose appointment as Trump's chief campaign manager had made White supremacists rejoice (Devaney November 14, 2016), had a contentious relationship with Trump. At first Trump said Bannon was "highly qualified." Then, on April 11, 2017, he erased Bannon's role in his campaign by uttering, "I'm my own strategist," but defended him in the aftermath of the Charlottesville clashes against charges of racism on August 15. However, the very next day, an interview Bannon had given criticized Trump's political strategy. On August 18, 2017, Trump fired Bannon. On August 19, Trump twitted kind words about Bannon and his return to *Breitbart News*: "I want to thank Steve Bannon for his service. He came to the campaign during my run against Crooked Hillary Clinton—it was great! Thanks S." That good will continued for two months, when Trump went from calling Bannon "a good friend of mine" to settling for "Sloppy Steve" once the world learned that Bannon had contributed to Michael Wolff's scathing account of the Trump White House, *Fury* (Keneally January 5, 2018).

In addition to internal turmoil, the Trump presidency also dealt with allegations of corruption concerning the FBI inquiry into Russian interference in the election, which led to impeachment hearings, and also Trump's refusal to release his tax reports. He would only do that in the last year of his presidency; the reports had some innovative claims, such as an annual deduction of US$750,000 for hairstyling.

Bolsonaro also repeatedly replaced ministers and faced charges of corruption either directly or involving members of his immediate family. The Ministry of Education was the stage of a veritable game of "musical chairs" (Reis June 18, 2020). The original minister, Ricardo Vélez, was fired in April 2019, a casualty of an internal power struggle. His replacement, Abraham Weintraub, was a controversial figure, who defended cutting funds for federal universities and proposed the end of philosophy and social sciences majors, arguing that they did not train students to have successful careers and were thus a waste of public funds. Weintraub recurrently misspelled and mispronounced words, which made him a constant source of mocking memes. In addition, when he gave a press conference to introduce the reduction of funds to education, he mistakenly referred to 30 percent as "3 percent." Weintraub left his position on June 18, 2020 for a post at the World Bank. He left the country with a diplomatic passport, an irregularity given that he was neither a diplomat nor did he have a governmental post by then.

Before he left, Weintraub was prominently featured on a bombastic video of a meeting President Bolsonaro had with all his ministers which had taken place on April 22, 2020 and was leaked to the press exactly a month later. On it, Bolsonaro refers to his followers as "cattle," the pejorative term the opposition gives to them. The minister of the environment, Ricardo Salles, advises that they take advantage of the turbulence brought on by the viral pandemic that had begun early in the year to change environmental laws that would eliminate indigenous land and protected areas. Weintraub calls the Supreme Court "a bunch of bums" who should be thrown in jail. That was the meeting that precipitated the ousting of Sergio Moro, minister of justice, who broke with the president when he objected to Bolsonaro's interference with the command of the Federal Police, purportedly to protect one of his sons from an investigation of corruption charges. The president uttered over 30 curse words during the meeting.

Weintraub repudiated the use of the term "indigenous people" and "gypsy people" during the meeting of April 22. He said there was only one people in Brazil, that is, the Brazilian people. Yet, when he was intimated to testify before the Supreme Court over his lack of decorum toward it, he remained silent. Later, when the "Fake News Operation" investigated his home and the homes of other presidential allies, Weintraub, who is Jewish, called it the "Brazilian kristallnacht." Jews in Brazil, the United States, and Israel objected to Weintraub's choice of words, calling them a vulgarization of the Nazi Holocaust (*Brazil 247* May 30, 2020).

Renato Feder, secretary of education from the state of Paraná, had his indication to replace Weintraub aborted when it was reported that he was under investigation for tax evasion. The next name on the list was Carlos Alberto Decotelli, a business professor, who presented himself as a technician rather than a politician and had ample support from the military and civil factions. However, he never got to take on the position due to accusations of plagiarism in his master's thesis and the denial of the Universidade Nacional de Rosario, in Argentina, that he had graduated from there with a doctoral degree, given that his dissertation had never been approved (wwww.dw.com). Several other replacements continued to take place, none more perilous than the ministry of health, given that the exits were precipitated by the ministers' disagreements with the president over how to respond to a viral pandemic that occurred in 2020 to 2021.

SUMMING UP

This conclusion reflects the key point of the present book: Whiteness and White supremacy have been the basis of the idea of nation in the United

States and Brazil. Therefore, rather than a surprise, the elections of Donald Trump and Jair Bolsonaro were continuations of centuries-old trends. In both countries, some groups have been excluded, so they keep trying to belong in ways that keep us asking, what is a nation?

This book is fruit of my argument that similarities between Donald Trump's and Jair Bolsonaro's governments abound. That is not to say they are identical. For starters, there are major differences on the constitutions of each nation. Consequently, their political systems are quite different. The U.S. presidential system, which focuses on two opposing candidates, varies from the Brazilian parliamentary system, which yields several candidates, allows the president and the vice president to be from distinct parties, and leads to the formation of multipartisan coalitions, all of which is inconceivable in the United States.[1]

The trajectories that Donald Trump and Jair Bolsonaro took to the presidency are also very different. Although both are firmly on the right, Bolsonaro's comparatively humbler beginnings, decades-old political career, military posts before that, and longing for the military dictatorship that governed Brazil for 21 years contrast with Trump's business style; despite his having been impeached for abuse of power and obstruction of congress, Trump is much more favorable of political solutions based on an economic than on a militaristic stance. Still, Trump's refusal to accept defeat in the 2020 presidential elections and failed attempts to change the results in his favor hinted at his possible fondness for dictatorships, which approximates him to Bolsonaro's style. Finally, the fact that I see similarities between the two does not mean that I consider them equal to each other. Evidently, Trump has much more power than Bolsonaro, a fact that is not lost on Bolsonaro, whose actions follow Trump's whim (Mitchell December 12, 2019).

Still, I maintain that the similarities outweigh the differences between the two. Both presented themselves as saviors—one, to restore his nation to "greatness"; the other, vaguely "to change everything" in his nation so that it would be "above everything." Both singled out the exclusion and subordination of minorities as a necessary pathway to achieve greatness. Behind Trump's allegations is the old view that only Whites belong in the United States, whereas Bolsonaro's appeal to put Brazil above everything without class or racial distinctions at the same time that verbal and physical attacks to minorities have increased closely resembles the period before compensatory policies started to benefit racial minorities and the poor. Yet once they were elected, both pushed for the construction of generic, raceless populations. For instance, Trump signed an executive order that condemned the mentioning of racism and sexism in employment because they are false, un-American charges that only serve to divide the country, thus ignoring the many deaths of Black men and women at the hands of the police and the attacks against protesters by White supremacy groups. The video of the murder of George Floyd by asphyxiation by a police officer in Minnesota in May 2020 was shared and seen throughout the world; it brought attention to the Black Lives Matter movement and catapulted countless demonstrations in the United States and abroad. However, President Trump seemed unfazed by the events; he resorted to calling demonstrators "agitators." In turn, Bolsonaro, his vice president, and one of his former ministers insisted that there is only the "Brazilian people"—not Afro-Brazilians, not Brazilian Indians, not "gypsies"—and no racism in Brazil. Never mind that the Black Lives Matter movement struck a chord in Brazil as well, where several cases similar to Floyd's are not uncommon.

If racial/ethnic diversity is ignored, what stands out is Whiteness disguised as sameness and invisibility. The dichotomy between "Whites" and "People of Color," ever so popular since the late twentieth century, helps to render Whiteness invisible by implying that Whites are devoid of color (Penha-Lopes 2010). Instead, Whiteness must be recognized as the race/color whose higher power grants it the privilege of being normative. As a result of that privilege, groups with less power end up bearing the brunt of social problems.

In the presidential election of 2020, millions of U.S. citizens clamored for change. Still, millions also voted for the maintenance of the status quo. The country is divided over issues of race, gender, and the economy. If change is really to come, the country must be willing to grapple with the fact that it was born out of the contradictory values of equality and inequality. The millions of votes cast amid a pandemic lead me to believe that, although racism is a reality, there are plenty of people who want to confront it. Historically, every effort to tackle racism in the United States has been interracial. Biden's past—as the vice president of the first Black U.S. president—and his present—as the first president with a Black vice president—raises hope that the candid conversation that should have happened in 1865 (end of the Civil War), 1877 (end of the Reconstruction), 1965 (Voting Rights Act), and 2008 (Obama's first election) may finally take place.

With Trump's political defeat and Bolsonaro's continued allegiance to him to the point of hinting at declaring war against the country under Biden (Alves November 10, 2020), Bolsonaro's success at reelection in 2022 is questionable. In the local elections of November 2020, there were already signs that Bolsonaro was losing his allure as a changemaker. After all, all of the mayoral candidates he backed lost, in Manaus, Recife, Belo Horizonte, São Paulo, and Rio de Janeiro. The thunderous defeat of Celso Russomanno in São Paulo is significant because Bolsonaro clashed with João Doria, the governor of the state, throughout the pandemic. In Rio, the incumbent mayor, Marcelo Crivella, is an Evangelical pastor whose uncle is the founder of the Universal Church of the Kingdom of God. Having diverged from

Bolsonaro during the pandemic, Crivella renewed his alliance with Bolsonaro as the mayoral elections approached, but ended up losing to Eduardo Paes, a center-right former mayor of Rio who was touted as the lesser of two evils. Bolsonaro's relatives also fared poorly: one of his ex-wives, Rogéria Bolsonaro, was defeated in the race for councilperson in Rio; a cousin of his managed only 4 percent of the votes for mayor of a town in the countryside of São Paulo (Phillips November 16, 2020). The conclusion is that mainstream political parties are making a comeback. In the words of Mauricio Santoro, a professor of political science at the State University of Rio de Janeiro, "The president is no longer the kingmaker he was in 2018, when his support was enough to get even unknown candidates elected" (Yahoo News November 16, 2020). Whether Bolsonaro meets the same fate as Trump, the fact is that both owe their previous success to the attitudes and behaviors of millions who, like them, have a narrow notion of nation.

NOTE

1. I am indebted to Sidney Greenfield and Kenneth Erickson for this comparison (personal communication, Columbia University Seminar on Brazil, December 19, 2019).

Afterword

In December 2019, reports of a virus epidemic in Wuhan, China, hit the traditional and social media. It was dubbed "the new coronavirus" after the spikes that shaped it had resembled a crown; later, the name was shortened to "Covid-19." There was uncertainty over whether it originated in pangolins or bats that were eaten by humans, but there was widespread concern over the speed of contaminations. Frequent air travel, characteristic of contemporary life, made the spread of the virus to the rest of the world a real threat. One implication of White supremacy in both the United States and Brazil has been the way the two countries have faced the virus.

In January 2020, there were signs that the virus had reached Europe and the United States. Although it was later reported that President Trump had been briefed in the first two months of the year of the possibility of a pandemic, he dismissed it. Interestingly enough, when Trump considered running for president in 2000, one of his campaign ideas "was a project to develop and stockpile treatments in anticipation of future pandemics or the use or release of biological agents by terrorists" (D'Antonio 2016, 250). And yet, once elected, he destroyed former president Obama's provisions for a pandemic in 2020.

By March, the contamination and death rates were alarmingly high throughout the world. European countries such as Italy and Germany closed their borders and confined their populations at home in an effort to contain the spread of the virus. In the United States, New York City was the epicenter as the virus spread to the rest of the country. Trump, however, insisted that he had "the Chinese virus" under control and saw no need to close businesses, as Europe had done. On March 16, he twitted, "The United States will be powerfully supporting those industries, like Airlines and others, that are particularly affected by the Chinese Virus. We will be stronger than ever before!" By then, Trump was feuding with the World Health Organization (WHO), whose director at first recommended constant hand sanitation, but not the use of facial masks. WHO and New York mayor Bill de Blasio criticized Trump over his use of the terms "Chinese virus" and "China virus" for fueling discrimination against Asians and Asian Americans, but he defended his words and continued to utter them. Trump also had a contentious relationship with Dr. Anthony Fauci, head of the Center for Disease Control (CDC), which recommended social distancing and the closing of nonessential business in order to decrease the possibility of human contact.

In January, there were two confirmed cases of Covid-19 in the United States, which prompted Trump to utter, "It's going to be just fine. We have it totally under control" (President Donald J. Trump January 22, 2020). In late February, the numbers had climbed to 24, still a manageable figure. However, by the end of March, research by the Coronavirus Resource Center at Johns Hopkins University counted 192,301 cases in the United States; 2.8 percent of those resulted in deaths (Pereira and Mitropoulos March 6, 2021). Much to Trump's chagrin, governors and mayors, first in New York, and then throughout the country, ordered the closing of nonessential businesses and public schools to encourage social distancing.

To be sure, with hospitals reaching full capacity, little was known about how to contain contamination. At a news briefing with Dr. Fauci, director of infectious diseases at the CDC, President Trump suggested that, if the best prevention against contamination was handwashing, soapy water be injected in people's bodies (including their lungs) to wash off the virus. That followed his suggestion that ultraviolet laser-like beams be shot at the victims. Asked by a journalist whether there was any evidence for that, Trump retorted, "I'm the president and you're fake news" (YouTube April 23, 2020). Trump said he was being "sarcastic" after much repercussion, but then he threatened to stop having news briefs about the pandemic. He also threatened to fire Dr. Anthony Fauci, who disagreed with him about the efficacy of hydroxychloroquine to cure the viral infection.

Whenever Trump disagreed with some statement, he called it "fake news." Perhaps because of that, Americans were much less likely to believe the news and became polarized along Democrat-Republican lines. As Russonello (May 11, 2020) put it,

A Pew Research Center survey released on Friday found that 63 percent of Democrats nationwide said they thought the news media's coverage of the outbreak had been generally helpful. But just 27 percent of Republicans agreed, including a meager 22 percent of conservative Republicans.

While close to three-quarters of Democrats said in the Pew poll that the media's virus coverage was getting them the information they needed, only 44 percent of Republicans said so. Two-thirds of Republicans said in the survey that the news media's coverage of the pandemic had been "more negative than it should be."

That partisan divide is contributing to a decline in the country's overall faith in journalism. Fifty-two percent of respondents said that they generally had little to no confidence that journalists would operate in the public's best interests. Two years ago, 55 percent of Americans told Pew that they had at least a decent amount of confidence.

On April 21, 2020, the United States reached one million cases of covid-19; 57,000 were confirmed dead.

In Brazil, Bolsonaro also quickly dismissed the coronavirus pandemic as "just a little flu" (*só uma gripezinha*), to which he was probably immune due to his "athletic constitution." Like Trump, he claimed the use of masks was unnecessary and a sign of weakness. The more contamination climbed, the more outrageous pronouncements Bolsonaro made. On March 9, when the number of deaths was close to zero, Bolsonaro stated that the pandemic was "superdimensioned." Two days later, he said that "other flus killed more."

Social distancing in Brazil began on March 14. On March 15, Bolsonaro claimed that "in 2009, 2010, there was a similar crisis." On March 17, he said the virus had created "a certain hysteria." On March 20, he famously said, "It is not a little flu that will bring me down." On March 22, he vowed, "The people will know that it was dupped by these governors and by a large part of the media." On March 24, he again personalized the pandemic by claiming that he would feel nothing if infected; if at all, it would not go beyond "a little cold" or "a little flu." On March 27, he denied that so many deaths had been caused by the virus, thus spreading the rumor that death certificates were being adulterated in order to inflate the numbers of deaths related to Covid-19. On March 29, he undermined the losses by saying that "everybody will die one day." On April 1, when mortality in Brazil had surpassed 1,000, he pondered that "a virus is like getting caught in the rain; you will get wet, but you will not drown." He made fun of journalists on April 2, asking them whether they were afraid of catching the virus. He falsely claimed, 10 days later, the "virus is going away." On April 20, with deaths close to 4,000, he declared, "I am not an undertaker." Finally, on April 28, with 71,887 cases and 5,017 deaths, Bolsonaro asked rhetorically, "So what? I am sorry. What do you want me to do? My name is Messias [Messiah], but I am not a miracle worker" (Uol April 28, 2020).

On April 16, 2020, Bolsonaro fired Luiz Henrique Mandetta, minister of health. A medical doctor, he refused to endorse Bolsonaro's claim that hydroxychloroquine cured Covid-19. He was replaced by another doctor, Nelson Teich, who, like Mandetta, at first seemed to be on Bolsonaro's side. However, at a meeting on April 22, which was recorded on video, Teich looked particularly uncomfortable with Bolsonaro's pronouncements. Teich quit on May 15, 2020 for refusing to agree that hydroxychloroquine was a valid treatment for Covid-19, since research and experience had shown that it was not and might be even lethal. He was the 11th minister to leave Bolsonaro's government. In his place, Bolsonaro installed General Eduardo Pazuello, an army general who is a veterinarian, not a medical doctor, and abode by Bolsonaro's orders.

Amid news of the spike in deaths due to the virus, on the week of May 3, 2020, Bolsonaro announced that he would host, on May 9, a barbecue in his residence in Brasília; a soccer game was also planned for that date. After much dismay from the part of antagonists, he said such an event was never to be, that he had uttered that only in jest, and that journalists were "idiots." Any similarity with Trump's treatment of the press may not be mere coincidence.

Soon, Brazil would reach the unenviable post of second in the world in Covid-19 cases. Bolsonaro's insistence in, on the one hand, denying the existence of the pandemic and, on the other, letting it run its course led Senior Supreme Court Justice Celso Mello to compare him with Hitler, on May 31, 2020. A few days earlier, the Human Rights Committee of the House of Representatives had denounced Bolsonaro to the United Nations for his praise of torture, which had characterized the military dictatorship in Brazil.

On July 15, 2020, Felipe Neto, a Brazilian internet comedian, published a video on *The New York Times*' website on which he listed the five reasons that make Jair Bolsonaro, not Donald Trump, "the worst president of the pandemic." In near-native American English pronunciation, he related how Bolsonaro had gone over the Supreme Court's order to wear masks, how he hopped from event to event shaking people's hands after having brushed his nose with his own hands, how he touted hydroxychloroquine as the miracle cure for Covid-19, and how he mentioned that it would be easy to install a dictatorship in Brazil. Finally, he showed clips of Bolsonaro's dismissive statements as the death toll went up. Neto reminded the public that Trump called Bolsonaro "a great friend," so he pleaded with American voters to take heed at the presidential election in November because if Trump lost, Bolsonaro's power would be destabilized (Neto July 15, 2020). Carlos Bolsonaro sued Neto for calling his father "genocidal," claiming that statement violated national security. His suit was dismissed on March 21, 2021.

Omitting the existence of a problem in order to pretend that it does not exist does not eliminate its consequences. The Covid-19 pandemic has shown that. The United States and Brazil ranked first and second in deaths. In March of 2021, the death toll in Brazil surpassed that in the United States; in that month alone, 58,924 persons lost their lives in Brazil, compared with 35,919 deaths in the United States (Galzo March 30, 2021). Brazil became the epicenter of the pandemic and was touted as a threat to the entire world. As of June 2021, the total death toll in Brazil was 488,228, and in the United States, 599,781 (*The New York Times* June 14, 2021; Valery June 14, 2021). In both countries, the largest numbers of victims were non-Whites (Afro-descendants, indigenous, and Latino(a)s). In the United States, Latino(a)s—especially the women—Blacks, and Asian Americans were among those who had suffered the most from job losses (Krogstad, Gonzalez-Barrera, and Noe-Bustamante April 3, 2020; Kochhar June 9, 2020). In Brazil, Blacks had higher infection and mortality rates than Whites (Valor Online April 11, 2020). Rather than a coincidence, that was the result of their historically lower quality of life due to inequalities in wages, access to health care and education, and political participation. Given the statistics, the flippant attitude that Trump and Bolsonaro had toward the spread of contaminations led some to conclude they were flirting with genocide.

In the end, the two purported saviors did little to save their countries from the pandemic. Trump's initial statement that the virus was under control and Bolsonaro's assurance that it was nothing more than a mild flu were followed by their accusation that China had purposely created the virus in order to conquer the world. Turning the pandemic into a political issue delayed the employment of measures to contain it and led to the pursuit of medical dead ends. It also framed the issue as an intense polarization between naysayers and alarmists. The refusal of both presidents to wear masks and to label those who do "losers," "weak," and less manly encouraged behavior that resulted in preventable contaminations.

The false contradiction Trump and Bolsonaro established between population health and economic robustness ultimately affected both and helped to cost Trump his reelection. The victory of the Joe Biden-Kamala Harris ticket in 2020 was a sign that the majority of voters was weary of Trump's idea of nation. The election broke the record of most votes ever cast and placed a woman in the White House as the nation's vice president. If that were not emblematic enough in the 100th anniversary of the granting of suffrage to (White) women, Kamala Harris, the vice president elect, is the first Afro-Indian American citizen to occupy such a high post; she is also the child of immigrants.

That is not enough, however, to declare the end of White supremacy; efforts to nullify the election results made that abundantly clear. A belief in the demise of White supremacy and the emergence of a new, all-inclusive nation would run the risk of repeating the mistake of concluding that the election and reelection of the first U.S. Black president in 2008 and 2012 were signs that the country had become "post-racial." In turn, Bolsonaro's declining popularity amid investigations of his role in the spread of the Covid-19 pandemic in Brazil may very well lower his chances of reelection in 2022, even though the ideas that made him popular in 2018 continue to be at play.

References

Abraham Lincoln Historical Society. "Lincoln's View on Slavery." Accessed October 26, 2019. http://www.abraham-lincoln-history.org/lincolns-view-on-slavery/.

Abramowitz, Alan I. *The Great Alignment: Race, Party Transformation, and the Rise of Donald Trump*. New Haven, CT and London: Yale University Press, 2018.

The Action Network. "Never Again Means Never Again!" Accessed October 4, 2020. https://actionnetwork.org/petitions/never-again-means-never-again#.

ADVFN. "Cotação do Dólar em Janeiro de 2018." Accessed March 24, 2020. https://br.advfn.com/moeda/dolar/2018/01

Affonso, Julia and Fausto Macedo. "Justiça Condena Bolsonaro por 'Quilombolas Não Servem nem para Procriar.'" *Estadão* October 3, 2017. Accessed February 7, 2019. https://politica.estadao.com.br/blogs/fausto-macedo/justica-condena-bolsonaro...

Aguiar, Adriana. "Na USP, Janaína Paschoal Diz que "Cobras" Tentam se Perpetuar no Poder." *Valor Econômico* April 4, 2016. Accessed January 29, 2020. https://valor.globo.com/politica/noticia/2016/04/04/na-usp-janaina-paschoal-diz-que-cobras-tentam-se-perpetuar-no-poder.ghtml

Aguirre, Jr., Adalberto and David V. Baker, eds. *Structured Inequality in the United States: Critical Discussions on the Continuing Significance of Race, Ethnicity, and Gender*. 2nd ed. Upper Saddle River, NJ: Pearson Prentice Hall, 2008.

Alagoas 24 Horas. "PDT de Ciro Gomes Anuncia 'Apoio Crítico' a Fernando Haddad no Segundo Turno." October 10, 2018. Accessed March 19, 2020. https://www.alagoas24horas.com.br/1185341/pdt-de-ciro-gomes-anuncia-apoio-critico-a-fernando-haddad-no-segundo-turno/

Allen, Jonathan and Amie Parnes. *Shattered: Inside Hillary Clinton's Doomed Campaign*. New York: Broadway Books, 2017.

Allende, Isabel. *Daughter of Fortune*. New York: Harper Perennial, 1999.

Alonso, Angela. "O Abolicionismo como Movimento Social." *Novos Estudos CEBRAP* 100, (November 2014). Accessed May 20, 2010. https://www.scielo.br/scielo.php?pid=S0101-33002014000300115&script=sci_arttext&tlng=pt

———. *Flores, Votos e Balas: O Movimento Abolicionista Brasileiro (1868–88)*. São Paulo: Companhia das Letras, 2015.

———. "A Comunidade Moral Bolsonarista e o Caso Olavo de Carvalho." Presentation at II Congresso ABRE (Associação de Brasilianistas na Europa), Paris, France, September 19, 2019.

Alves, Hellen. "VÍDEO: Bolsonaro Ameaça Guerra contra EUA de Biden na Defesa da Amazônia." November 10, 2020. Accessed November 10, 2020. https://www .diariodocentrodomundo.com.br/video-bolsonaro-ameaca-guerra-contra-eua-de -biden-na-defesa-da-amazonia/

American Institute for Public Opinion. *Gallup Political Index*. Princeton, NJ: Gallup International, Inc, 1965.

Amnesty International. "Brazil: Spike in Killings by Rio Police as Country Faces UN Review." May 4, 2017. Accessed January 27, 2020. https://www.amnesty.org /en/latest/news/2017/05/brazil-spike-in-killings-by-rio-police-as-country-faces-un -review/

Anderson, Benedict. *Imagined Communities: Reflections on the Origin and Spread of Nationalism*. London: Verso, 1991.

Anderson, Carol. *One Person, No Vote: How Voter Suppression Is Destroying Our Democracy*. New York: Bloomsbury Publishing, 2018.

Anderson, Terry. *The Pursuit of Fairness*: *A History of Affirmative Action*. New York: Oxford University Press, 2004.

Andrews, Evan. "10 Things You May Not Know About the Mexican-American War." History.com. August 29, 2018. Accessed October 15, 2019. https://www.history .com/news/10-things-you-may-not-know-about-the-mexican-american-war.

Araújo, Ubiratan Castro de. "A Política dos Homens de Cor no Tempo da Independência." *Estudos Avançados* 18, no. 50 (January/April) (2004). https://doi .org/10.1590/S0103-40142004000100022

Arcanjo, Daniela and Joelmir Tavares. "Ofensas a Japoneses Amplia Rol de Falas Preconceituosas de Bolsonaro contra Grupos." *Folha de São Paulo* Janeiro 26, 2020, A4, A8.

Associated Press. "Protesters Gather at 'Saturday Night Live' Studio to Oppose Donald Trump Hosting." *Hollywood Reporter* November 4, 2015. Accessed June 25, 2020. https://www.hollywoodreporter.com/news/donald-trump-snl-con- troversy-protesters-837264.

Azanha, Gilberto. "As Terras Indígenas Terena no Mato Grosso do Sul." *Revista de Estudos e Pesquisas*, FUNAI 2, no. 1 (July 2005): 61–111. Accessed May 22, 2020. http://www.funai.gov.br/arquivos/conteudo/cogedi/pdf/Revista-Estudos -e-Pesquisas/revista_estudos_pesquisas_v2_n1/2.%20As%20terras%20indigenas %20Terena%20no%20Mato%20Grosso%20do%20Sul.pdf

Bailey, Sarah Pulliam. "White Evangelicals Voted Overwhelmingly for Trump, Exit Polls Show." *Washington Post* November 9, 2016. Accessed December 19, 2019. https://www.washingtonpost.com/news/acts-of-faith/wp/2016/11/09/exit-polls -show-white-evangelicals-voted-overwhelmingly-for-donald-trump/

Baker, Peter C. "The Tragic, Forgotten History of Black Military Veterans." *The New Yorker*. November 27, 2016. Accessed December 4, 2019. https://www.newyorker

.com/news/news-desk/the-tragic-forgotten-history-of-black-military-veterans. https://www.washingtonpost.com/news/acts-of-faith/wp/2016/11/09/exit-polls -show-white-evangelicals-voted-overwhelmingly-for-donald-trump/.

Balakrishnan, Gopal. "The National Imagination." In *Mapping the Nation*, edited by Gopal Balakrhishnan, 198–213. London: Verso, 1999.

Baltzell, E. Digby. *The Protestant Establishment: Aristocracy & Caste in America*. New York: Random House, 1964.

Baraviera, Verônica de Carvalho Maia. "A Questão Racial na Legislação Brasileira." Trabalho final apresentado ao Curso de Especialização em Direito Legislativo realizado pela Universidade do Legislativo Brasileiro – UNILEGIS e Universidade Federal do Mato Grosso do Sul – UFMS como requisito para obtenção do título de Especialista em Direito Legislativo. Brasília, 1985. Accessed April 8, 2020. https://www2.senado.leg.br/bdsf/bitstream/handle/id/82/Veronica_de_Carvalho .pdf

Barrett, James E. and David Roediger. "How White People Became White." In *White Privilege: Essential Readings on the Other Side of Racism*, 4th ed., edited by Paula S. Rothenberg, 39–44. New York: Worth, 2012.

BBC. "US Election: Full Transcript of Donald Trump's Obscene Videotape." October 9, 2016. Accessed July 5, 2020. https://www.bbc.com/news/election-us-2016 -37595321.

Beason, Tyrone. "The Angry Us: Voters Are Sick and Tired of Politics as Usual." *The Seattle Times* July 14, 2016. Accessed June 30, 2020. https://www.seattle-times.com/pacific-nw-magazine/the-angry-us-voters-are-sick-and-tired-of-politics -as-usual/.

Belloni, Luiza. "O que Foi o 'Kit Gay', Material Escolar sobre Homossexualidade Criticado por Bolsonaro e Inês Brasil." *Huffpost* August 29, 2017. Accessed January 7, 2019. https://www.huffpostbrasil.com/2017/08/29/o-que-foi-o-kit-gay -material-escolar-sobre-homossexualidade-criticado-por-bolsonaro-e-ines-brasil_a _23188320/.

Belth, Nathan. *A Promise to Keep: A Narrative of the American Encounter with Anti-Semitism*. New York: The New York Times Book Company, Inc., 1979.

Bento, Maria Aparecida Silva. "Branqueamento e Branquitude no Brasil." In *Psicologia Social do Racismo: Estudos sobre Branquitude e Branqueamento no Brasil*, 2nd ed., edited by Iray Carone and Maria Aparecida Silva Bento, 25–57. Petrópolis, RJ: Editora Vozes, 2003.

Beran, Chelsea. "Before They Were Presidents…They Were Lawyers." *Law Technology Today* February 15, 2016. Accessed June 6, 2020. https://www.law-technologytoday.org/2016/02/before-they-were-presidents-they-were-lawyers/

Berenson, Tessa. "Donald Trump Calls For 'Complete Shutdown' of Muslim Entry to U.S." *Time* December 7, 2017. Accessed November 10, 2020. https://time.com /4139476/donald-trump-shutdown-muslim-immigration/.

Bernardo, Nairim. "9 Mitos e uma Verdade sobre Tiradentes e a Inconfidência Mineira." *Nova Escola* March 7, 2018. Accessed May 10, 2020. https://novaescola .org.br/conteudo/4914/9-mitos-e-uma-verdade-sobre-tiradentes-e-a-inconfidencia -mineira

Bertoni, Estêvão. "Eleições 2018: Veja como os Partidos se Posicionaram no Segundo Turno." *Veja* October 11, 2018. Accessed March 19, 2020. https://veja .abril.com.br/politica/eleicoes-2018-veja-como-os-partidos-se-posicionaram-no -segundo-turno/

Bertulio, Dora Lucia de Lima. "Direito e Relações Raciais: Uma Introdução Crítica ao Racismo." Master's thesis, Centro de Ciências Jurídicas, Universidade Federal de Santa Catarina, 1989.

Betts, Jennifer. "What Does LGBTQIA+ Stand for?" *Your Dictionary* n.d. Accessed June 10, 2021. https://abbreviations.yourdictionary.com/what-does-lgbtqia-stand -for-full-acronym-explained.html.

Bezerra, Juliana. "Lei do Ventre Livre." *Toda Matéria.* n.d. a. Accessed May 18, 2020. https://www.todamateria.com.br/lei-do-ventre-livre-1871/.

———. "Lei dos Sexagenários (1885)." *Toda Matéria.* n.d. b. Accessed May 19, 2020. https://www.todamateria.com.br/lei-dos-sexagenarios/ .

Bigelli, Alexandre. "Revolução Constitucionalista: Em 1932, Elite Paulista Reage à Ditadura." *Uol Educação* July 7, 2014. Accessed May 13, 2020. https://educa-cao.uol.com.br/disciplinas/historia-brasil/revolucao-constitucionalista-de-1932-2 -movimento-foi-contra-getulio-vargas.htm?

Biggestuscities.com. "Minneapolis, Minnesota Population History 1880–2018." January 20, 2017. Accessed September 20, 2020. https://www.biggestuscities.com /city/minneapolis-minnesota.

Biografias. "Dante de Oliveira." Accessed June 2, 2020. *Educação UOL.* https:// educacao.uol.com.br/biografias/dante-de-oliveira.htm

Biography.com. "Earl Warren." April 17, 2019 (September 29, 2014). Accessed December 4, 2019. https://www.biography.com/political-figure/earl-warren.

———. "Ben Carson." January 14, 2020 (March 21, 2018). Accessed November 9, 2020. https://www.biography.com/political-figure/ben-carson.

Bittencourt, Julinho. "Morreu Carlos Alberto Caó de Oliveira, por Jean Willys." *Revista Forum* February 4, 2018. Accessed June 2, 2020. https://revistaforum.com .br/politica/morreu-carlos-alberto-cao-de-oliveira-por-jean-willys/

Black Demographics. "New York City." 2020. Accessed June 21, 2020. https://black-demographics.com/cities-2/new-york-nj-ny/.

Blank, Rebecca M. "An Overview of Trends in Social and Economic Well Being, by Race." In *America Becoming: Racial Trends and their Consequences*, Volume 1, edited by Faith Mitchell, William Julius Wilson, Neil J. Smelser, 21–39. National Research Council, Commission on Behavioral and Social Sciences and Education. National Academies Press, 2001.

Bloom, Jack M. *Class, Race, and the Civil Rights Movement: The Changing Political Economy of Southern Racism.* Bloomington, IN: Indiana University Press, 1987.

Bobo, Lawrence. "Laissez-Faire Racism, Racial Inequality, and the Role of the Social Sciences." In *Rethinking the Color Line: Readings in Race and Ethnicity*, 4th ed., edited by Charles A. Gallagher, 155–164. New York: McGraw-Hill, 2008.

——— and James R. Kluegel. "Opposition to Race-Targetting: Self-interest, Stratification Ideology, or Racial Attitudes?" *American Sociological Review* 58, no. 4 (August 1993): 443–464.

_____, James R. Kluegel, and Ryan A. Smith. "Laissez-Faire Racism: The Crystallization of a Kinder, Gentler Antiblack Ideology." In *Racial Attitudes in the 1990s: Continuity and Change*, edited by Steven Tuch and Jack K. Martin, 15–44. New York: Praeger, 1997.

_____ and Ryan A. Smith. "From Jim Crow Racism to Laissez-Faire Racism: The Transformation of Racial Attitudes." In *Beyond Pluralism: The Conception of Groups and Group Identities in America*, edited by Wendy F. Katkin, Ned Landsman, and Andrea Tyree, 182–220. Urbana, IL: University of Illinois Press, 1998.

Bolsonaro, Flávio. "Flávio Bolsonaro Vota contra a Lei de Cotas nos Concursos Públicos." *YouTube* October 21, 2011. Accessed January 17, 2020. https://www .bing.com/videos/search?q=bolsonaro+contra+cotas&view=detail&mid=E17EF7F FCA527EE8BFFEE17EF7FFCA527EE8BFFE&FORM=VIRE

Bonilla-Silva, Eduardo. *Racism without Racists: Color-Blind Racism and the Persistence of Racial Inequality in America*. Lanham, MD: Rowman & Littlefield, 2003.

———. "From Biracial to Tri-Racial: The Emergence of a New Racial Stratification System in the United States." In *Skin/Deep: How Race and Complexion Matter in the "Color-Blind" Era*, edited by Cedric Herring, Verna M. Keith, and Hayward Derrick Horton, 224–239. Urbana and Chicago, IL: University of Illinois Press, 2004.

Brasil 247. "Posse de Bolsonaro: Imprensa É Tratada como Lixo. Franceses e Chineses Abandonam Cobertura." January 1, 2019. Accessed January 2, 2019. https://www.brasil247.com/midia/posse-de-bolsonaro-imprensa-e-tratada-como -lixo-franceses-e-chineses-abandonam-cobertura

———. "Instituto Brasil-Israel Condena Uso de Referências Nazistas pelo Governo Bolsonaro." May 30, 2020. Accessed May 30, 2020. https://www.brasil247.com/ brasil/instituto-brasil-israel-condena-uso-de-referencias-nazistas-pelo-governo- bolsonaro

———. "Depois de Almoçar na Embaixada, Bolsonaro Cumprimenta Trump por Independência dos EUA e o Chama de Grande Estadista." July 4, 2020. Accessed July 4, 2020. https://www.brasil247.com/regionais/brasilia/depois-de-almocar-na -embaixada-bolsonaro-cumprimenta-trump-por-independencia-dos-eua-e-o-chama -de-grande-estadista?amp=&utm_source=onesignal&utm_medium=notification &utm_campaign=push-notification.

Bremmer, Ian. "Jair Bolsonaro: Brazil's New Test." *Time Magazine: The 100 Most Influential People* April 29/May 6, 2019, p. 92.

Brêtas, Pollyanna. "O que Mudou Após os Cinco Anos da PEC da Doméstica." *Extra* June 2, 2020, p. 9.

Brown, DeNeen. "How Harry S. Truman Went from Being a Racist to Desegregating the Military." *The Washington Post* July 26, 2018. https://www.washingtonpost .com/news/retropolis/wp/2018/07/26/how-harry-s-truman-went-from-being-a-rac- ist-to-desegregating-the-military/. Accessed December 4, 2019.

Brown, Heather. "What Is The History Behind Minnesota's Somali-American Community?" *CBS Minnesota* July 23, 2019. Accessed September 20, 2020.

https://minnesota.cbslocal.com/2019/07/23/minnesota-somali-american-popula-tion-good-question/.

Brooks, Rebecca Beatrice. "Who Fought in the Revolutionary War?" History of Massachusetts Blog. November 17, 2017. Accessed July 5, 2019. https://history ofmassachusetts.org/who-fought-revolutionary-war/.

———. "Continental Soldiers in the Revolutionary War." History of Massachusetts Blog. December 26, 2017. Accessed September 28, 2019. https://historyofmassac husetts.org/continental-soldiers-revolutionary-war/.

Brum, Elaine. "Mulheres contra a Opressão." *El País* September 24, 2018. Accessed March 19, 2020. https://brasil.elpais.com/brasil/2018/09/24/opinion/1537805079 _256045.html

Bump, Philip. "In 1927, Donald Trump's Father Was Arrested after a Klan Riot in Queens." *The Washington Post* February 29, 2016. Accessed June 21, 2020. https:// www.washingtonpost.com/news/the-fix/wp/2016/02/28/in-1927-donald-trumps -father-was-arrested-after-a-klan-riot-in-queens/.

Bunker, Theodore. "Kellyanne Conway May Help Trump Win Women Voters." *Newsmax* July 16, 2016. Accessed July 16, 2020. https://www.newsmax.com/ Headline/kellyanne-conway-help-trump-win/2016/08/25/id/745157/.

Burstein, Paul. "Public Opinion, Demonstrations, and the Passage of Antidiscrimination Legislation." *Public Opinion Quarterly* 43, no. 2 (Summer 1979): 157–172. https:// doi.org/10.1086/268508. Accessed October 11, 2020.

California Newsreel. "Episode Two: The Story We Tell." *Race: The Power of an Illusion*. California Newsreel and Regents of the University of California, 2003. http://newsreel.org/transcripts/race2.html. Accessed September 5, 2019.

Calmes, Jackie and Alexei Barrionuevo. "Amid Crises, Obama Lands in South America." *The New York Times* March 19, 2011. https://www.nytimes.com/2011 /03/20/world/americas/20obama-brazil.html Accessed January 13, 2020.

Campos, João Pedroso de. "Vitória de Dilma em 2014 Foi 'Fraude Eleitoral', Diz Marina." *Veja* November 27, 2017. Accessed February 12, 2020. https://veja.abril .com.br/politica/vitoria-de-dilma-em-2014-foi-fraude-eleitoral-diz-marina/

Carandiru. Directed by Héctor Babenco. Columbia Pictures do Brasil, 2003.

Carone, Iray. "Breve Histórico de uma Pesquisa Psicossocial sobre a Questão Racial Brasileira." In *Psicologia Social do Racismo: Estudos sobre Branquitude e Branqueamento no Brasil*. 2nd ed., edited by Iray Carone and Maria Aparecida Silva Bento, 13–23. Petrópolis, RJ: Editora Vozes, 2003.

Carvalho, Ilona Szabó de. "How to Curb Violence and Drugs." Presentation at Columbia University Seminar on Brazil, New York, October 29, 2019.

Carvalho, Leandro. "Trabalho Escravo nas Minas"; *Brasil Escola*. Accessed May 10, 2020. https://brasilescola.uol.com.br/historiab/trabalho-escravo-nas-minas.htm

Casanova, Amanda. "What Does the Term 'Evangelical' Really Mean? Here are 10 Things to Know." *Christianity.com* June 15, 2018. Accessed July 18, 2020. https://www.christianity.com/church/denominations/what-does-the-term-evangeli-cal-really-mean-here-are-10-things-to-know.html.

Castano, Aicha El Hammar. "Far-right Candidate Jair Bolsonaro's Win in Brazil Could Signal Close Relationship with Trump: ANALYSIS." *ABC News* November

1, 2018. Accessed March 12, 2020. https://abcnews.go.com/International/candidate-jair-bolsonaros-win-brazil-signal-close-relationship/story?id=58822707

Catraca Livre. "Bolsonaro Diz que Nazismo É de Esquerda e É Corrigido." April 2, 2019. Accessed February 15, 2020. https://catracalivre.com.br/cidadania/bolsonaro-diz-que-nazismo-e-de-esquerda-e-e-corrigido/

Chalmers, David M. *Hooded Americanism: The First Century of the Ku Klux Klan, 1865–1965*. Garden City, NY: Doubleday & Company, Inc., 1965.

———. *And the Crooked Places Made Straight: The Struggle for Social Change in the 1960s*. Baltimore: The Johns Hopkins University Press, 2013.

Chamberlain, Samuel. "In First Executive Order, Trump Tells Agencies to Ease ObamaCare Burden." *Fox News* January 20, 2017. Accessed November 1, 2020. https://www.foxnews.com/politics/in-first-executive-order-trump-tells-agencies-to-ease-obamacare-burden.

Cheney, Kyle. "No, Clinton Didn't Start the Birther Thing. This Guy Did." *Politico* September 16, 2016. Accessed July 3, 2020. https://www.politico.com/story/2016/09/birther-movement-founder-trump-clinton-228304.

Cheng, Amrit. "The Muslim Ban: What Just Happened?" *ACLU* December 6, 2017. Accessed November 10, 2020. https://www.aclu.org/blog/immigrants-rights/muslim-ban-what-just-happened

Chicago Tribune. "What Trump's Election Could Mean to Auto Industry." November 11, 2016. Accessed July 1, 2020. https://www.chicagotribune.com/autos/ct-trumps-win-republican-congress-auto-industry-20161111-story.html.

Chiu, Allyson. "'Stunning in Ugliness and Tone': Trump Denounced for Attacking Somali Refugees in Minnesota." *The Washington Post* October 12, 2019. Accessed October 12, 2019. https://www.washingtonpost.com/nation/2019/10/11/trump-somali-refugees-minneapolis-rally/.

Cieglinski, Amanda. "Durante Governo Lula, Expansão do Acesso ao Ensino Superior se Deu com Apoio das Particulares." December 24, 2010. Accessed January 17, 2020. https://educacao.uol.com.br/noticias/2010/12/24/durante-governo-lula-expansao-do-acesso-ao-ensino-superior-se-deu-com-apoio-das-particulares.htm

Ciência sem Fronteiras. Accessed January 17, 2020. www.cienciasemfronteiras.gov.br/web/csf.

Cipriani, Juliana. "Por 61 Votos a 20, Senado Aprova Impeachment da Presidente Dilma Rousseff." *Estado de Minas* August 31, 2016. https://www.em.com.br/app/noticia/politica/2016/08/31/interna_politica,799471/por-61-votos-a-20-senado-aprova-impeachment-de-dilma-rousseff.shtml Accessed January 13, 2020.

CNN. "2016 Presidential Candidates." June 2016. Accessed June 30, 2020. https://edition.cnn.com/interactive/2015/05/politics/2016-election-candidates/.

———. "Presidential Results." 2016. Accessed September 28, 2020. https://www.cnn.com/election/2016/results/president.

Cohen, Michael. *Disloyal: A Memoir: The True Story of the Former Personal Attorney to President Donald J. Trump*. New York: Skyhorse, 2020.

Cohn, Nate. "More Hispanics Declaring Themselves White." *New York Times* May 21, 2014. Accessed January 26, 2017. https://www.nytimes.com/2014/05/22/

upshot/more-hispanics-declaring-themselves-white.html?_r=0 http://www.monarquia.org.br/PDFs/CONSTITUICAODOIMPERIO.pdf.

Collins, Patricia Hill. *Black Feminist Thought: Knowledge, Consciousness, and the Politics of Empowerment (Perspectives on Gender)*. London: HarperCollins, 1990.

Contins, Marcia. 2004. "Estratégias de Combate à Discriminação Racial no Contexto da Educação Universitária no Rio de Janeiro." In *Ação Afirmativa na Universidade: Reflexão sobre Experiências Concretas Brasil-Estados Unidos*, edited by Angela Randolpho Paiva, 109–148. Rio de Janeiro, Editora PUC-Rio, 2004.

———. *Lideranças Negras*. Rio de Janeiro: Aeroplano, 2005.

Costa, Iraci del Nero da. "As Populações das Minas Gerais no Século XVIII: Um Estudo de Demografia Histórica." *Revista Crítica Histórica* Ano II, no. 4 (December 2011): 176–197. http://www.revista.ufal.br/criticahistorica/attachments /article/122/As%20popula%C3%A7%C3%B5es%20das%20Minas%20Gerais %20no%20s%C3%A9culo%20XVIII.pdf

Cox, Oliver C. *Caste, Class, and Race: A Study in Social Dynamics*. Garden City, NY: Doubleday, 1948.

Cpdoc. "Imigração." n.d. Accessed May 22, 2020. https://cpdoc.fgv.br/sites/default/ files/verbetes/primeirarepublica/IMIGRA%C3%87%C3%83O.pdf

Daily News. "Clown Runs for President." June 17, 2015, cover page.

Daniel, G. Reginald. *Race and Multiraciality in Brazil and the United States: Converging Paths?* University Park: Pennsylvania State University Press, 2006.

——— and Jennifer Kelekay. "From Loving v. Virginia to Barack Obama: The Symbolic Tie That Binds." *Creighton Law Review* 50, no. 3 (2017): 641–668.

Danner, Chas. "Poll: Nearly Two Thirds of Americans Believe Trump Is Unqualified to Be President." *New York Magazine,* June 26, 2016. Accessed December 15, 2019. nymag.com/intelligencer/2016/06/poll-nearly-23-of-voters-say-trump-unq ualified.html

D'Antonio, Michael. *The Truth about Trump*. New York: Thomas Dunne Books, 2016.

De Ferrari, Ignazio. "The Dissolution of Congress and the Future of Peru's Democracy." *IPI Global Observatory* November 5, 2019. Accessed January 8, 2020. https://theglobalobservatory.org/2019/11/dissolution-congress-and-future-of -perus-democracy/.

Devaney, Tim. "KKK, American Nazi Party Praise Trump's Hiring of Bannon." *The Hill* November 14, 2016. Accessed April 10, 2020. https://thehill.com/blogs/blog -briefing-room/305912-kkk-american-nazi-party-praise-trumps-hiring-of-bannon.

Diário do Centro do Mundo. ""Brasil Acima de Tudo: Patriotas Carregam Faixa que Homenageia Donald Trump." January 1, 2019. Accessed January 2, 2019. https:// www.diariodocentrodomundo.com.br/essencial/brasil-acima-de-tudopatriotas-carregam-faixa-que-homenageia-bolsonaro-e-trump/.

Dias, Paulo Eduardo e Luís Adorno. "Negros são Oito de Cada 10 Mortos pela Polícia no Brasil, Aponta Relatório." *Uol* October 18, 2020. https://noticias.uol.com.br/ cotidiano/ultimas-noticias/2020/10/18/oito-a-cada-10-mortos-pela-policia-no-brasil-sao-negros-aponta-relatorio.htm.

Direitos Brasil. "As Leis Trabalhistas no Brasil e a CLT: Entenda." Accessed May 29, 2020. https://direitosbrasil.com/as-leis-trabalhistas-no-brasil/.

Dobyns, Lloyd. "Fighting... Maybe for Freedom, but Probably Not." *CW Journal* (Autumn 2007). Accessed September 28, 2019. https://www.history.org/Foundation /journal/Autumn07/slaves.cfm.

Domingues, Petrônio. "Os 'Pérolas Negras': A Participação do Negro na Revolução Constitucionalista de 1932." *Afro-Ásia* 29/30 (2003): 199–245.

———. "Movimento Negro Brasileiro: Alguns Apontamentos Históricos." *Tempo* 12, no. 23 (2007). Accessed May 29, 2020. https://doi.org/10.1590/S1413 -77042007000200007.

Douglass, Frederick. "What to the Slave Is the Fourth of July?" In *Narrative of the Life of Frederick Douglass, an American Slave, Written by Himself*, edited by William L. Andrews and William S. McFeely, 116–127, 1997 [1852].

Du Bois, W. E. B. *The Souls of Black Folk*. New York: Penguin Books, 1903 [1989].

———. "The Talented Tenth." In *The Negro Problem*, edited by Booker T. Washington. New York: J. Pott & Company, 1903.

———. "The Souls of White Folk." Chapter 2 in *Darkwater: Voices from within the Veil*. New York: Harcourt, Brace and Company, 1920.

Durham, Philip and Everett L. Jones. *The Negro Cowboys*. Lincoln, NE: University of Nebraska Press, 1965.

Dw.com "Dilma Rousseff É Cassada pelo Senado." August 31, 2016. https://www.dw .com/pt-br/dilma-rousseff-é-cassada-pelo-senado/a-19516550 Accessed January 13, 2020.

Ebiography.com. "Fernando Henrique Cardoso." Accessed March 4, 2020. https:// www.ebiografia.com/fernando_henrique_cardoso/.

Edelman, Adam. 2016. "A Look at Trump's Most Outrageous Comments about Mexicans as He Attempts Damage Control by Visiting with Country's President." Accessed January 5, 2019. https://www.nydailynews.com/news/politics/trump -outrageous-comments-mexicans-article-1.2773214.

The Editors of Encyclopaedia Britannica. "United States Presidential Election of 1876." October 31, 2019. Accessed October 3, 2020. https://www.britannica.com/ event/United-States-presidential-election-of-1876.

Elliott, Ward E. Y. *The Rise of Guardian Democracy: The Supreme Court's Role in Voting Rights Disputes, 1845–1969*. Cambridge, MA: Harvard University Press, 1974.

Equipe HuffPost. "Horário Eleitoral: Como É Feita a Divisão do Tempo de TV." *HuffPost* July 20, 2018. Accessed March 2, 2020. https://www.huffpostbrasil.com /2018/07/20/entenda-como-e-feita-a-divisao-do-tempo-de-tv-no-horario-eleitoral _a_23485856/.

Erickson, Kenneth. Commentary on "Presidential Elections, Whiteness, and the Right in Brazil and the U.S." Presentation by Vânia Penha-Lopes at Columbia University Seminar on Brazil, December 19, 2019.

Espiritu, Yen Le. *Asian American Panethnicity: Bridging Institutions and Identities*. Philadelphia, PA: Temple University Press, 1992.

Exame. "João Doria Jr. Assume 'O Aprendiz' e Promete Ser Sutil." October 10, 2010. Accessed December 10, 2019. https://exame.com/carreira/joao-doria-jr-assume -aprendiz-promete-ser-sutil-549551/.

———. "Bolsonaro Assumirá Papel de Líder Populista do Brasil, Diz Bannon a Jornal." October 29, 2018. Accessed February 17, 2020. https://exame.abril .com.br/brasil/bolsonaro-assumira-papel-de-lider-populista-do-brasil-diz-bannon-a -jornal/.

———. "'Não Existe Racismo no Brasil', Diz Mourão ao Comentar Morte no Carrefour.'" November 20, 2020. Accessed November 22, 2020. https://exame .com/brasil/nao-existe-racismo-no-brasil-diz-mourao-ao-comentar-morte-no -carrefour/.

Extra. "Jair Bolsonaro É Apresentado como pré-candidato à Presidência da República." March 2, 2016. Accessed January 16, 2020. https://extra.globo.com /noticias/brasil/jair-bolsonaro-apresentado-como-pre-candidato-presidencia-da -republica-18791859.html.

———. "Ministros São Empossados." January 2, 2019, p. 8.

———. "Sem Papas na Língua: Metralhadora Giratória de Bolsonaro Não Para." July 31, 2019, p. 3.

Feagin, Joe R. "Introduction." In *Dark Water: Voices from Within the Veil,*" edited by W. E. B. Du Bois. New York: Humanity Books, 2003.

———."Systemic Racism: A Comprehensive Perspective." In *Racist America: Roots, Current Realities, and Future Reparations.* 4th ed., edited by Joe R. Feagin and Kimberley Ducey, 1–34. New York: Routledge, 2019.

Feingold, Henry L. *Zion in America: The Jewish Experience from Colonial Times to the Present.* New York: Hippociene Books, Inc., 1981.

Fellet, João. "Olavo de Carvalho, o 'Parteiro' da Nova Direita que Diz Ter Dado à Luz Flores e Lacraias." *BBC News Brasil* December 15, 2016. Accessed March 10, 2020. https://www.bbc.com/portuguese/brasil-38282897.

———. "Quem São os Discípulos de Olavo de Carvalho que Chegaram ao Governo e Congresso." *BBC News Brasil* January 10, 2019. Accessed June 7, 2020. https:// www.terra.com.br/noticias/brasil/quem-sao-os-discipulos-de-olavo-de-carvalho -que-chegaram-ao-governo-e-congresso,9cf7544337fefb60db43a947ddb59fadn8 ieal33.html.

Ferling, John. "Myths of the American Revolution." January 2010. Accessed September 28, 2019. https://www.smithsonianmag.com/history/myths-of-the -american-revolution-10941835/.

Fernandes, Cláudio. "O que Foi o Estado Novo?" *Brasil Escola.* Accessed May 28, 2020. https://brasilescola.uol.com.br/o-que-e/historia/o-que-foi-estado-novo.htm.

Fernandes, Marcella. "Fora do País, Bolsonaro Ganhou em Tóquio, Lisboa, Montevidéu, Istambul e Miami." *HuffPost Brasil* October 28, 2018. Accessed March 20, 2020. https://www.huffpostbrasil.com/2018/10/28/fora-do-pais-bolso- naro-ganhou-em-toquio-lisboa-montevideu-istambul-e-miami_a_23574273/.

Fernandez, Alexia. "Billy Bush's Wife Sydney Davis Files for Divorce 10 Months After Their Separation: Report." *People* July 13, 2018. Accessed July 5, 2020. https://people.com/tv/billy-bushs-wife-sydney-davis-files-divorce/.

FGV CPDOC. "Partido Democrata Cristão (PDC- 1985–1993)." Accessed January 7, 2020. http://www.fgv.br/cpdoc/acervo/dicionarios/verbete-tematico/partido -democrata-cristao-pdc-1985-1993.

———. "A Era Vargas: Dos Anos 20 a 1945." Accessed May 29, 2020. https://cpdoc .fgv.br/producao/dossies/AEraVargas1/anos37-45/QuedaDeVargas.

Folha de S. Paulo. "'Negro de Direita', Presidente da Fundação Palmares Disse que Escravidão Foi Benéfica." November 27, 2019. Accessed June 4, 2020. https:// www1.folha.uol.com.br/ilustrada/2019/11/presidente-da-fundacao-palmares -nomeado-por-bolsonaro-diz-que-brasil-tem-racismo-nutella.shtml.

Foner, Philip. *Blacks in the American Revolution.* Westport, CT: Greenwood Press, 1976.

Ford, Matt. "Trump's Press Secretary Falsely Claims: 'Largest Audience Ever to Witness an Inauguration, Period'." *The Atlantic* January 21, 2017. Accessed October 17, 2020. https://www.theatlantic.com/politics/archive/2017/01/inauguration-crowd-size/514058/.

Frankenberg, Ruth. *White Women, Race Matters: The Social Construction of Whiteness.* Minneapolis, MN: University of Minnesota Press, 1995.

Frazão, Dilva. "Domitila de Castro Canto e Melo: Amante de Dom Pedro I." Ebiography November 1, 2019. Accessed May 18, 2020. https://www.ebiografia .com/domitila_de_castro_canto_e_melo/.

Frazier, E. Franklin. *Black Bourgeoisie.* New York: Simon and Schuster, 1957.

Freire Institute. "Paulo Freire: Biography." 2020. Accessed January 15, 2020. https:// www.freire.org/paulo-freire/paulo-freire-biography.

French, Jan Hoffman. "Rethinking Police Violence in Brazil: Unmasking the Public Secret of Race." *Latin American Politics and Society* 55, no. 4 (Winter 2013): 161–181.

Frostenson, Sarah. "A Crowd Scientist Says Trump's Inauguration Attendance Was Pretty Average." *Vox* January 24, 2017. Accessed October 17, 2020. https://www .vox.com/policy-and-politics/2017/1/24/14354036/crowds-presidential-inaugurations-trump-average.

Fryer Jr., Roland G. "Guess Who's Been Coming to Dinner? Trends in Interracial Marriage over the 20th Century." In *Rethinking the Color Line: Readings in Race and Ethnicity,* 4th ed., edited by Charles A. Gallagher, 377–383. New York: McGraw-Hill, 2008.

Fu, Vincent Kang. "How Many Melting Pots? Intermarriage, Pan Ethnicity, and the Black/Non-Black Divide in the United States." *Journal of Comparative Family Studies* 38, no. 2 (Spring 2007): 215–237. https://doi.org/10.3138/jcfs.38.2.215.

Fuentes-Rohwer, Luis and Guy-Uriel Charles. "The Electoral College, the Right to Vote, and Our Federalism: A Comment on a Lasting Institution." *Florida State University Law Review* 29 (2001): 879–924. Accessed September 28, 2020. https://scholarship.law.duke.edu/cgi/viewcontent.cgi?article=5565&context=faculty_scholarship.

Fusion. "Death of Eduardo Campos a Blow to Brazil's Politically Disenchanted Youth." *Splinter* August 14, 2014. Accessed February 11, 2020. https://splinternews .com/death-of-eduardo-campos-a-blow-to-brazil-s-politically-1793842248.

Gabbatt, Adam. "Golden Escalator Ride: The Surreal Day Trump Kicked off his Bid for President." *The Guardian* June 14, 2019. Accessed June 29, 2020. https://www.theguardian.com/us-news/2019/jun/13/donald-trump-presidential-campaign-speech-eyewitness-memories.

Gallego, Esther Solano. "La Bolsonarisación de Brasil." *Documentos de Trabajo Ielat* no. 1, April 2019, 4–41. Accessed March 24, 2020. https://ielat.com/wp-content/uploads/2019/03/DT_121_Esther-Solano-Gallego_Web_abril-2019.pdf.

———. "Conversando com Eleitores de Bolsonaro: Os Porquês do Voto." Presentation at II Congreso ABRE (Associação de Brasilianistas na Europa), Paris, France, September 19, 2019.

Gallagher, Charles A. "Color-blind Privilege: The Social and Political Functions of Erasing the Color Line in Post-Race America." In *Rethinking the Color Line: Readings in Race and Ethnicity,* 4th ed., edited by Charles A. Gallagher, 100–108. New York: McGraw-Hill, 2009.

Galzo, Wessley. "Brasil Lidera Número de Mortes Diárias por Covid-19 no Mundo em Março." *CNN Brasil* March 20, 2021. Accessed June 14, 2021. https://www.cnnbrasil.com.br/saude/2021/03/30/brasil-e-o-pais-que-mais-registra-mortes-diarias-por-covid-19-em-marco.

Gamboa, Suzanne. "Donald Trump Announces Presidential Bid By Trashing Mexico, Mexicans." *NBC News* June 16, 2015. Accessed June 20, 2020. https://www.nbcnews.com/news/ latino/donald-trump-announces-presidential-bid-trashing-mexico-mexicans-n376521.

Gans, Herbert J. "Symbolic Ethnicity: The Future of Ethnic Groups and Cultures in America." *Ethnic and Racial Studies* 2 (January 1979): 1–20.

———. "The Possibility of a New Racial Hierarchy in the Twenty-First-Century United States." In *The Cultural Territories of Race: Black and White Boundaries*, edited by Michèle Lamont, 371–390. Chicago and New York: University of Chicago Press and Russell Sage Foundation, 1999.

Garaeis, Vítor Hugo. "A História da Escravidão no Brasil." *Geledés* July 13, 2012. Accessed April 16, 2020. https://www.geledes.org.br/historia-da-escravidao-negra-brasil/.

Garcia, Gustavo, Fernanda Calgaro, Filipe Matoso, Laís Lis, and Mateus Rodrigues. "Senado Aprova Impeachment, Dilma Perde Mandato e Temer Assume." *G1* August 31, 2016. Accessed January 6, 2019. http://g1.globo.com/politica/processo-de-impeachment-de-dilma/noticia/2016/08/senado-aprova-impeachment-dilma-perde-mandato-e-temer-assume.html.

Garcia, Janaina and Nathan Lopes. "Cunha é Condenado por Moro a 15 Anos e 4 Meses de Prisão." *Uol* March 30, 2017. Accessed February 11, 2020. https://noticias.uol.com.br/politica/ultimas-noticias/2017/03/30/moro-condena-eduardo-cunha-a-15-anos-e-4-meses-de-reclusao.htm?cmpid=copiaecola.

Garrow, David J. *Protest at Selma: Martin Luther King, Jr., and the Voting Rights Act of 1965*. New Haven, CT: Yale University Press, 1978.

Gazeta do Povo. "Prometeu, Tem que Cumprir." November 26, 2014. Accessed February 12, 2020. https://www.gazetadopovo.com.br/vida-publica/eleicoes/2014/prometeu-tem-que-cumprir-efehym6ty2qaiqbo00lnzw5la/.

———. "Resultados para Presidente no Exterior em Nova York (Exterior)." October 7, 2018. Accessed March 20, 2020. https://especiais.gazetadopovo.com.br/eleicoes /2018/resultados/municipios-exterior/nova-york-ex/presidente/.

———. "A História de Jair Bolsonaro." October 28, 2018. Accessed January 8, 2020. https://especiais.gazetadopovo.com.br/eleicoes/2018/historia-de-jair-bolsonaro/.

Gearan, Anne. "Trump Sees a Lot to Like in Brazil's Unapologetically Far-right, Nationalist Leader." *The Washington Post* March 19, 2019. Accessed April 3, 2020. https_www.washingtonpost.com/?url=https%3A%2F%2Fwww.washingtonpost.com%2Fpolitics%2Ftrump-sees-a-lot-to-like-in-brazils-unapologetically-far-right-nationalist-leader%2F2019%2F03%2F19%2Fbcd1542c-4a4d-11e9-9663-00ac73f49662_story.html.

Geier, Ben. "Donald Trump Has a New Nickname for Hillary Clinton." April 18, 2016. Accessed January 3, 2019. http://fortune.com/2016/04/18/trump-clinton -nickname/.

Geledés. "Abdias Fala da Frente Negra Brasileira." September 16, 2011. Accessed May 28, 2020. https://www.geledes.org.br/abdias-fala-da-frente-negra-brasileira/.

Glazer, Nathan. *Affirmative Discrimination: Ethnic Inequality and Public Policy.* New York: Basic Books, 1975.

Goldberg, Michelle. "Mazel Tov, Trump. You've Revived the Jewish Left." *The New York Times* August 19, 2019. Accessed August 19, 2019. https://www.nytimes.com /2019/08/24/opinion/sunday/trump-jews.html.

Goldi Productions. "The First Peoples of Canada." 2007. Accessed October 6, 2019. https://www.firstpeoplesofcanada.com/fp_groups/fp_groups_origins.html.

Gonzalez-Barrera, Ana. "Hispanics with Darker Skin Are More Likely to Experience Discrimination than those with Lighter Skin." *Pew Research Center* July 2, 2019. Accessed July 25, 2020. https://www.pewresearch.org/fact-tank/2019/07/02/hispanics-with-darker-skin-are-more-likely-to-experience-discrimination-than-those -with-lighter-skin/.

Greenfield, Sidney. Commentary on "Presidential Elections, Whiteness, and the Right in Brazil and the U.S." Presentation by Vânia Penha-Lopes at Columbia University Seminar on Brazil, December 19, 2019.

Grenell, Alexis. "White Women, Come Get Your People." *New York Times* October 6, 2018. Accessed November 20, 2018. https://www.nytimes.com/2018/10/06/ opinion/lisa-murkowski-susan...

Griffin, Andrew. "Omarosa Book Summary: The Most Shocking Allegations from the Book that Has Outraged Donald Trump." *Independent* August 15, 2018. Accessed November 9, 2020. https://www.independent.co.uk/news/world/americas/trump-omarosa-book-summary-review-latest-tweets-white-house-unhinged -a8493286.html.

Grin, Monica and Marcos Chor Maio. "O Antirracismo da Ordem no Pensamento de Afonso Arinos de Melo Franco." *Topoi* 14, no. 26 (January/July 2013): 33–45. https://www.scielo.br/pdf/topoi/v14n26/1518-3319-topoi-14-26-00033.pdf.

The Guardian. "Brazil's Far-right Presidential Candidate Denies Links to Steve Bannon after Son's Claims." October 12, 2018. Accessed March 11, 2020. https:// www.theguardian.com/world/2018/oct/11/brazil-steve-bannon-jair-bolsonaro.

Guardianangels.org. Accessed July 1, 2020.

Guimarães, Antonio Sérgio. *Racismo e Antirracismo no Brasil*. São Paulo: Editora 34, 1999.

Guimarães, Eduardo. "Cadeirante É Agredido por Eleitores de Aécio por Usar Estrela do PT." *Blog da Cidadania* October 17, 2014. Accessed January 15, 2020. https:// blogdacidadania.com.br/2014/10/cadeirante-e-agredido-por-eleitores-de-aecio-por -usar-estrela-do-pt/.

Guinier, Lani and Gerald Torres. "The Ideology of Colorblindness." In *Rethinking the Color Line: Readings in Race and Ethnicity*, 4th ed., edited by Charles A. Gallagher, 109–113. New York: McGraw-Hill, 2009.

G1. "Salário Mínimo em 2018: Veja o Valor." January 4, 2018. Accessed March 24, 2020. https://g1.globo.com/economia/noticia/salario-minimo-em-2018-veja-o -valor.ghtml.

———. "Bolsonaro Diz que Liberou Visto porque Turistas Americanos Não Vão ao Brasil Buscar Emprego." March 19, 2019. Accessed April 1, 2020. https://g1.globo .com/politica/noticia/2019/03/19/bolsonaro-diz-que-liberou-visto-porque-turistas -americanos-nao-vao-ao-brasil-em-busca-de-emprego.ghtml.

Halley, Jean, Amy Eshleman, and Ramya Mahadevan Vijaya. *Seeing White: An Introduction to White Privilege and Race*. Lanham, MD: Rowman & Littlefield, 2011.

Hamasaki, Sonya. "Pussyhat Project Tops off Women's March on Washington." *CNN* January 20, 2017. Accessed November 6, 2020. https://www.cnn.com/2017 /01/20/politics/pussyhat-project-washington-march-trnd/index.html.

Higham, John. "American Anti-Semitism Historically Reconsidered." In *Anti-Semitism in the United States*, edited by Leonard Dinnerstein, 63–77. New York: Holt, Rinehart & Winston, 1971.

Historiaresumos.com. "Atos Institucionais do Brasil: Ai-1, Ai-2, Ai-3 e Ai-4 (Resumo)." Accessed January 7, 2020. https://www.historiaresumos.com/atos -institucionais-ai-1-ai-2-ai-3-ai-4/.

History Editors. "Trail of Tears." September 30, 2019. Accessed October 14, 2019. https://www.history.com/topics/native-american-history/trail-of-tears.

———. "Donald Trump Is Inaugurated." January 4, 2018. Accessed October 17, 2020. https//www.history.com/this-day-in-history/donald-trump-is-inaugurated.

———. "Women's March." January 5, 2018. Accessed November 6, 2020. https:// www.history.com/this-day-in-history/womens-march.

Hochschild, Arlie Russell. *Strangers in Their Own Land: Anger and Mourning on the American Right*. New York: The New Press, 2018.

———. "No Country for White Men." In *Readings for Sociology,* 9th ed., edited by Garth Massey and Timothy O'Brien, 225–235. New York: W. W. Norton & Company, 2019.

Holanda, Sérgio Buarque de. *Raízes do Brasil*. São Paulo: Companhia das Letras, 2002 [1936].

Honorato, Maylson. "Movimento Negro de AL Lembra 13 de Maio como o Dia da Inauguração do Racismo." *Globo.com* May 13, 2020. Accessed May 20, 2020.

https://gazetaweb.globo.com/portal/noticia/2020/05/movimento-negro-de-al-lembra-13-de-maio-como-o-dia-da-descoberta-do-racismo_105383.php.

Howard, Adam. "What's behind Trump's 'Pocahontas' Attack on Sen. Elizabeth Warren?" *MSNBC* May 16, 2016. Accessed September 21, 2020. http://www.msnbc.com/msnbc/whats-behind-trumps-pocahontas-attack-warren.

Hubby, Kristen. "How Many Americans Actually Vote?" April 20, 2018. Accessed September 28, 2020. https://www.dailydot.com/debug/voter-turnout-2016/.

Hughey, Matthew W. "White Lives Matter?" *Contexts* (June 2016). https://doi.org/10.1177/1536504217714256.

Humberto, Cláudio. "Brasil Pode Ter Mais de 100 Partidos em 2020." *Folha de Londrina* November 25, 2019. Accessed February 20, 2020. https://www.folhadelondrina.com.br/colunistas/claudio-humberto/brasil-pode-ter-mais-de-100-partidos-em-2020-2974825e.html.

Hutchinson, Pamela. "#MeToo and Hollywood: What's Changed in the Industry a Year on?" *The Guardian* October 8, 2018. Accessed July 6, 2020. https://www.theguardian.com/world/2018/oct/08/metoo-one-year-on-hollywood-reaction.

IBGE (Instituto Brasileiro de Geografia e Estatística). "Territórios Brasileiros e Povoamento>>Negros>>População Negra no Brasil." 2020. Accessed May 20, 2020. https://brasil500anos.ibge.gov.br/territorio-brasileiro-e-povoamento/negros/populacao-negra-no-brasil.

Influence Watch.org. "Carmen Perez." Accessed November 6, 2020. https://www.influencewatch.org/person/teresa-shook/.

———. "Linda Sarsour." Accessed November 6, 2020. https://www.influencewatch.org/person/linda-sarsour/.

———. "Teresa Shook." Accessed November 6, 2020. https://www.influencewatch.org/person/teresa-shook/.

Instituto Brasil-Israel. "Guilherme Cohen, do Judeus Pela Democracia, É o Entrevistado do Novo Episódio do Podcast do IBI." February 13, 2020. Accessed February 13, 2020. http://institutobrasilisrael.org/noticias/noticias/guilherme-cohen-do-judeus-pela-democracia-e-o-entrevistado-do-novo-episodio-do-podcast-do-ibi?fbclid=IwAR0JtGsBOfQrraK0IyNxJ6txDqiDygUaTNsTDSgElqfOxVYsB0egV3gQ098.

Iraheta, Diego. "Adelio Bispo de Oliveira: Quem É o Homem que Esfaqueou Jair Bolsonaro." *HuffPost* September 6, 2018. Accessed March 2, 2020. https://www.huffpostbrasil.com/2018/09/06/adelio-bispo-de-oliveira-quem-e-o-homem-que-esfaqueou-jair-bolsonaro_a_23519490/.

Jackson, David and Erin Kelly. "Ben Carson Drops out of GOP Presidential Race." *USA Today* March 4, 2016. Accessed March 2, 2020. https://www.usatoday.com/story/ news/2016/03/04/ben-carson- republican-presidential-race/80047678/.

Jacobs, Jennifer and Misyrlena Egkolfopoulou. "Jared Kushner Says African-Americans Must 'Want to Be Successful.'" *Bloomberg* October 26, 2020. Accessed November 16, 2020. https://www.bloomberg.com/news/articles/2020-10-26/kushner-says-african-americans-must-want-to-be-successful.

Jewett, Tom. "Jefferson on Native Americans." 2019. Accessed October 6, 2019. https://www.varsitytutors.com/earlyamerica/jefferson-primer/jefferson-native-americans.

Jewish Virtual World. "Virtual Jewish World: New York State, United States." *Jewish Virtual Library* 1998–2020. Accessed June 21, 2020. https://www.jewishv irtuallibrary.org/new-york-state-jewish-history.

Jordan, Winthrop. *The Americans*. Boston, MA: McDougal Littell, 1996.

Jornal GGN. "Bolsonaro Anuncia o Fim da Corrupção no Brasil." October 7, 2020. Accessed November 22, 2020. https://jornalggn.com.br/noticia/bolsonaro-anuncia -o-fim-da-corrupcao-no-brasil/.

Junge, Benjamin. "'Our Brazil Has Become a Mess': Nostalgic Narratives of Disorder and Disinterest as a 'Once-Rising Poor' Family from Recife, Brazil, Anticipates the 2018 Elections." *Journal of Latin American and Caribbean Anthropology* 00, no. 0 (2019): 1–18.

_____, and Sean Mitchell. "From the New Middle Class to the Rise of Popular Conservatism: Data from Recife, Rio de Janeiro, and São Paulo." Presentation at Columbia University Seminar on Brazil, February 21, 2019.

Junqueira, Alfredo. "Vestibulares das Universidades Estaduais do Rio Voltam a Ter Sistema de Cotas." *O Dia Online* June 6, 2009. Accessed June 9, 2009. http://odia .terra.com.br/portal/educacao/html/2009/6/vestibulares_das_universidades_estad-uais_do_rio_voltam_a_ter_sistema_de_cotas_15352.html.

Jus Vigilantibus. "As Constituições do Brasil." *Jusbrasil* 2008. Accessed April 10, 2020. https://jus-vigilantibus.jusbrasil.com.br/noticias/117944/as-constituicoes-do -brasil.

Kadanus, Kelli. "Bancada da Bala Pode Eleger um Presidente da República em 2018." *Gazeta do Povo* October 4, 2018. Accessed May 23, 2021. https://www .gazetadopovo.com.br/politica/republica/eleicoes-2018/bancada-da-bala-pode -eleger-um-presidente-da-republica-em-2018-5m11eeyph6qnrfiixk9z011f6/.

Keneally, Meghan. "A Timeline of Trump and Bannon's Turbulent Relationship." *ABC News* January 5, 2018. Accessed July 15, 2020. https://abcnews.go.com/ Politics/timeline-trump-bannons-turbulent-relationship/story?id=52137016.

Kessler, Glenn, Salvador Rizzo, and Meg Kelly. "President Trump Has Made 13,435 False or Misleading Claims over 993 Days." *Washington Post* October 14, 2019. Accessed November 10, 2019. https://www.washingtonpost.com/ politics/2019/10/14/president-trump-has-made-false-or-misleading-claims-over -days.

Khan, Shehab. "Donald Trump's Father 'Repeatedly Tried to Hide His Family's German Heritage.'" *The Independent* November 30, 2017. Accessed June 21, 2020. https://www.independent.co.uk/news/world/americas/us-politics/donald-trump -fred-german-heritage-swedish-gwenda-blair-a8083366.html.

King, Jr, Martin Luther. "Nobel Lecture by MLK." December 11, 1964. *The King Center*. Accessed December 6, 2019. https://thekingcenter.org.

Kivisto, Peter. *Americans All: Racial and Ethnic Relations in Historical, Structural, and Comparative Perspectives*. Belmont, CA: Wadsworth Publishing Company, 1995.

Kluegel, James R. and Eliot R. Smith, 1983. "Affirmative Action Attitudes: Effects of Self-Interest, Racial Affect, and Stratification Beliefs on Whites' Views." *Social Forces* 61, 3 (March 1983): 797–824, https://doi.org/10.1093/sf/61.3.797.

Knowles, Louis L. and Kenneth Prewitt. "The Report of the National Advisory Commission on Civil Disorders: A Comment." In *Structured Inequality in the United States: Critical Discussions on the Continuing Significance of Race, Ethnicity, and Gender.* 2nd ed., edited by Adalberto Aguirre, Jr. and David V. Baker, 14–21. Upper Saddle River, NJ: Pearson Prentice Hall, 2008.

Kochhar, Rakesh. "Hispanic women, immigrants, young adults, those with less education hit hardest by COVID-19 job losses." *Pew Research Center* June 9, 2020. Accessed May 22, 2021. https://www.pewresearch.org/fact-tank/2020/ 06/09/hispanic-women-immigrants-young-adults-those-with-less-education-hit-hardest-by-covid-19-job-losses/.

Koister, Martijn and Flávio Eiró. "Understanding Politics in Present-day Brazil: Assessing Candidates and Imagining the State." Presentation at Columbia University Seminar on Brazil, November 14, 2019.

Krogstad, Jens Manuel, Ana Gonzalez-Barrera, and Luis Noe-Bustamante. "U.S. Latinos among Hardest Hit by Pay Cuts, Job Losses Due to Coronavirus." *Pew Research Center* April 3, 2020. Accessed August 13, 2020. https://www.pewresearch.org/fact-tank/2020/04/03/u-s-latinos-among-hardest-hit-by-pay-cuts-job -losses-due-to-coronavirus/.

Lanning, Michael. *African Americans in the Revolutionary War.* New York: Kensington Publishing, 2000.

Lasch, Christopher. *The Culture of Narcissism: American Life in an Age of Diminishing Expectations.* New York: W.W. Norton, 1979.

Lawson, Stephen F. *Black Ballots: Voting Rights in the South.* New York: Columbia University Press, 1976.

LeCount, Ryan Jerome. "Visualizing the Increasing Effect of Racial Resentment on Political Ideology among Whites, 1986 to 2016." *Socius: Sociological Research for a Dynamic World* 4 (2018):1–2.

Lenzi, Tié. "Quais São os Partidos Políticos do Brasil?" Accessed February 20, 2020. https://www.todapolitica.com/partidos-politicos-brasil/.

Levine, Barry and Monique El-Faizy. *All the President's Women: Donald Trump and the Making of a Predator.* New York: Hachette Books, 2019.

Lewis, Simon. "Twitter Erupts Over Donald Trump's Embrace of Daughter Ivanka at RNC." *Time* July 21, 2016. Accessed July 6, 2020. https://time.com/4418524/ ivanka-trump-donald-daughter-touching-reaction/.

Lipsitz, George. *The Possessive Investment in Whiteness: How White People Profit from Identity Politics.* Philadelphia, PA: Temple University Press, 2006.

Llaneras, Kiko. "Bolsonaro Divide o Brasil: Arrasa nas Cidades mais Brancas e mais Ricas." *El País* October 30, 2018. Accessed March 20, 2020. https://brasil.elpais .com/brasil/2018/10/29/actualidad/1540828734_083649.html.

Logan, John R. "Who Are the Other African Americans? Contemporary African and Caribbean Immigrants in the United States." In *Rethinking the Color Line: Readings in Race and Ethnicity,* 4th ed., edited by Charles A. Gallagher, 1343– 1352. New York: McGraw-Hill, 2009.

Louault, Frédéric. "Subverter a Ordem Democrática: Estratégias Legitimadoras dos Movimentos de Direita Radical na Europa e nas Américas." Presentation at II Congresso ABRE (Associação de Brasilianistas na Europa), Paris, France, September 19, 2019.

Luisa, Ingrid. "4 Coisas que te Ensinaram Errado sobre a Inconfidência Mineira." *Super Interessante* April 20, 2018. Accessed May 11, 2020. https://super.abril.com.br/historia/4-coisas-que-te-ensinaram-errado-sobre-a-inconfidencia-mineira/.

Lusher, Adam. "Donald Trump's Father 'Told Staff' to 'Get Rid of Blacks' when Running Property Firm with his Son, FBI Dossier Claims." *The Independent* February 16, 2017. Accessed June 21, 2020. https://www.independent.co.uk/news/world/americas/donald-trump-father-fred-fbi-dossier-trump-management-company-racist-get-rid-of-blacks-dont-rent-to-a7583851.html.

Lustosa, Isabel. *Dom Pedro I*. São Paulo: Companhia das Letras, 2006.

Macdonald, Gareth. "Trump Vows to Bring Drug Production Back to the U.S." 2017. Accessed January 5, 2019 https://www.in-pharmatechnologist.com/Article/2017/01/12/Trump-vows-to-bring-drug-production-back-to-US.

Marchao, Talita. "Bolsonaro Indicar Filho Como Embaixador nos EUA É Nepotismo?" *UOL* July 11, 2019. Accessed November 12, 2020. https://noticias.uol.com.br/politica/ultimas-noticias/2019/07/11/bolsonaro-indicar-filho-como-embaixador-nos-eua-e-nepotismo.htm.

Married Biography. "Kellyanne Conway." June 17, 2020. Accessed July 15, 2020. https://marriedbiography.com/kellyanne-conway-biography/.

Massey, Douglas S. and Nancy A. Denton. *American Apartheid: Segregation and the Making of the Underclass*. Cambridge, MA: Harvard University Press, 1993.

Mathias, Roberta. "A Nossa Bandeira Jamais Será Vermelha: Que Cores Queremos em Nossa Bandeira?" *Vertentes do Cinema* December 13, 2019. Accessed January 15, 2020. https://vertentesdocinema.com/a-nossa-bandeira-jamais-sera-vermelha/.

Matoso, Filipe. "Governo Dilma Tem Aprovação de 9% e Reprovação de 70%, Diz Ibope." *G1*, December 15, 2015. Accessed September 4, 2016. http://g1.globo.com/politica/noticia/2015/12/governo-dilma-tem-aprovacao-de-9-e-reprovacao-de-70-diz-ibope.html.

Máximo, Wellton. "Com 100% das Urnas Apuradas, Bolsonaro Obteve 57,7 Milhões de Votos." *Agência Brasil* October 28, 2018. Accessed March 5, 2020. https://agenciabrasil.ebc.com.br/politica/noticia/2018-10/com-100-das-urnas-apuradas-bolsonaro-teve-577-milhoes-de-votos

McAdam, Doug. *Political Process and the Development of Black Insurgency, 1930–1970*. Chicago, IL: University of Chicago Press, 1982.

Me Too. "About." 2018. Accessed July 6, 2020. https://metoomvmt.org/about/.

Megale, Bela. "Bolsonaro Pediu Fim da Lei que Garante Atendimento a Vítimas de Estupro." *Época* October 12, 2018. Accessed January 8, 2020. https://epoca.globo.com/bela-megale/bolsonaro-pediu-fim-da-lei-que-garante-atendimento-vitimas-de-estupro-23152056.

Megerian, Chris. "What Donald Trump Has Said through the Years about where President Obama Was Born." *LA Times* September 16, 2016. Accessed January 3, 2019. https://www.latimes.com/politics/la-na-pol-trump-birther-timeline-20160916-snap-htmlstory.html.

Meia Hora. "Ataque a Zumbi e a Negros." June 4, 2020, p. 9.

Melo, Débora. "Ciro Gomes sobre Apoio no 2° Turno: 'Ele Não, sem Dúvida.'" *HuffPost Brasil* October 7, 2018. Accessed March 19, 2020. https://www.huffpostbrasil.com/2018/10/07/ciro-gomes-sobre-apoio-no-2o-turno-ele-nao-sem-duvida_a_23553739/.

Memorial da Democracia. "1965 27 de Outubro: Ato 2 Fecha Partidos e Veta Eleição Direta." 2015–2017. Accessed January 11, 2020. http://memorialdademocracia.com.br/card/ato-2-fecha-partidos-e-veta-eleicao-direta.

Mendes, Adriana. "'Nosso Presidente', Afirma Mourão sobre Trump." *Extra* August 8, 2019, p. 11.

Merica, Dan. "Trump's Labor Dept. Pick Admits to Employing Undocumented Worker." *CNN* February 7, 2017. Accessed November 9, 2020. https://www.cnn.com/2017/02/06/politics/andrew-puzder-labor-department-trump-undocumented-worker/index.html.

Messenberg, Débora. "A Direita que Saiu do Armário: A Cosmovisão dos Formadores de Opinião dos Manifestantes de Direita Brasileiros." *Sociedade e Estado* 32, no. 3 (September/December 2017). Accessed March 10, 2020. http://www.scielo.br/scielo.php?pid=S0102-69922017000300621&script=sci_arttext.

Migalhas. "Hélio Bicudo e Janaina Paschoal Pedem Impeachment de Dilma." September 1, 2015. Accessed January 29, 2020. https://www.migalhas.com.br/Quentes/17,MI226205,71043-Helio+Bicudo+e+Janaina+Paschoal+pedem+impeachment+de+Dilma.

Minnesota Compass. "Somali Population: Minnesota, 2013–2017." 2020. Accessed September 20, 2020. https://www.mncompass.org/demographics/cultural-communities/somali.

Mitchell, Sean. Commentary on "Fake News: Desinformação e Discurso de Ódio na Erosão da Democracia Brasileira." Presentation at Columbia University Seminar on Brazil, New York, December 12, 2019.

Moore, Deborah Dash. *B'nai B'rith and the Challenge of Ethnic Leadership*. Albany, NY: SUNY Press.

Moreira, Regina da Luz. "E Ele Voltou... O Brasil no Segundo Governo Vargas." FGV CPDOC, 2020. Accessed May 29, 2020. https://cpdoc.fgv.br/producao/dossies/AEraVargas2/artigos/PreparandoaVolta/ParlamentarAusente.

Mori, Leticia. "Eleições 2018: Como Votos em Branco e Nulos Podem Beneficiar Bolsonaro no 2° Turno." *BBC News Brasil* October 16, 2018. Accessed March 19, 2020. https://www.bbc.com/portuguese/brasil-45831774.

Morris, Aldon D. *The Scholar Denied: W. E. B. Du Bois and the Birth of Modern Sociology*. Los Angeles, CA: University of California Press, 2015.

Moura, Maurício and Juliano Corbellini. *A Eleição Disruptiva: Por que Bolsonaro Venceu*. Rio de Janeiro: Editora Record, 2019.

Moynihan, Daniel Patrick. "The Negro Family: The Case for National Action." United States Department of Labor, March 1965. Accessed May 20, 2021. http://www.dol.gov/dol/aboutdol/history/webid-moynihan.htm.

Murse, Tom. "US Presidents With No Political Experience." *Though.Co* January 16, 2020. Accessed June 21, 2020. https://www.thoughtco.com/does-president-need-political-experience-4046139.

Murthy, Dhiraj. "Towards a Sociological Understanding of Social Media: Theorizing Twitter." *Sociology* 46, no. 6 (December 2012): 1059–1073.

Myrdal, Gunnar. *An American Dilemma*. New York: Routledge, 1944.

National Archives. "Declaration of Independence: A Transcript." Accessed July 5, 2019. https://www.archives.gov/founding-docs/declaration-transcript.

National Congress of American Indians. "Demographics." June 1, 2020. Accessed July 4, 2020. http://www.ncai.org/about-tribes/demographics.

NBC. "The Celebrity Apprentice." Accessed June 29, 2020. https://www.nbc.com/the-celebrity-apprentice.

NBC News. "Melania Trump: 'I'm Honored to Be Your First Lady.'" January 20, 2017. Accessed October 30, 2020. https://www.nbcnews.com/video/watch-donald-trump-s-full-inaugural-address-859186755817.

Neto, Felipe. "Donald Trump Isn't the Worst Covid President. Just Ask Brazilians." *New York Times* Opinion. *YouTube* July 15, 2020. Accessed July 15, 2020. https://www.youtube.com/watch?v=XvK6Y_txWEE

Neves, Márcio. "Protesto anti-Dilma Reúne Milhares em SP; ato Registrou Brigas e Agressão." *UOL* November 15, 2014. Accessed February 12, 2020. https://noticias.uol.com.br/politica/ultimas-noticias/2014/11/15/protesto-anti-dilma-em-sp-reune-2500-e-e-marcado-por-brigas-e-agressao.htm.

Newport, Frank. "American Jews, Politics and Israel." *Gallup* August 27, 2019. Accessed July 14, 2020. https://news.gallup.com/opinion/polling-matters/265898/american-jews-politics-israel.aspx.

Ngai, Mae M. *Impossible Subjects: Illegal Aliens and the Making of Modern America*. Princeton, NJ: Princeton University Press, 2004.

1News Brasil. "Filho de Bolsonaro Pede Orações Após Pai Ser Esfaqueado." September 6, 2018. Accessed March 10, 2020. https://www.1news.com.br/noticia/523258/noticias/apos-facada-jair-bolsonaro-e-levado-as-pressas-para-hospital-e-passa-por-cirurgia-301-06092018.

Noe-Bustamante, Luis, Antonio Flores and Sono Shah. "Facts on Hispanics of Cuban Origin in the United States, 2017." *Pew Research Center* September 16, 2019. Accessed May 19, 2021. https://www.pewresearch.org/ hispanic/fact-sheet/u-s-hispanics-facts-on-cuban-origin-latinos/.

Nogueira, Luiz Fernando Veloso. "Expectativa de Vida e Mortalidade de Escravos: Uma Análise da Freguesia do Divino Espírito Santo do Lamim – MG (1859–1888)." *Histórica* nº. 51 (December 2011). Accessed May 19, 2020. http://www.historica.arquivoestado.sp.gov.br/materias/anteriores/edicao51/materia01/.

Nogueira, Oracy. "Preconceito Racial de Marca e Preconceito Racial de Origem: Sugestão de um Quadro de Referência para a Interpretação do Material sobre Relações Raciais no Brasil." *Tempo Social* 19, no. 1 (1954): 287–308.

Nossa Política. "Geisel: Bolsonaro É "um Mau Militar." *Nossapolitica.net* December 29, 2017. Accessed January 7, 2020. https://nossapolitica.net/2017/12/geisel-bolsonaro-mau-militar/.

Noticias.uol.com.br. "Após Morte no Carrefour, Bolsonaro Diz Ser Daltônico: 'Todos Têm a Mesma Cor.'" November 21, 2020. Accessed November 22, 2020.

https://noticias.uol.com.br/ultimas-noticias/agencia-estado/2020/11/21/apos-morte
-no-carrefour-bolsonaro-diz-ser-daltonico-todos-tem-a-mesma-cor.htm.

NPR. "Bolsonaro Visits The U.S." March 17, 2019. Accessed April 1, 2020. https://
www.npr.org/2019/03/17/704209684/bolsonaro-visits-the-u-s.

O Dia. "Aprovação do Governo Dilma Cai de 36 para 31%, Aponta Pesquisa." June
19, 2014. Accessed February 11, 2020. https://odia.ig.com.br/noticia/brasil/2014
-06-19/aprovacao-do-governo-dilma-cai-de-36-para-31-aponta-pesquisa-cni-ibope
.html.

O Globo. "O Primeiro Discurso aos Colegas de Congresso." January 2, 2019, p.10.

———. "Pouca Diversidade e Coesão Ideológica no Primeiro Escalão do Novo
Governo." January 2, 2019, p. 15.

Oliveira, Eduardo. "A Idéia de Império e a Fundação da Monarquia Constitucional
no Brasil (Portugal-Brasil, 1772–1824)." *Tempo* 9, no. 18 (January/June 2005).
Accessed May 14, 2020. https://doi.org/10.1590/S1413-77042005000100003.

Oliveira, Fabricio. "Bolsonaro Publica Desculpas a Maria do Rosário após Ordem
Judicial." *Regional Press* June 14, 2019. Accessed on December 18, 2019. https://
www.rp10.com.br/2019/06/bolsonaro-publica-desculpas-a-maria-do-rosario-apos
-ordem-judicial/.

Oliveira, Laiana Lannes de. "A Frente Negra Brasileira: Política e Questão Racial
nos anos 1930." Master's thesis in Political History, Universidade do Estado do
Rio de Janeiro, 2002.

Oliver, Melvin L. and Thomas M. Shapiro. *Black Wealth/White Wealth: A New
Perspective on Racial Inequality*. New York: Routledge, 1995.

On the Issues. "Donald Trump on Jobs: 2016 Republican nominee for President; 2000
Reform Primary Challenger for President." Accessed January 9, 2019. http://www
.ontheissues.org/2016/Donald_Trump_Jobs.htm.

O Povo Online. "Nordestinos São Alvo de Preconceito após Resultado do 1° Turno
das Eleições; Prática É Crime." October 8, 2018. Accessed March 19, 2020. https://
www.opovo.com.br/noticias/politica/2018/10/nordestinos-sao-alvo-de-preconceito
-apos-fim-do-1-turno-das-eleicoes.html.

Otta, Lui Aiko. "Em Entrevista a Rádio, Damares Aconselha Pais de Meninas a Fugir
do País para Evitar Violência." *Estadão* February 15, 2019. Accessed May 20,
2020. https://brasil.estadao.com.br/noticias/geral,em-entrevista-a-radio-damares
-aconselha-pais-de-meninas-a-fugir-do-pais-para-evitar-violencia,70002722916.

Oyama, Thaís. *Tormenta: O Governo Bolsonaro: Crises, Intrigas e Segredos*. São
Paulo: Companhia das Letras, 2020.

Pauls, Elizabeth Prine. "Trail of Tears." Encyclopaedia Britannica. Accessed October
14, 2019. https://www.britannica.com/event/Trail-of-Tears.

Park, Robert Ezra and Herbert Adolphus Miller. *Old World Traits Transplanted*. New
York: Harper, 1921.

Pedroso, Osni. "Deputado Jair Bolsonaro: Sou Contra Quotas Raciais." *YouTube*
March 7, 2014. Accessed January 17, 2020. https://www.youtube.com/watch?v
=WkpVd0U--fc.

Penha-Lopes, Vânia. "What Next? On Race and Assimilation in the United States and
Brazil." *Journal of Black Studies* 26, no. 6 (1996): 809–826.

———. "It's a Family Affair: Parenting, Domestic Participation, and Gender among Black Men." Unpublished doctoral dissertation, Department of Sociology, New York University, 1999.

———. "Whites Are Also People of Color." viagensdapoetisa.blogspot.com, June 3, 2010.

———. "Race and Ethnic Identity Formation in Brazil and the U.S.: Three Case Studies." *Afro-Hispanic Review* 29, 2 (Fall 2010): 251–262.

———. *Pioneiros: Cotistas na Universidade Brasileira*. Jundiaí: Paco Editorial, 2013.

———. *Confronting Affirmative Action in Brazil: University Quota Students and the Quest for Racial Justice*. Lanham, MD: Lexington Books, 2017.

Peoples, Steve. "Ben Carson on Donald Trump's Heels, Poll Suggests." *CBC* September 15, 2015. Accessed June 30, 2020. https://www.cbc.ca/news/world/carson-versus-trump-1.3229721.

Pereira, Ivan and Arielle Mitropoulos. "A Year of COVID-19: What Was Going on in the US in March 2020." *ABC News* March 6, 2021. Accessed May 21, 2021. https://abcnews.go.com/ Health/year-covid-19-us-march-2020/story?id=76204691.

Pereira, Moacir. "Dilma É Reeleita com 51,64% dos Votos." October 26, 2014. Accessed February 11, 2020. http://wp.clicrbs.com.br/moacirpereira/2014/10/26/dilma-lidera-apuracao-com-5132-dos-votos/?topo=67,2,18,,,67&2,18,,,67.

Perissinotto, Renato M. *Classes Dominantes e Hegemonia na República Velha*. Campinas: Unicamp, 1994.

Pessoa, Gabriela Sá and Paulo Saldaña. "Janaina Paschoal É a Deputada Estadual mais Votada da História." *Folha de São Paulo* October 7, 2018. Accessed April 8, 2020. https://www1.folha.uol.com.br/poder /2018/10/janaina-paschoal-e-a-deputada-estadual-mais-votada-da-historia.shtml.

Phillips, Tom. "Setback for Bolsonaro after Poor Results in Brazil Local Elections." *The Guardian* November 16, 2020. Accessed November 29, 2020. https://www.theguardian.com /world/2020/nov/16/setback-for-bolsonaro-after-poor-results-in-brazil-local-elections.

Pinho, Patrícia de Santana. "White but Not Quite: Tones and Overtones of Whiteness in Brazil." *Small Axe* 29 (July 2009): 39–56.

Piza, Edith. "Porta de Vidro: Entrada para a Branquitude." In *Psicologia Social do Racismo: Estudos sobre Branquitude e Branqueamento no Brasil,* 2nd ed., edited by Iray Carone and Maria Aparecida Silva Bento, 59–90. Petrópolis, RJ: Editora Vozes, 2003.

Poder360. "No 2º Turno, Bolsonaro Venceu em 15 Estados e no DF; Haddad, em 11." October 28, 2018. Accessed March 5, 2020. https://www.poder360.com.br/eleicoes/no-2o-turno-bolsonaro-venceu-em-16-estados-haddad-em-11/.

Polenberg, Richard. *One Nation Divisible: Class, Race, and Ethnicity in the United States Since 1938*. New York: Penguin, 1991.

Plummer, Deborah L. *Some of My Best Friends Are…: The Daunting Challenges and Untapped Benefits of Cross-racial Friendships*. New York: Penguin Press, 2019.

Postman, Neil. *Amusing Ourselves to Death: Public Discourse in the Age of Show Business*. New York: Penguin, 1985.

Presidência da República. "Lei Nº 3.353, de 13 de Maio de 1888." Accessed May 20, 2020. http://www.planalto.gov.br/ccivil_03/leis/lim/LIM3353.htm.

―――. Constituição da República Federativa do Brasil de 1967. Accessed May 31, 2020. http://www.planalto.gov.br/ccivil_03/Constituicao/Constituicao67.htm.

―――. Constituição da República Federativa do Brasil de 1988. Accessed June 3, 2020. http://www.planalto.gov.br/ccivil_03/Constituicao/Constituicao.htm.

Presidency of the Republic of Brazil. "Elections 2018: Understand how Brazilian Elections Work." Accessed January 11, 2020. http://www.brazil.gov.br/about-brazil/news/2018/08/understand-how-brazilian-elections-work.

Presidentes do Brasil. Accessed May 25, 2020. https://presidentes-do-brasil.info/brasil-republica/republica-velha.html.

Previdelli, Amanda. "Protesto contra Copa faz Dilma Chamar Reunião de Emergência." *Huff Post* January 27, 2014. Accessed February 11, 2020. https://www.huffpostbrasil.com/2014/01/27/protesto-contra-copa-faz-dilma-chamar-reuniao-de-emergencia_n_4673601.

Pronotícia. "Revolta da Chibata." May 17, 2016. Accessed May 25, 2020. https://www.pronoticia.com/educacao/historia/revolta-chibata.html.

Puente, Maria. "Omarosa Gets Job in Trump White House as 'Public Liaison' Leader." *USA Today* January 4, 2017. Accessed November 6, 2020. https://www.usatoday.com/story/life/people/2017/01/04/omarosa-gets-job-trump-white-house-public-liaison-leader/96167028/.

Putti, Alexandre. "São Paulo É o Estado que Mais Mata Pessoas Trans no Brasil, Mostra Relatório." *Carta Capital* January 29, 2020. Accessed January 29, 2020. https://www.cartacapital.com.br/diversidade/sao-paulo-e-o-estado-que-mais-mata-pessoas-trans-no-brasil-mostra-relatorio/.

Pye, Michael. *Maximum City: The Biography of New York*. McClelland & Stewart Ltd, 1993.

Queiroga, Louise. "Embaixada da Alemanha Explica o Nazismo e É Contestada por Brasileiros." *O Globo* September 17, 2018. Accessed February 15, 2020. https://oglobo.globo.com/sociedade/embaixada-da-alemanha-explica-nazismo-e-contestada-por-brasileiros-2-23074988.

Rahn, Will. "Steve Bannon and the Alt-right: A Primer." *CBC News* August 19, 2016. Accessed July 16, 2020. https://www.cbsnews.com/news/steve-bannon-and-the-alt-right-a-primer/.

Ramalho, Renan. "STF Arquiva Inquérito contra Bolsonaro por Falas sobre Preta Gil." *G1* May 27, 2015. Accessed February 3, 2020. http://g1.globo.com/politica/noticia/2015/05/stf-arquiva-inquerito-contra-bolsonaro-por-falas-sobre-preta-gil.html.

Raymond, Adam K. and Matt Stieb. "Trump Hired Them, Then He Called Them Incompetent." *New York Magazine* February 13, 2020. Accessed April 10, 2020. https://nymag.com/intelligencer/2020/02/dumb-as-a-rock-9-times-trump-insulted-people...

Real, Evan. "Kellyanne Conway's 'Trump Revolutionary Wear' Inauguration Outfit Sets Twitter Abuzz." *Us Weekly* January 20, 2017. Accessed October 26, 2020. https://www.usmagazine.com/celebrity-news/news/the-internet-reacts-to-kellyanne-conways-inaguration-outfit-w462120/.

Redação Pragmatismo. "'Mamadeira Erótica de Haddad': A Fake News que Viralizou nas Redes Sociais." *Pragmatismo Político* October 5, 2018. Accessed January 16, 2020. https://www.pragmatismopolitico.com.br/2018/10/mamadeira -erotica-de-haddad-fake-news.html.

Redação RBA. "Exterior: Aécio Vence em Miami e Israel; Dilma Triunfa na Palestina e em Cuba." October 27, 2014. Accessed February 11, 2020. https://www.redeb-rasilatual.com.br/eleicoes-2014/2014/10/exterior-aecio-vence-nos-eua-e-em-israel -dilma-triunfa-na-palestina-8178/.

———. "Apoiador de Bolsonaro Mata Mestre de Capoeira a Facadas em Salvador." October 8, 2018. Accessed March 28, 2020. https://www.redebrasilatual.com.br/ eleicoes-2018/2018/10/violencia-apoiador-de-bolsonaro-mata-capoeirista-em-salvador/.

Rede Brasil Atual. "Em 27 Anos como Deputado, Bolsonaro Tem Dois Projetos Aprovados." May 6, 2018. Accessed January 8, 2020. https://www.redebrasilatual .com.br/politica/2018/05/em-27-anos-como-deputado-bolsonaro-tem-dois-proje-tos-aprovados/.

Rede TV! "'Mariana Godoy Entrevista' Recebe Jair Bolsonaro Nesta Sexta-feira." October 27, 2017. Accessed February 2, 2020. https://tvuol.uol.com.br/video /mariana-godoy-entrevista-recebe-jair-bolsonaro-nesta-sextafeira-27-04028D1 C3460D0996326/.

Reference.com. "Why Did the American Civil War Start?" Accessed October 26, 2019. https://www.reference.com/history/did-american-civil-war-start -88285c53d1f5f74c.

———. "How Many U.S. Presidents Have There Been?" Accessed June 6, 2020. https://www.reference.com/history/many-u-s-presidents-d217fa6dc09ecfd4.

Reilly, Mollie. "Former Miss Universe Says Trump Called Her 'Miss Piggy,' 'Miss Housekeeping.'" *HuffPost* May 23, 2016. Accessed July 14, 2020. https://www .huffpostbrasil.com/entry/alicia-machado-donald-trump_n_57431d11e4b00e0 9e89f8aa4?ri18n=true.

Reis, Yolanda. "A Dança da Cadeira de Bolsonaro: Todos os Ministros Substituídos desde o Começo do Governo." *Rolling Stone* June 18, 2020. Accessed November 29, 2020. https://rollingstone.uol.com.br/ /noticia/danca-da-cadeira-de-bolsonaro-t odos-os-ministros-substituidos-desde-o-comeco-do-governo/.

Reiter, Bernd. *The Dialectics of Citizenship: Exploring Privilege, Exclusion, and Racialization.* East Lansing, MI: Michigan University Press, 2013.

Resende, Erica Simone A. *Americanidade, Puritanismo e Política Externa: A (Re) produção da Ideologia Puritana e a Construção da Identidade nas Práticas Discursivas da Política Externa Norte-americana.* Rio de Janeiro: Contracapa, 2012.

Revista Forum. "Maria do Rosário Doa Indenização Recebida de Bolsonaro para Combate à Violência contra as Mulheres." November 19, 2019. Accessed November 19, 2019. https://revistaforum.com.br/politica/ /maria-do-rosario-do a-indenizacao-recebida-de-bolsonaro-para-combate-a-violencia-contra-mulheres/.

Reyes, Luis O. "The Puerto Rican Education Pipeline: New York City, New York State, and the United States." *Center for Puerto Rican Studies Hunter College, CUNY* (January 2017): 1–6. Accessed May 19, 2021. https://centropr.hunter.cuny .edu/sites/default/files/data_briefs/RB2016-12_EDUCATION.pdf

Rezzutti, Paulo. "As Escapadas de D Pedro II." *Tok de História* October 10, 2014. Accessed May 18, 2020. https://tokdehistoria.com.br/tag/baronesa-de-sorocaba/.

Riley, Glenda. *Divorce: An American Tradition*. New York: Oxford University Press, 1991.

Robertson. Lori and Robert Farley. "Fact Check: The Controversy over Trump's Inauguration Crowd Size." *USA Today* January 24, 2017. Accessed October 17, 2020. https://www.usatoday.com/story/news/politics/2017/01/24/fact-check-inauguration-crowd-size/96984496/.

Rodrigues, André Figueiredo and Jonis Freire. "O Preço dos Escravos e suas 'Cores' nas Escravarias dos Inconfidentes Mineiros da Comarca do Rio das Mortes, nas Minas Gerais de 1789 a 1791." *Estudos Ibero-Americanos* 44, no. 3 (September-December 2018): 548–562. https://doi.org/10.15448/1980-864X.2018.3.29237.

Roediger, David. *The Wages of Whiteness: Race and the Making of the American Working Class*. New York: Verso Press, 1991.

Romanews. "Juiz Autoriza Transferência de Esfaqueador de Bolsonaro." March 2, 2020. Accessed March 2, 2020. https://www.romanews.com.br/noticias/juiz-autoriza-transferencia-de-esfaqueador-de-bolsonaro/71230/.

Roos, Dave. "Why Was the Electoral College Created?" *History.com* July 10, 2020. Accessed October 4, 2020. https://www.history.com/news/electoral-college-founding-fathers-constitutional-convention.

———. "5 Presidents Who Lost the Popular Vote but Won the Election." *History.com* July 23, 2020. Accessed October 4, 2020. https://www.history.com/news/presidents-electoral-college-popular-vote.

Roper Center. "How Groups Voted in 2008." 2020. Accessed November 24, 2020. https://ropercenter.cornell.edu/how-groups-voted-2008.

Ross, Andrew S. and Damian J. Rivers. "Discursive Deflection: Accusation of "Fake News" and the Spread of Mis- and Disinformation in the Tweets of President Trump." *Social Media + Society* (April-June 2018): 1–12. Accessed July 16, 2020. https://journals.sagepub.com/doi/pdf/10.1177/2056305118776010.

Rossi, Amanda. "Eleições 2018: O Peso de Cada Região do Brasil na Votação para Presidente." *BBC News Brasil* October 8, 2018. Accessed October 9, 2018. https://www.bbc.com/portuguese/brasil-45780864.

———. Julia Dias Carneiro, and Juliana Gragnani. "#EleNão: A Manifestação Histórica Liderada por Mulheres no Brasil Vista por Quatro Ângulos." *BBC News* September 30, 2018. Accessed October 9, 2018. https://www.bbc.com/portuguese/brasil-45700013.

Rubin, Lillian B. *Families on the Fault Line: America's Working Class Speaks about the Family, the Economy, Race and Ethnicity*. New York: Harper Perennial, 1994.

Russo Jr., Carlos. "Por que Roy Cohn É o Paradigma de Olavo de Carvalho?" *Jornal Opção* March 10, 2019. Accessed June 22, 2020. https://www.jornalopcao.com.br/opcao-cultural/por-que-roy-cohn-e-o-paradigma-de-olavo-de-carvalho-169569/.

Russonello, Giovanni. "In a Polarized Era, Even the Coronavirus's Death Toll Is in Dispute. A Pew Study Points to Why." *New York Times on Politics* May 11, 2020. Accessed May 11, 2020. nytdirect@nytimes.com.

Ryan, Camille. "Computer and Internet Use in the United States: 2016." U.S. Census Bureau August 2018. Accessed November 26, 2020. https://www.census.gov/content/dam/Census/library/publications/2018/acs/ACS-39.pdf.

Saflate, Vladimir. "Lá Onde Está o seu Maior Perigo." *Folha de São Paulo* April 8, 2016.

Sago, Renata, Bem Markus, and Jude Joffe-Block. "Sick of Political Parties, Unaffiliated Voters Are Changing Politics." *NPR* February 28, 2016. Accessed June 30, 2020. https://www.npr.org/2016/02/28/467961962/sick-of-political-parties-unaffiliated-voters-are-changing-politics.

Saint-Clair, Clóvis. *Bolsonaro: O Homem que Peitou o Exército e Desafia a Democracia*. Rio de Janeiro: Máquina de Livros, 2018.

Salles, Fernanda. "Homem que Esfaqueou Capoeirista Desmente que Seja Eleitor de Bolsonaro." *Terça Livre* October 11, 2018. Accessed March 28, 2020. https://www.tercalivre.com.br/homem-que-esfaqueou-capoeirista-desmente-que-seja-eleitor-de-bolsonaro/.

Sanches, Mariana. "Perfil: Janaína Paschoal e a 'República da Cobra' que Tomou Conta das Redes." *O Globo* April 6, 2016. Accessed January 29, 2020. https://oglobo.globo.com/brasil/perfil-janaina-paschoal-a-republica-da-cobra-que-tomou-conta-das-redes-19026078.

Sarmiento, Isabella Gomez. "After Controversial Leaders Step Down, The Women's March Tries Again in 2020." *NPR* January 17, 2020. Accessed November 7, 2020. https://www.npr.org/2020/01/17/797107259/after-controversial-leaders-step-down-the-womens-march-tries-again-in-2020.

Sassine, Vinicius. "O Boletim de Bolsonaro nas Escolas Militares que Frequentou nos Anos 70 e 80." *Época* November 19, 2018. Accessed January 6, 2020. https://epoca.globo.com/o-boletim-de-bolsonaro-nas-escolas-militares-que-frequentou-nos-anos-70-80-23243285.

Schenawolf, Harry. "Black Soldiers in the Continental Army." *Revolutionary War Journal*, May 9, 2013. Accessed September 28, 2019. www.revolutionarywarjournal.com/blacks-in-the-continental-army/.

Schneider, Christopher J. "Social Media and e-Public Sociology." In *The Public Sociology Debate: Ethics and Engagement*, edited by Ariane Hanemaayer and Christopher J. Schneider, chapter 8. Vancouver, BC: UBC Press, 2014.

Schreiber, Mariana. "'Bolsonaro Gosta do STF quando lhe Dá Decisão Positiva. Se É Negativa, Prefere Não Brincar de Democracia', Diz Professora da FGV." *BBC News Brasil* May 30, 2020. Accessed May 30, 2020. https://www.bbc.com/portuguese/brasil-52857992.

Schwarcz, Lilia Moritz. *Sobre o Autoritarismo Brasileiro*. São Paulo: Companhia das Letras, 2019.

Scirea, Bruna. "'Contundente de Forma Irônica: Conheça Janaina Paschoal, a Autora do Pedido de Impeachment." *Diário Gaucho* April 15, 2016. Assessed January 20, 2020. http://diariogaucho.clicrbs.com.br/rs/noticia/2016/04/contundente-de-forma-ironica-conheca-janaina-paschoal-a-autora-do-pedido-de-impeachment-5779284.html.

Senra, Ricardo. "'Ele Soa como Nós': Ex-líder da Ku Klux Klan Elogia Bolsonaro, mas Critica Proximidade com Israel." *Terra* October 16, 2018. Accessed October 16, 2018. https://www.terra.com.br/noticias/eleicoes/ele-soa-como-nos-ex-lider-da -ku-klux-klan-elogia-bolsonaro-mas-critica-proximidade-com-israel,abbbd712a ab704bdb1d5461c491529ec8p1ypmd7.html?fbclid=IwAR0IDhLSQ7tTVSLoXuZ 8Wfjk3ttcRGg7jVKcQ6dTSgIhEHzahMTyneFTwvk.

Shalders, André. "Bolsonaro nos EUA: O que Esperar do Primeiro Encontro do Presidente Brasileiro com Trump." *BBC News Brasil* March 19, 2019. Accessed November 27, 2020. https://www.bbc.com/portuguese/international-47621289.

Shapiro, Esther and Richard Alan Shapiro. *Dynasty*. Los Angeles, CA: Aaron Spelling Productions, 1981–1989.

Shear, Michael. "Trump Sexual Misconduct Accusations Repeated by Several Women." *New York Times* December 11, 2017. Accessed July 4, 2020. https:// www.nytimes.com/2017/12/11/us/politics/trump-accused-sexual-misconduct .html.

Silva, Débora. "História do Partido Socialismo e Liberdade (PSOL)." *Estudo Prático* November 7, 2015. Accessed March 2, 2020. https://www.estudopratico.com.br/ historia-do-partido-socialismo-e-liberdade-psol/

Silva, Sandro Dutra e. "'Heroes' of the Sertão: The Bandeirantes as a Symbolic Category for the Study of Brazilian West Colonization." *Revista Territórios & Fronteiras* 11, no. 1 (January-July 2018): 60–76.

Silva, Vinicius Carlos da. "Diretas Já." *Portal São Francisco*. Accessed June 2, 2020. https://www.portalsaofrancisco.com.br/historia-do-brasil/diretas-ja.

Silver, Michael G. "Eugenics and Compulsory Sterilization Laws: Providing Redress for the Victims of a Shameful Era in United States History." In *Structured Inequality in the United States: Critical Discussions on the Continuing Significance of Race, Ethnicity, and Gender,* 2nd ed., edited by Adalberto Aguirre, Jr. and David V. Baker, 340–350. Upper Saddle River, NJ: Pearson Prentice Hall, 2008.

Silvério, Valter Roberto. "Negros em Movimento: A Construção da Autonomia pela Afirmação de Direitos." In *Levando a Raça a Sério: Ação Afirmativa e Universidade*, edited by Joaze Bernardino e Daniela Galdino, 39–69. Rio de Janeiro: DP & A Editora, 2004.

Silverstein, Jason. "White House Website Removes Pages for LGBT Rights, Climate Change, Regulations, Spanish." *New York Daily News* January 24, 2017. Accessed October 28, 2020. https://www.nydailynews.com/news/politics/white -house-removes-lgbt-climate-change-spanish-webpages-article-1.2954157.

Simões, Eduardo. "Junho/2016: Laudo Mostra que Dilma Não Participou de Irregularidades." *Exame* July 6, 2016. Accessed July 6, 2016. https://exame .abril.com.br/brasil/laudo-mostra-que-dilma-nao-participou-de-irregularidades/ ?fbclid=IwAR1jYgud-Mg5Qn1D6wteC7txq2Wk83lNIZY27K2hWITzOmjFj6q7 1mQ4v1A.

Sims, Alexandra and Andrew Buncombe. "Who Voted for Donald Trump? Mostly White Men and Women, Voting Data Reveals." *Independent* November 9, 2016. Accessed October 4, 2020. https://www.independent.co.uk/news/world/americas

/us-politics/who-voted-donald-trump-white-men-and-women-most-responsible-new-president-elect-voting-data-reveals-a7407996.html.

Smidt, Corwin. *American Evangelicals Today*. Rowman & Littlefield, 2013.

Smith, Anthony. "Donald Trump's Star of David Hillary Clinton Meme Was Created by White Supremacists." 2016. Accessed January 4, 2019. https://mic.com/articles/147711/donald-trump-s-star-of-david-hillary-clinton-meme-was-created-by-white-supremacists#.8Yo8CHqng.

Smith, David Norman. "Authoritarianism Reimagined: The Riddle of Trump's Base." *The Sociological Quarterly* 60, no. 2 (2019): 210–223. https://doi.org/10.1080/00380253.2019.1593061.

———— and Eric Hanley. "The Anger Games: Who Voted for Donald Trump in the 2016 Election, and Why? *Critical Sociology* 44, no. 2 (2018): 195–212.

———— and Eric Hanley. "Whiter Than White: Patterns of Race, Class, and Prejudice in the Divided Midwest." In *Political Landscapes of Donald Trump*, edited by Barney Warf. New York: Routledge, 2020.

Snipp, C. Matthew. "The First Americans." In *Race and Ethnicity in Society: The Changing Landscape*, 4th ed., edited by Elizabeth Higginbotham and Margaret L. Andersen, 52–59. Boston, MA: Cengage Learning, 2016.

Só História. "Inconfidência Mineira." Accessed May 10, 2020. https://www.sohistoria.com.br/ef2/inconfidencia/.

Sokoloff, Natalie. *Black Women and White Women in the Professions: Occupational Segregation by Race and Gender, 1960–1980*. New York: Routledge, 1992.

Sonneland, Holly K. and Nicki Fleischner. "Chart: How U.S. Latinos Voted in the 2016 Presidential Election." *Americas Society/Council of the Americas* November 10, 2016. Accessed October 4, 2020. https://www.as-coa.org/articles/chart-how-us-latinos-voted-2016-presidential-election.

Sousa, Judite. *Político Esfaqueado ou É Morto ou É Eleito*. Alfragide, Portugal: Oficina do Livro, 2019.

Souza, Jessé. *Subcidadania Brasileira: Para Entender o País além do Jeitinho Brasileiro*. Rio de Janeiro: Editora Casa da Palavra, 2018.

————. *A Elite do Atraso: Da Escravidão a Bolsonaro*. Rio de Janeiro: GMT Editores, 2019.

Sperling, Nicole. "Ava DuVernay's Fight to Tell the True Story of the Central Park Five." *Vanity Fair* May 17, 2019. Accessed July 1, 2020. https://www.vanityfair.com/hollywood/2019/05/the-true-story-of-the-central-park-five.

Statista Research Department. "Percentage of Housing Units with Telephones in the United States from 1920 to 2008." September 30, 2010. Accessed November 25, 2020. https://www.statista.com/statistics/189959/housing-units-with-telephones-in-the-united-states-since-1920.

Steinberg, Stephen. "How Jewish Quotas Began." *Commentary* September 1971. Accessed December 2, 2019. https://www.commentarymagazine.com/articles/how-jewish-quotas-began/.

————. *The Ethnic Myth: Race, Ethnicity, and Class in America*. New York: Atheneum, 1981.

Steinbuch, Yaron and Ruth Brown. "Omarosa Fired, 'Physically Dragged' from the White House." *New York Post* December 13, 2017. Accessed November 6, 2020. https://nypost.com/2017/12/13/omarosa-is-leaving-the-white-house/.

Steinbugler, Amy. "Loving across Racial Divides." In *Race and Ethnicity in Society: The Changing Landscape*, 4th ed., edited by Elizabeth Higginbotham and Margaret L. Andersen, 208–213. Boston, MA: Cengage Learning, 2016.

Strauss, Valerie. "The Trump Administration Has a Lot to Learn about African American History. Here's a Reading List." *The Washington Post* March 7, 2017. Accessed January 25, 2020.https://www.washingtonpost.com/news/answer-sheet/wp/2017/03/07/trump-administration-has-a-lot-to-learn-about-african-american-history-heres-a-reading-list/.

Struck, Jean-Philip. "Há 50 Anos, Brasil Deixava de Ser 'Estados Unidos do Brasil.'" *DW* March 15, 2017. Accessed June 2, 2020. https://www.dw.com/pt-br/h%C3%A1-50-anos-brasil-deixava-de-ser-estados-unidos-do-brasil/a-37946427.

Strum, Philippa. *Mendez v. Westminster: School Desegregation and Mexican-American Rights*. Lawrence, KS: University Press of Kansas, 2010.

Swift, Nicky. "President Trump's Awkward Moments with Ivanka." *YouTube* June 23, 2018. Accessed July 6, 2020. https://www.youtube.com/watch?v=6h8XzB6-m1s.

Tabuchi, Hiroki. "Coal Mining Jobs Trump Would Bring Back No Longer Exist." *New York Times* March 29, 2017. Accessed January 5, 2019. https://www.nytimes.com/2017/03/29/business/coal-jobs-trump-appalachia.html.

Takala, Rudy. "Trump Slams CNN: 'Clinton News Network.'" *Washington Examiner* September 18, 2016. Accessed July 16, 2020. https://www.washingtonexaminer.com/trump-slams-cnn-clinton-news-network.

Tannenbaum, Frank. *Slave and Citizen: The Negro in the Americas*. New York: Vintage Books, 1947.

Taparata, Evan. "The US Has Come a Long Way since its First, Highly Restrictive Naturalization Law." *Public Radio International* July 4, 2016. Accessed December 1, 2019. https://www.pri.org/stories/2016-07-04/us-has-come-long-way-its-first-highly-restrictive-naturalization-law.

Tavares, Joelmir. "Quilombos Citados por Bolsonaro Rebatem Crítica." *Folha de São Paulo* May 3, 2018. Accessed February 3, 2020. https://www1.folha.uol.com.br/poder/2018/05/quilombos-citados-por-bolsonaro-rebatem-critica.shtml.

Taylor, Kate. "Porn Star Stormy Daniels Is Taking a Victory Lap after Michael Cohen's Guilty Plea. Here's a Timeline of Trump's Many Marriages and Rumored Affairs." *Business Insider* August 25, 2018. Accessed June 29, 2020. https://www.businessinsider.com/trump-melania-stormy-daniels-affairs-marriages+//////-time-line-2018-3.

Teixeira, Daniel Bustamante. "As Jornadas de Junho de 2013 e a Crise da Democracia." *Revista IHU Online* July 11, 2018. Accessed February 11, 2020. http://www.ihu.unisinos.br/78-noticias/580737-as-jornadas-de-junho-de-2013-e-a-crise-da-democracia.

Telles, Edward E. *Race in Another America: The Significance of Skin Color in Brazil.* Princeton, NJ: Princeton University Press, 2004.

———— and René Flores. "Not Just Color: Whiteness, Nation, and Status in Latin America." *Hispanic American/ Historical Review* 93, no. 3 (2013): 411–451.

Tenpas, Kathryn Dunn. "Tracking Turnover in the Trump Administration." *Brookings* November 2020. Accessed November 28, 2020. www.brookings.edu/research/ tracking-turnover-in-the-trump-administration/.

Terra.com.br. "Dilma: Manifestações contra a Copa São o Preço da Democracia." June 4, 2014. Accessed February 11, 2020. https://www.terra.com.br/noticias/ brasil/politica/dilma-manifestacoes-contra-copa-sao-o-preco-da-democracia,1f01 d243ec466410VgnCLD200000b1bf46d0RCRD.html.

————. Relembre quem já Foi Demitido no Governo Bolsonaro." January 29, 2020. Accessed June 7, 2020. https://www.terra.com.br/noticias/relembre-quem-ja-foi -demitido-no-governo-bolsonaro,6b5447208171253ca2473eb20b74306a7bma8pp r.h.

The Dialogue. "High Rates of Violence Against Women in Latin America Despite Femicide Legislation: Possible Steps Forward." October 15, 2018. Accessed June 8, 2020. https://www.thedialogue.org/blogs/2018/10/high-rates-of-violence -against-women-in-latin-america-despite-femicide-legislation-possible-steps -forward/.

The Economist. "Brazil Takes off." November 12, 2009. https://www.economist.com /leaders/2009/11/12/brazil-takes-off Accessed January 13, 2020.

————. "Rankings: The World Economy 2017." https://worldinfigures.com/rankings /topic/8 Accessed January 13, 2020.

The Editors of the Encyclopaedia Britannica. "Richard Wright." September 25, 2020. Acessed November 16, 2020. https://www.britannica.com/biography/Richard -Wright-American-writer.

The Guardian. "The Guardian View on Dilma Rousseff's Impeachment: A Tragedy and a Scandal." April 18, 2016. Accessed April 18, 2016. https://www.the-guardian.com/commentisfree/2016/apr/18/the-guardian-view-on-dilma-rousseffs -impeachment-a-tragedy-and-a-scandal?fbclid=IwAR2BqU3JHHNV44Ox2liik N4bzX56LW_L1usTg1I2FulcGyp7CZDXlleDV_U.

The New York Times. "Donald Trump's Cabinet Is Complete. Here's the Full List." May 11, 2017. Accessed October 28, 2020. https://www.nytimes.com/interactive /2016/us/politics/donald-trump-administration.html.

————. "Coronavirus in the U.S.: Latest Map and Case Count." June 14, 2021. Accessed June 14, 2021. https://www.nytimes.com/interactive/2021/us/covid -cases.html.

The Social Dilemma. Directed by Jeff Orlowski. Netflix, 2020.

The White House. "Remarks by President Obama and President Lula Da Silva of Brazil." Accessed January 13, 2020. https://obamawhitehouse.archives.gov/the -press-office/remarks-president-obama-and-president-lula-da-silva-brazil .

————. "Executive Order on Combating Race and Sex Stereotyping." September 22, 2020. Accessed October 25, 2020. https://www.whitehouse.gov/presidential -actions/executive-order-combating-race-sex-stereotyping/.

Tiagoleite and michele Vogel. "Jair Bolsonaro Pode Ficar Fora dos Debates na Televisão por 'Motivo Estranho.'" *Blasting News* March 21, 2018. Accessed February 20, 2020. https://br.blastingnews.com/politica/2018/03/jair-bolsonaro -pode-ficar-fora-dos-debates-na-televisao-por-motivo-estranho-002450621.html.

Time Staff. "Here's Donald Trump's Presidential Announcement Speech." *Time* June 16, 2015. Accessed June 29, 2020. https://time.com/3923128/donald-trump -announcement-speech/.

———. "Jeb Bush Drops Out of Presidential Race." *Time* February 20, 2016. Accessed June 30, 2020. https://time.com/4231664/jeb-bush-drops-out-president/.

———. "Read Donald Trump's Full Inauguration Speech." January 20, 2017. Accessed October 17, 2020. https://time.com/4640707/donald-trump-inauguration -speech-transcript/.

Todamateria.com.br. "Constituição de 1937." Accessed April 10, 2020. https://www .todamateria.com.br/constituicao-de-1937/.

Today in Civil Liberty History. "'To Secure These Rights': Truman's Civil Rights Committee Delivers Historic Report, October 27, 1949." Accessed December 4, 2019. http://todayinclh.com/?event=to-secure-these-rights-trumans-civil-rights -committees-report-released.

Toral, André Amaral de. "A Participação dos Negros Escravos na Guerra do Paraguai." *Estudos Avançados* 9 no. 24, May/August, 1995. Accessed May 19, 2020. https:// www.scielo.br/scielo.php?script=sci_arttext&pid=S0103-40141995000200015

Trading Places. Directed by John Landis. West Hollywood, CA: Paramount Pictures, 1983.

Tran, Van C., Jennifer Lee, and Tiffany J. Huang. "Revisiting the Asian Second-generation Advantage." *Ethnic and Racial Studies* 42, no. 13 (2019): 2248–2269. https://doi.org/10.1080/01419870.2019.1579920.

TRE-RJ. "Justificativa Eleitoral." Accessed March 20, 2020. https://www.tre-rj.jus.br /site/servicos_eleitor/justificativa/justificativa.jsp.

Trump, Donald J. *Twitter* October 29, 2018, 8:29 a.m.

Trump, Mary L. *Too Much and Never Enough: How My Family Created the World's Most Dangerous Man.* New York: Simon & Schuster, 2020.

Tribuna. "Homem que Esfaqueou Bolsonaro É Doente Mental e Pode ter Pena Reduzida." April 10, 2019. Accessed March 2, 2020. https://www.tribunapr.com.br /noticias/brasil/homem-que-esfaqueou-bolsonaro-e-doente-mental-e-pode-ter-pena -reduzida/.

Tyson, Alec and Shiva Maniam. "Behind Trump's Victory: Divisions by Race, Gender, Education." November 9, 2016. Accessed July 16, 2020. https://www .pewresearch.org/fact-tank/2016/11/09/behind-trumps-victory-divisions-by-race -gender-education/.

Uchoa, Pablo. "Kennedy Cogitou Ação Militar contra Goulart." *BBC News Brasil* March 27, 2014. Accessed March 27, 2014. https://www.bbc.com/ portuguese/noti cias/2014/03/140327_kennedy_goulart_pai_pu.

Último Segundo. "Bolsonaro É Inocentado em Acusação de Racismo contra Quilombolas." June 7, 2019. Accessed February 15, 2020. https://ultimosegundo

.ig.com.br/politica/2019-06-07/bolsonaro-e-inocentado-em-acusacao-de-racismo -contra-quilombolas.html.

UOL. "Quando uma Eleição Presidencial Vai para o Segundo Turno?" September 9, 2018. Accessed March 4, 2020. https://noticias.uol.com.br/politica/eleicoes/2018 /noticias/2018/09/23/quando-uma-eleicao-presidencial-vai-para-o-segundo-turno .htm.

———. "'Sou Messias, Mas Não Faço Milagres,' Diz Bolsonaro sobre Recorde de Mortes." April 28, 2020. Accessed November 30, 2020. https://noticias.uol.com.br /saude/ultimas-noticias/redacao/2020/04/28/sou-messias-mas-nao-faco-milagres -diz-bolsonaro-sobre-recorde-de-mortes.htm.

United States Census Bureau. "1920 Census: Volume 1. Population, Number and Distribution of Inhabitants." 1921. Accessed May 18, 2021. https://www.census .gov/ library/publications/1921/dec/vol-01-population.html.

———. "Quick Facts: New Orleans City, Louisiana." Accessed June 30, 2020. https://www.census.gov/quickfacts/fact/table/neworleanscitylouisiana#.

———. "Income, Poverty and Health Insurance Coverage in the U.S.: 2018." December 4, 2019. Accessed May 18, 2021. https://www.census.gov/newsroom/ press-releases/2018/income-poverty.html.

U.S. History.com. "U.S. Population, Land Area and Density, 1790–2000." Accessed October 6, 2019. https://www.u-s-history.com/pages/h986.html.

Valente, Rubens. "Bolsonaro Era Agressivo e Tinha 'Excessiva Ambição', Diz Ficha Militar." *Folha de São Paulo* May 16, 2017. Accessed January 7, 2020. https:// www1.folha.uol.com.br/poder/2017/05/1884332-bolsonaro-era-agressivo-e-tinha -excessiva-ambicao-diz-ficha-militar.shtml.

Valery, Gabriel. "Brasil Lidera Mortes por Covid-19 em 2021. Total de Vítimas se Aproxima de 490 Mil." *Rede Brasil Atual* June 14, 2021. Accessed June 14, 2021. https://www.redebrasilatual.com.br/saude-e-ciencia/2021/06/brasil-lidera-mortes -por-covid-19-em-2021-total-de-vitimas-se-aproxima-de-490-mil/.

Valor Online. "Coronavírus É Mais Letal entre Negros no Brasil, Apontam Dados do Ministério da Saúde." April 11, 2020. Accessed May 22, 2021. https://g1 .globo.com/bemestar/coronavirus/ noticia/2020/04/11/coronavirus-e-mais-letal-e ntre-negros-no-brasil-apontam-dados-do-ministerio-da-saude.ghtml

Veja. "Dilma se Pronuncia sobre os Protestos no Brasil; Leia a Íntegra do Discurso." June 21, 2013. Accessed February 11, 2020. https://veja.abril.com.br/brasil/dilma -se-pronuncia-sobre-os-protestos-no-brasil-leia-a-integra-do-discurso/.

———. "Bolsonaro Lamenta Atos de Violência e Diz Não Ter Controle de Apoiadores." October 10, 2018. https://veja.abril.com.br/politica/bolsonaro -lamenta-atos-de-violencia-e-diz-nao-ter-controle-de-apoiadores/.

———. "Haddad Ganha na França e Alemanha; Bolsonaro, na Suíça e Inglaterra." October 28, 2018. Accessed March 20, 2020. https://veja.abril.com.br/politica/had dad-ganha-na-franca-e-alemanha-bolsonaro-na-suica-e-inglaterra/.

———. "Almanaque Bolsonaro." January 2, 2019. São Paulo: Editora Abril.

Venceslau, Pedro and Ricardo Galhardo. "Judeus Reclamam do Uso de Símbolos por Bolsonaro." *Estadão* August 25, 2019. Accessed August 25, 2019. https://

politica.estadao.com.br/noticias/geral,judeus-reclamam-do-uso-de-simbolos-por-bolsonaro,70002981346.

Verdery, Katherine. "Whither 'Nation' and 'Nationalism'?" In *Mapping the Nation*, edited by Gopal Balakrhishnan, 226–234. London: Verso, 1999.

Vi o Mundo.com. "Com Vitória Esmagadora no Nordeste, Dilma Rousseff É Reeleita por Pequena Margem; Aécio Perde onde é mais Conhecido, Minas e Rio; Apoiadores Gritam 'Fora Rede Globo'." October 14, 2014. Accessed February 11, 2020. https://www.viomundo.com.br/politica/dilma-reeleita-presidente-brasil-com.html.

Vieira, Tamara. "Processo de Integração do Negro na Sociedade Brasileira enquanto Cidadão: Análise do Processo de Transformação do Escravo em Cidadão (Região Sudeste, 1870–1930)." Laboratório de Cultura e Estudos Afrobrasileiros/LEAFRO. Londrina: Universidade Estadual de Londrina. Accessed May 20, 2020. http://www.uel.br/eventos/semanacsoc/pages/arquivos/GT%204/Tamara%20Vieira.pdf.

Wall Street. Directed by Oliver Stone. Los Angeles, CA: 20th Century Fox, 1987.

Wang, Frances Kai-Hwa. "50 Years Later, Challenging the 'Model Minority Myth' Through #ReModelMinority." *NBC News*, January 11, 2016. Accessed December 6, 2019. https://www.nbcnews.com/news/asian-america/50-years-later-challenging-model-minority-myth-through-remodelminority-n493911.

Washington, Booker T. *Up from Slavery*. New York: Doubleday, 1901.

Waters, Mary C. *Ethnic Options: Choosing Identities in America*. Berkeley, CA: University of California Press, 1990.

Weiner, Juli. "Financially Embattled Thousandaire" and Journalism's Other Top Donald Trump Epithets." *Vanity Fair* April 20, 2011. Accessed July 6, 2020. https://www.vanityfair.com/news/2011/04/financially-embattled-thousandaire-and-journalisms-other-top-donald-trump-epithets.

When They See Us. Directed by Ava DuVernay. Netflix, 2019.

Wilkins, Roy, with Tom Mathews. *Standing Fast: The Autobiography of Roy Wilkins*. New York: Viking Press, 1982.

Williams, Zoe. "Feminazi: The Go-to Term for Trolls out to Silence Women." *The Guardian* September 15, 2015. Accessed March 26, 2020. https://www.theguardian.com/world/2015/sep/15/feminazi-go-to-term-for-trolls-out-to-silence-women-charlotte-proudman.3.

Wills, Garry. *Negro President: Jefferson and the Slave Power*. Boston, MA: Mariner Books, 2005.

Wilson Center. "'We Are Committed to Restoring Confidence in the Country and its Institutions': A Conversation with his Excellency Hamilton Mourão Vice President of the Federative Republic of Brazil." April 9, 2020.

Wilson, Valerie and William Rodgers III. "Black-White Wage Gaps Expand with Rising Wage Inequality." *Economic Policy Institute* September 20, 2016. Accessed July 3, 2020. https://www.epi.org/publication/black-white-wage-gaps-expand-with-rising-wage-inequality/#epi-toc-7.

Wilson, William Julius. *When Work Disappears: The World of the New Urban Poor*. New York: Random House, 1996.

Wolf, Tom. The "Me" Decade and the Third Great Awakening." *New York* August 23, 1976. Accessed June 22, 2020. https://nymag.com/news/features/45938/.

Woodward, Bob. Fear: *Trump in the White House*. New York: Simon & Schuster, 2018.

World Bank. "The World Bank in Brazil." October 14, 2019. https://www.worldbank .org/en/country/brazil/overview Accessed January 13, 2020.

Wu, Ellen D. "Imperatives of Asian American Citizenship." In *Race and Ethnicity in Society: The Changing Landscape,* 4th ed., edited by Elizabeth Higginbotham and Margaret L. Andersen, 60–66. Boston, MA: Cengage Learning. YEAR.

Wu, Frank H. " Why Vincent Chin Matters." *The New York Times* June 22, 2012. https://www.nytimes.com/2012/06/23/opinion/why-vincent-chin-matters.html. Accessed October 19, 2019.

Wyllys, Jean and Fernando Solis. "Fake News: Desinformação e Discurso de Ódio na Erosão da Democracia Brasileira." Presentation at Columbia University Seminar on Brazil, New York, December 12, 2019.

Yahoo News. "Bolsonaro Says Brazil Polls a Win for 'Conservative Wave.'" https:// news.yahoo.com/bolsonaro-says-brazil-polls-win-

Yan, Holly, Devon M. Sayers, and Steve Almasy. "Virginia Governor on White Nationalists: They Should Leave America." *CNN* August 14, 2017. Accessed November 10, 2020. https://www.cnn.com/2017/08/13/us/charlottesville-white -nationalist-rally-car-crash/index.html.

York, Chris. "Quem é Stephen Bannon, Assessor de Trump Acusado de Racismo." *HuffPost* November 16, 2016. Accessed July 15, 2020. https://exame.com/mundo/ stephen-bannon-racismo-antissemita/.

YouTube. "G20: Barack Obama and the President of Brazil (Lula)." April 2, 2009. https://www.youtube.com/watch?v=wdZ8iZ3wvQw Accessed January 13, 2020.

———. "CQC - O Povo Quer Saber - Jair Bolsonaro 28/03/2011 [HD]." March 29, 2011. Accessed January 10, 2019. https://www.youtube.com/watch?v=XHj _yoggvMo.

———. "A Nossa Bandeira Jamais Será Vermelha." August 15, 2015. Accessed January 15, 2020. https://www.youtube.com/watch?v=DLrSUbH8Yzg.

———. "Donald Trump: Jeb Bush Is a Nervous Wreck." February 8, 2016. Accessed June 30, 2020. https://www.youtube.com/watch?v=m_7xXIAfMTA.

———. "[NocauteTV] Nossa Bandeira Nunca Será Vermelha." November 17, 2016. Accessed January 15, 2020. https://www.youtube.com/watch?v=QLl6zwdun7E.

———. "Janaína Paschoal Chora e Pede Desculpas." August 30, 2016. Accessed January 29, 2020. https://www.youtube.com/watch?v=L0hk0FeNz7w.

———. "Haddad (PT) - Governo PT / Steve Bannon / Depoimento de Pessoas Torturadas - Presidente 2018 - 16/10." October 16, 2018. Accessed November 7, 2020. https://www.youtube.com/ /watch?v=929o3Rui4WI.

———. "Trump Torches the Press: 'I'm the President and You're Fake News.'" April 23, 2020. Accessed November 30, 2020. https://www.youtube.com/ watch?v=d7pXNy0Yumc.

Zanona, Melanie. "Obama Rips Trump over Auto Industry Comments." November 7, 2016. Accessed July 1, 2020. https://thehill.com/policy/transportation/304741 -obama-rips-trump-over-auto-industry-comments.

Index

About the Author

Vânia Penha-Lopes is professor of Sociology at Bloomfield College, cochair of the Brazil Seminar at Columbia University (2008 to present), and a former member of the executive committee of the Brazilian Studies Association (BRASA) (2010–2014). A native of Rio de Janeiro, Brazil, Dr. Penha-Lopes graduated with honors from the Universidade Federal do Rio de Janeiro, with a bachelor's degree in Social Sciences (1982), and from New York University, with a master's degree in Anthropology (1987) and a PhD in Sociology (1999). As a postdoctoral fellow at the Universidade do Estado do Rio de Janeiro (2006–2007), she did research on the first graduating class of Brazilian university quota students. She has received a number of awards, including the Carter G. Woodson Institute Predoctoral Fellowship in Afro-American and African Studies, from the University of Virginia (1996–1998), and the Scholarship for Study Abroad, from the Encyclopaedia Britannica do Brasil (1982), of which she was the youngest recipient. Dr. Penha-Lopes has lectured extensively on comparative race relations, African American fatherhood, and racism in Brazil, and has been interviewed for articles in *Época, Diverse Issues in Higher Education, O Estado de São Paulo*, and *The Washington Post*. She is the author of *Racismo Lá e Cá: 60 Crônicas* (2020), *Confronting Affirmative Action: University Quota Students and the Quest for Racial Justice* (2017), and *Pioneiros: Cotistas na Universidade Brasileira* (2013), and coeditor of *Religiosidade e Performance: Diálogos Contemporâneos* (2015). On social media, she can be found at www.vania-penhalopes.com; on Facebook, @vaniapenhalopes.phd; on YouTube, on the "Racismo Lá e Cá" channel; and on Instagram, vaniapenhalopes_phd.

www.ingramcontent.com/pod-product-compliance
Lightning Source LLC
Chambersburg PA
CBHW022308280326
41932CB00010B/1020